Contradictions of
the Welfare State

Studies in Contemporary German Social Thought
Thomas McCarthy, general editor

Alfred Schmidt, *History and Structure: An Essay on Hegelian-Marxist and Structuralist Theories of History*, 1981

Hans-Georg Gadamer, *Reason in the Age of Science*, 1982

Joachim Ritter, *Hegel and the French Revolution: Essays on the Philosophy of Right*, 1982

Theodor W. Adorno, *Prisms*, 1982

Theodor W. Adorno, *Against Epistemology: A Metacritique*, 1983

Hans Blumenberg, *The Legitimacy of the Modern Age*, 1983

Jürgen Habermas, *Philosophical-Political Profiles*, 1983

Jürgen Habermas, editor, *Observations on "The Spiritual Situation of the Age,"* 1983

Michael Theunissen, *The Other: Studies in the Social Ontology of Husserl, Heidegger, Sartre, and Buber*, 1984

Helmut Peukert, *Science, Action, and Fundamental Theology: Toward a Theology of Communicative Action*, 1984

Claus Offe, *Contradictions of the Welfare State*, 1984

Contradictions of the Welfare State

Claus Offe

Edited by John Keane

The MIT Press

Cambridge, Massachusetts

361.6
032 c

First MIT Press edition, 1984

© 1984 by Claus Offe and John Keane

Library of Congress Cataloging in Publication Data
Offe, Claus.
  Contradictions of the welfare state.
  (Studies in contemporary German social thought)
  Bibliography: p.
  Includes index.
  1. Welfare state—Addresses, essays, lectures. ·
2. Democracy—Addresses, essays, lectures. 3. Socialism
—Addresses, essays, lectures. I. Keane, John,
1949– . II. Title. III. Series.
JC325.O33 1984   361.6′5   83–18772
ISBN 0–262–15027–1
ISBN 0–262–65014–2 (pbk.)

Printed and bound in Great Britain

Contents

Figures

Acknowledgements

The author, editor and publishers would like to thank the copyright holders below for their kind permission to reproduce the following material:

Westdeutscher Verlag for ' "Crises of crisis management": elements of a political crisis theory', which appeared in M. Jänicke (ed.), *Herrschaft und Krise* (Opladen 1973); and for 'Social policy and the theory of the state', which was published in C. V. Ferber and F. X. Kaufman (eds.), *Kölner Zeitschrift für Soziologie und Sozialpsychologie*, special issue, **19** (1977).

Surkampf Verlag for ' "Ungovernability": the renaissance of conservative theories of crisis', which was first published in Jürgen Habermas (ed.), *Stichworte sur Geistigen Situation der Zeit* (Frankfurt 1979). The English translation reproduced in this volume is © 1983 by Massachusetts Institute of Technology.

New German Critique for permission to use their earlier translation of 'Theses on the theory of the state'.

Basil Blackwell Publishers Ltd for 'Some contradictions of the modern welfare state'.

Studies in Political Economy for 'The separation of form and content in liberal democracy'.

Das Argument, Zeitschrift für Philosophie und Socialwissenschaften, **128,** edited by Frigga Haug and Wolfgang Fritz Hau (1981), for 'Political culture and Social Democratic administration'.

Zeitschrift für Verbraucherpolitik and Suhrkampf Verlag for 'Alternative strategies in consumer policy'.

Editor's preface

This volume consists of a selection of the most important essays written by Claus Offe during the last decade. They cover a wide range of subjects related to the present crisis of the welfare state, including the failure of social democracy, the rise of the New Right, corporatism, social policy, political parties, trade unions and new social movements, and the future of democratic socialism. The collection also includes a closely edited interview with Claus Offe, conducted especially for this volume by David Held and myself during the latter months of 1982. It should be emphasized that the essays selected and arranged here have been published and originally presented in a variety of contexts – as research summaries and conference papers, as contributions to books and journals, and (in one case) as a radio broadcast. I have not attempted to render these essays into a falsely homogeneous whole; accordingly, their varying difficulty and rather divergent styles persist. While quite a few of the essays are already available in English, their republication in one volume seemed to be justified by the widespread interest in Claus Offe's writings, by the well-known difficulty of procuring them, and by the growing uncertainty about the future of welfare state capitalism. Several essays are published here for the first time in English. Every other existing translation has been checked carefully and either amended or retranslated entirely.

I should like to express my gratitude to Claus Offe, whose convivial assistance made this project all the more pleasurable. I am indebted to Andrew Buchwalter and Jon Rothschild for their help in the translation work. I am very grateful to Sarah Conibear and Claire L'Enfant at Hutchinson for their highly competent and helpful editorial assistance. For their critical advice and encouragement in preparing this volume, I should also like to express my thanks to Boris Frankel, Ian Gough, David Held, Matjaž Maček, Paul Mier, Chantal Mouffe, James O'Connor, Anne Rogers, Anne Sassoon, David Wolfe and Nancy Wood.

John Keane
London
1983

Foreword

The majority of the essays in this volume were written during years in which the future of the entire political arrangements associated with the welfare state were much less the object of doubts and public debates than they have become today. In as much as all of them anticipate, explore and seek to systematize these doubts, their collation and republication seemed to have some justification. The various arguments presented in this collection have been edited, revised and sometimes expanded, although not to the extent necessary to eliminate their points of overlap and divergent emphases. More recent references and data have not been added to update the texts, most of which rely to an obvious, and perhaps disproportionate extent on the West German social-scientific and political debates of recent years. Thanks are due to Hutchinson for their interest in publishing this collection and, most of all, to John Keane. He has not only translated nearly all of the essays that were written in German, but also edited those written originally in my own Teutonic English. I also benefited from his thoughtful comments and friendly advice at many points. During the past year, the Netherlands Institute for Advanced Study (NIAS) has kindly provided me with the time and facilities to rethink and rework some of these essays.

Claus Offe
Wassenaar
The Netherlands
1983

Introduction

John Keane

The limits of crisis management

These essays on the 'contradictions' of the welfare state appear at a
time of considerable uncertainty about its future. Everywhere, and
from all sides, there are mounting attacks on the orthodox welfare
state policies of stimulating private investment, reducing unemployment, securing 'national defence' and administering various
social needs. All that seemed settled and certain about these
policies during the last four decades has become controversial. The
conditions of international political stability and profitable
economic growth, upon which all West European and North
American welfare states relied during this period, have been
seriously eroded. At the same time, welfare state interventions
have become the object of new types of social and political resistance. Nowadays, few are willing to project a certain future for the
welfare state.

The origins and consequences of this disruption of the post-war
settlement are of central concern to Claus Offe, whose political
writings appear here for the first time in one volume in English.[1]*
For readers unfamiliar with these writings, the following remarks
may serve as a brief guide to several of their most important arguments. To begin with, it should be emphasized that this volume is
not a work of normative political philosophy. Offe's critique of the
welfare state does not take sides in the growing philosophical controversies about social justice, needs, rights and the state's responsibility for the welfare of the community.[2] Although concerned to
precisely define and critically analyse the growth and functioning of
the welfare state at a rather generic level, he does not speak directly
for or against the view that it is a guarantor of well-being and
citizenship rights within a more 'just' and 'egalitarian' society. Nor

---

* Superior figures refer to the Notes and references at the end of each chapter.

does Offe accept those narrowly descriptive approaches – strongly evident in much of the welfare state literature – which narrate the historical landmarks of state policies or specify their growth and operation using quantitative indicators of expenditures on particular public policies.[3] Offe rejects these normative and narrowly descriptive approaches. His theoretical and empirical research is unique, in so far as it attempts to carefully analyse and explain the mechanisms and conditions that lead to systematic *failures* in welfare state policy-making and administration. Offe's desire to clarify the *limits* of the welfare state merges with his overall understanding of the role of social scientific inquiry. While social science is incapable of directly prescribing valid political norms, he proposes that it can nevertheless engage in a form of 'indirect' normative criticism of the system of welfare state capitalism. Social scientific inquiry is capable of questioning the false 'common sense' beliefs that presently serve to sustain this system. Thereby, social science can promote an awareness among social groups of the need for more adequate and desirable decision-making arrangements. According to Offe, this form of indirect normative criticism is possible only in so far as the contemporary social sciences disengage from their present role as pragmatic servants of power. Charged with the function of stimulating democratic action and promoting public awareness of the deficiencies of the present system of welfare state capitalism, the social sciences must abandon their attempt to become providers of clear-cut advice and 'practical' information to policy-makers and administrators. They must instead orient themselves to raising discussion about *crisis tendencies* and, thus, to deliberately identifying *more* problems than the ruling elites in politics, administration and business are capable of accommodating and 'solving'.[4]

Guided by this interpretation of the *critical* function of the social sciences, Offe uses a revised version of systems theory to analyse the present difficulties of the welfare state. This systems-theoretical approach, which draws upon Marxism and the work of the leading German systems theorist, Niklas Luhmann, is especially evident in his earlier writings (see essay one in this volume). Late capitalist societies are analysed as systems structured by three interdependent but differently organized subsystems. These subsystems include the structures of *socialization* (such as the household) which are guided by normative rules; the commodity production and exchange relationships of the capitalist *economy*; and the welfare *state*, organized by the mechanisms of political and administrative power and coercion. The welfare state is interpreted, from this perspective, as a multi-functional and heterogeneous set of political and administrative institutions whose purpose is to manage the structures of socialization and the capitalist economy. Offe rejects the narrow and conventional understanding of the welfare state as the provider of social services.[5] He argues that, since the end of the Second World War, the political subsystem has performed a co-ordinating role which is central to the whole social system. Welfare states have been broadly defined by the goal of 'crisis management', that is, the regulation of the processes of socialization and capital accumulation within their adjacent or 'flanking' subsystems. For example, welfare states have sought to guarantee the survival of privately-controlled exchange processes by minimizing their self-paralysing tendencies. In turn, this economic strategy has depended upon the formal recognition of the actual power of trade unions in the process of collective bargaining and public policy-making and administration. Welfare state administrations have also sought to correct and regulate the processes of socialization through, for example, legal transfers of resources to various groups whose life chances had been damaged systematically by market exchange processes.

Offe points out that the former popularity and effectiveness of these welfare state policies of crisis management has been derived, to some extent, from their multi-functional character and reliance upon various techniques of intervention, such as bureaucratic regulation, monetary transfers and professional expertise. This need of the welfare state to pursue many goals, often through conflicting strategies, has become one of its fundamental sources of weakness in the present period. Its vulnerability is highlighted by the critical systems-theoretical approach, which draws attention to the mutual 'interference' and conflict-ridden interactions between the socialization, economic and political subsystems of late capitalism. Simply stated, Offe's inquiries focus upon the persistent 'boundary disputes' between these different subsystems. The consequence of this analysis, to anticipate Offe's arguments, is that the 'epicentre' of the present contradictions of the welfare state is no longer traced back to the economy and its class struggles (as in many recent Marxist discussions).[6] Instead, these contradictions are seen to derive from the antagonistic *relationship* between the three sub-systems of late capitalism and, more precisely, from the *inability* of the administrative-political system to separate itself from its 'flank-ing' subsystems in such a way that it can facilitate their undisturbed and independent functioning. Offe argues that welfare states are rapidly ceasing to be a viable solution to the socio-political problems generated by late capitalist societies because the systems of economic and social life are not in harmony with the require-ments of the administrative-political system. The 'panacea' of state intervention and regulation itself becomes controversial. Welfare state systems generate more policy failures, political conflict and social resistance than they are capable of resolving; the crisis management strategies of the welfare state themselves become subject to new forms of crisis tendency.

Decommodification

This thesis, which has strongly influenced the writings of Habermas,[7] proposes that the limitations of the welfare state are neither passing phenomena nor random events which have a con-tingent origin. On the contrary, their systematic and deep-seated character derives from fundamental contradictions within the mode of operation of all welfare state systems. These contradictions implicate welfare states in a process of cumulative self-obstruction. Of decisive importance – the 'primary contradiction' – is the fact that the various branches of the welfare state are compelled to perform two incompatible functions *vis-à-vis* the economic sub-system: commodification and decommodification.[8] On the one hand, Offe argues, the policy-making and administering activities of the welfare state are constrained and limited by the dynamics of the sphere of economic production. Welfare state policies are supposed to be 'negatively subordinated' to the process of capitalist accumulation. The fact that property in labour power and capital is for the most part private means that welfare state institutions are unable to directly organize the production process according to political criteria. This independence of the capitalist-controlled economy is reinforced by the constant threat of private capital exercising its power *not* to invest – whose aggregate exercise, as we know from the present period, is synonymous with economic crisis. The administrators of the welfare state therefore have a 'self-interest' in giving preferential treatment to the capitalist economy, because the healthy functioning of this economic subsystem (capi-talist investment and 'full employment' of labour) is a crucial condition of the 'mass loyalty' to the welfare state and, indirectly, the vital source of its revenues (which are generated through indirect and direct taxation, tariffs and borrowing from banks). Dependent upon the processes of commodity production and exchange, which are beyond its immediate power to control and organize directly, welfare state administrators must therefore be concerned with preserving the 'private' power and scope of these commodification processes. In sum, the welfare state is required to be a *self-limiting* state.

Offe reasons that this imperative of respecting capital's independent powers of investment and control over the economy cannot in practice be realized. The Keynesian welfare state must 'positively subordinate' itself to the capitalist economy. It is required to both *intervene* in this subsystem and create, through non-market or *decommodified* means, the pre-conditions of its successful functioning. That the welfare state must play a more 'positive' and interventionist role *vis-à-vis* the capitalist economy is evidently a consequence of the latter's self-crippling, cyclical dynamics. In Offe's view, the processes of capitalist accumulation cannot be reproduced through the 'silent compulsion of economic relations' (Marx). Rather, capitalist exchange processes exhibit a constant tendency to paralyse the commodity form of value; the likelihood that elements of labour power and capital will find opportunities for employment and exchange on the market is continually threatened.

In view of the recent controversies about the present crisis of the capitalist world system, it is surprising that Offe does not analyse the self-paralysis of the commodity form in any great detail. Whether, for example, these self-paralysing tendencies are the product of squeezes on the rate of profit due to the improved bargaining power of organized labour, a consequence of monopoly capital's search for investment outlets on a global scale, or the outcome of demand saturation and declining rates of productivity resulting from the exhaustion of the potentials of scientific and technical innovation, remains an obscure point in his analysis. Referring generally to the 'cyclical dynamics' or 'anarchic' character of capitalist accumulation processes, his thesis tends to rely upon a version of the familiar Marxian theory of the 'socialization of production' (essays two and three). Capitalist economic processes are said to accelerate the growth of forms of *collective* action to remedy the consequences of the operations of *individual* units of capital. In other words, the 'movement of private capital' systematically produces collectively-experienced outcomes, such as the decay of inner cities caused by capitalist disinvestment and real estate policies, the pollution of regional ecosystems, and a rise in unemployment levels due to the capitalist 'modernization' of industry. While these outcomes can obstruct or threaten the privately-controlled exchange process, they *cannot* be remedied or neutralized by the actions of individual units of capital.

The implication is that the overall survival of the 'unregulated' sphere of capitalist exchange depends upon the continuous application of forms of 'collective regulation'. These self-paralysing tendencies of the capitalist economy also threaten the effectiveness, popularity and fiscal viability of state policies, which are thereby forced to transcend and therefore contradict their self-limiting character. The welfare state must seek to universalize opportunities for the 'free' or unregulated exchange of labour and capital by *intervening* within that exchange process. The maintenance and generalization of 'private' exchange relationships depends upon decommodified (i.e., non-market, state) policies which effectively and efficiently promote the investment of capital and the saleability of labour power through public infrastructure investment, mandatory schemes of joint decision-making and social policy, and the application of various administrative regulations and incentives. In a word, welfare state policies are required to do the impossible: they are forced to reorganize and restrict the mechanisms of capitalist accumulation in order to allow those mechanisms to spontaneously take care of themselves.

This contradiction between commodification and decommodification helps to explain why very few areas of life are now outside the sphere of welfare state policy-making and administration. It also helps to explain why this state performs a multiplicity of roles, some of which have openly 'decommodifying' effects. At any one point in time, Offe contends, the welfare state seeks to maintain the economic dominance of capital, to challenge and erode its power, and to compensate for its disruptive and disorganizing consequences. The intrusion of decommodifying welfare state policies into the economic subsystem is a particularly significant development, for it indicates that the processes of commodity production and exchange are being directly eroded and threatened. Compared with the 'liberal' phase of capitalist development, and in relation to the total social labour power available, the scope and power of wage-labour–capital relationships have been considerably decreased; processes of commodity production and exchange are both dominant *and* recessive. Within the economy, the freedom of capital to invest and deploy labour power in the interests of profitable accumulation has been weakened, because the 'factors of production' (nature, labour power, capital) once assumed as given have increasingly become the object of specific state policies. The exploitation of labour power and other categories of the population by market processes dominated by capital has become more complicated and, therefore, less predictable and certain.

Offe does not consider whether the present transnational migration of industrial capital to the peripheral capitalist countries is a direct response by capital to this encroachment upon its power.[9] He prefers to indicate (essays four and six) that the welfare state has increased the 'means of resistance' that are available to social groups in their attempts to minimize the exploitative effects of capital's control over the means of production. For example, state-subsidized housing makes it possible for low income groups to live in better (and otherwise unaffordable) accommodation; the universal provision of health or dental services weakens the significance of factors of chance, profitability or ability to pay in matters of bodily care; the corporate pollution of the local environment ceases to be a private affair, and instead becomes a matter subject to state regulation; various forms of labour protection legislation, unemployment insurance and social security benefits increase the chances of male and female workers successfully resisting their employers and the disciplinary effects of the 'reserve army of labour' mechanism; and so on.

It can be suggested, in response, that this thesis is excessively generic, and that it therefore underestimates the importance of the new forms of social inequality and unfreedom instituted by welfare state policies. For example, the specification of minimum standards of social security provision for citizens typically depended upon the distinction between 'insurance' and 'welfare assistance'. Means-testing, stigma and inadequate and uneven provision were important features of welfare assistance for the 'undeserving poor'. Second-class citizenship and 'poverty traps', in other words, have always been an endemic feature of the post-war extension of 'citizenship rights'. There is also some evidence that Offe understates the degree to which legal-bureaucratic and professional forms of state intervention *weaken* clients' capacity for self-help by continually redefining and monitoring their 'needs'. As a consequence of state intervention, workers and other groups are indeed acknowledged to have the status of 'citizens' – citizens who are, none the less, expected to assume the role of passive objects of administrative care and surveillance.[10] Finally, by making the welfare *state* coterminous with decommodified welfare provision *in toto*, Offe's thesis neglects the continuing importance of non-state forms of provision. Private enterprise, charitable and 'voluntary' forms of welfare regulation are not merely 'survivors' of an earlier age, and thus cannot be subsumed under the general rubric of 'state intervention'. The links between state and non-state forms of social administration often involve intricate relations of interdependency, and must be theorized as such.

Offe's novel and suggestive thesis nevertheless remains plausible. He argues forcefully that policies of state intervention, designed to secure and enhance the capitalist-directed processes of commodification, in fact directly or indirectly threaten the collective power of capital. State policies considerably decommodify the daily lives of the population by replacing 'contract' with political status and 'property rights' with 'citizen rights'. This daring thesis has far-reaching implications, and explains why he refuses to speak of the welfare state as a Leviathan-like instrument for the 'reproduction of the relations of production'. He argues that, contrary to the claims of state-derivationist and functionalist Marxism, welfare state policies do not necessarily or automatically 'serve' the 'interests' of the capitalist class. Indeed, in the contemporary period, the continuation of the capitalist economy is no longer vitally dependent – as it was in the 'liberal' phase of capitalism – upon the creation and *expansion* of exchange relations *vis-à-vis* pre-capitalist 'remnants'. On the contrary, capitalist exchange processes are increasingly faced with the inverse problem of behaving *defensively*. They are compelled to shield themselves against the growth of forms of administrative and political power which are not *immediately* determined by the processes of commodity production and exchange.

The fiscal problems of the state

The entanglement of the welfare state within this contradictory development is deepened, Offe proposes, by several closely-related difficulties. At least three of these 'subsidiary contradictions' are identified in this collection of essays. They can be usefully introduced here, because they clarify his more general claim that the effectiveness and legitimacy of the interventionist welfare state are *systematically* restricted.

One important source of this ineffectiveness and illegitimacy, Offe explains, is the chronic fiscal problem of the welfare state.[11] This state's attempts to administer its economic and socialization subsystems has become extraordinarily expensive. The continuous expansion of state budgets is due indirectly to the fact that the viability of capitalist growth (especially within the oligopoly sector of the economy) depends upon ever larger investment projects, huge research and development subsidies, and a continuous rise in the costs of providing 'social overheads', such as health, transportation and energy systems. In order to encourage private capital investment, welfare states must 'socialize' these continuously increasing costs and outlays. One consequence of this is that the borrowing and taxation powers of the state tend to impinge upon the profitability of the capitalist sector. The likelihood of permanent fiscal deficits also grows because there is a contradiction between the ever-expanding costs associated with the welfare state's 'socialization' of production and the continuing *private* control over investment and the appropriation of its profits.

Under conditions of welfare state capitalism, thus, state expenditures persistently tend to outrun state revenues. The point may even be reached where capital openly resists the taxing and borrowing powers of the welfare state and where, consequently, it may be in this state's 'self-interest' to rationalize or 'cut back' its *own* expenditure patterns. These permanent fiscal deficits are evidently difficult to control or reduce. Offe does not consider whether the constant and dangerous growth of armaments production and militarism is partly responsible for these permanent fiscal problems of the welfare state – a lacuna, it may be added, that is symptomatic of his more general failure to analyse the external ordering of welfare states within the global system of nation-state power and conflict. Despite this weakness, his discussion of the inertia of welfare state overspending is highly provocative. In his view (which is also found among neo-conservative critics of the welfare state, as essay two indicates), the identification of the welfare state as an important socializer of the costs of production produces an addictive effect. Various power groups within the economic and socialization subsystems come to regard the state as if it were an unlimited liability insurance company. It is supposed to be capable of underwriting all possible risks, 'needs' and failures. This addiction effect tends to be exacerbated by the difficulty of co-ordinating and controlling state expenditures centrally. The cost-benefit accounting of these expenditures, a portion of which are used up in feeding state institutions themselves, is also a notoriously difficult task. Finally, attempts by state administrators to reduce the size of the public purse by increasing the effective rates of corporate taxation are also very dangerous.[12] Any state strategy oriented to the diversion of greater portions of value into what business considers 'unproductive' expenditures runs the risk, particularly under the present conditions of economic stagnation, of producing flights of capital – of increasing the possibility that capital will engage in a general investment strike.

Planning failures

This ability of capital to exercise a private power of veto against the welfare state's policy-making and administrative activities continually endangers their fiscal viability. It also contradicts and threatens their coherence and self-consistency. Welfare state planning systematically produces unforeseen difficulties, 'bottlenecks', policy reversals and challenges to its effectiveness and legitimacy. Offe does admit that disjoined, incremental types of state planning may be a necessary feature of all 'complex' societies. Under the specific conditions of welfare state capitalism, however, the attempt by the state to 'finely tune' and co-ordinate its economic and socialization subsystems is typically marked by an *excess* of failures and unplanned outcomes. In some measure, this surplus of planning failures is a consequence of various forms of organized resistance to state power. In particular, long-range bureaucratic planning is continually pushed and pulled by social and political forces. Social turbulence and political resistance is continually internalized *within* the welfare state apparatus. Disputes over wages and conditions within the state sector; the international transfer of capital; the struggles of trade unions against capitalist enterprises; and the opposition of social movements to state decisions are *specific* and *concrete* forms of resistance that tend to hinder or 'privatize' attempts by the welfare state to engage in 'public' planning guided by *general* or synoptic rules.

This limit upon welfare state planning is compounded by the typical lack of co-ordination between various state bureaucracies, and by the inability of the administrative branches of the state to secure their independence from the rules and outcomes of representative democratic institutions and party competition. As a consequence of all these factors, welfare state policies are marked by clumsy and fluctuating patterns of intervention, withdrawal and compromise. This 'muddling through', which encourages state administrators to rely upon often ineffective discretionary policies and indirect controls and incentives, is only aggravated by the fact that one set of priorities of the welfare state (its attempt to maintain the privately-steered accumulation process) is typically accommodated *within* every other form of policy planning and public administration. Because the welfare state is committed to giving preferential treatment to the capitalist economy, there is a high probability of planning failures within other policy areas. Thus, there is a contradiction between the welfare state's attempt to rationally plan its 'decommodifying' activities and the continuing private control over capital investment within the economy. By virtue of their powers of (non-)investment, the elements of capital can define and limit the boundaries of 'realistic' public planning and administration. The guiding criterion of private control of production for profit is not easily subjected to external controls, and this means that state planning can only ever be partial and incomplete. The welfare state is supposed to fulfil all its self-designated tasks (recognizing the power of trade unions, ensuring economic growth, national 'defence', the provision of collective commodities, the amelioriation of existing patterns of social inequality, etc.) without encroaching upon the private power of capital, a move that would violate the logic of the capitalist economy as a profit-oriented system of commodification. In other words, the welfare state has to refrain from planned interventions within the privately controlled accumulation process, upon whose cyclical dynamics and disruptive consequences, however, this state's planning and administration continue to depend.

Offe is convinced that this contradiction constitutes a serious limit to state policy-making. He therefore rejects those evolutionary accounts of the history of the welfare state which suppose that, in contrast with the erratic and inconsistent character of earlier state policies, the contemporary welfare state can be described as a coherent complex of measures guided by synoptic calculations.[13] In his view, the welfare state cannot function in this self-consistent and comprehensive way. It is not a class-conscious political organ which self-consciously and comprehensively arranges its economic and socialization subsystems, delivering planned gains to selected beneficiaries at the expense of selected losers. Welfare state institutions are incapable of becoming an 'ideal collective capitalist' (Engels). Victimized by an economic subsystem whose organizing principle is private control over investment and production, welfare state planning is marked by a surplus of 'compatibility problems' and disjointed and self-contradictory measures.[14] It is this routine 'anarchy' and 'ineffectiveness' that encourages the administrative apparatus to become dependent upon powerful and organized social interests (for example, employers' associations, professional organizations, trade unions), whose co-operation is vital for social order and effective administrative planning. It is also for this reason (essays seven and eleven) that the traditional liberal-democratic institutions of conflict articulation and resolution – elections, political parties, legislatures, judiciaries – are increasingly supplemented or replaced by informal 'corporatist' schemes of functional representation and bargaining. According to Offe, the effectiveness of welfare state policies comes to depend increasingly upon informal and publicly inaccessible negotiations between state planners and the elites of powerful social interest groups.

Mass loyalty problems

There are good reasons for doubting whether the popular *legitimacy* of this latter form of welfare state policy-making can be sustained. Offe's concern with the contradictions of the welfare state forces him to re-examine a problem first raised in the German sociological tradition by Max Weber and the *Verein für Sozialpolitik*, namely, whether state policies can effectively legitimate the socio-political institutions of organized capitalist societies. He proposes that the contradictions of the welfare state mentioned above are in fact intensified by permanent and deep-seated legitimation difficulties. Under welfare capitalist conditions, mass loyalty to the existing system of administrative and political power tends to disintegrate to a serious extent. The normative rules and resources necessary for the functioning of this system of state power are not produced in sufficient quantities by existing processes of socialization.

This thesis is rather incomplete, and it is for that reason not one of the most convincing arguments presented in this volume. Offe speaks of mass loyalty as a 'regulatory resource', as the ability of the

structures, processes and policy outcomes of the political-administrative system to be 'genuinely accepted' (essay one). It should be
mentioned that the reference to *genuine* (as distinct from false or
enforced) loyalty is not systematically analysed in these essays.
Unlike Habermas, for instance, Offe is not concerned with the
subject of moral-practical reasoning and the conditions under which
'interests' and normative validity claims can be considered as
warranted or 'true'.[15] Moreover, Offe does not engage current
advances within the analysis of ideology and discourse. This is one
reason why he undervalues the contemporary importance of certain
ideological discourses (for example, nationalism and militarism)
and strategies of consensus building (such as plebiscitarian leadership). Especially problematic is his failure to systematically
consider whether, in the present period of social and political disorganization, there can emerge widespread nostalgia for decaying
ideological traditions, a nostalgia which can, in turn, be strategically
nurtured and manipulated by the ruling groups of dominant institutions.

Offe's thesis none the less remains important and provocative.
He insists that welfare state capitalist systems can legitimate their
relations of command and obedience only to a very limited degree.
The welfare state is thereby caught within a further contradiction:
the more its policies 'close in' on the systems of socialization and
economic life, the more they tend to be regarded by various actors
within those domains as heteronomous and illegitimate. Several
explanations for this permanent legitimation problem are proposed
in this volume. First, there is the suggestion that the 'liveliness' or
meaningfulness of pre-modern traditions (such as Christianity and
patriarchal family life) is seriously eroded by contemporary processes of commodification and decommodification. The operations
of the economic and political subsystems destroy the 'naturalness'
of these traditions. In contrast to the 'liberal' phase of capitalism,
these traditions can no longer so easily serve as sources of mass
loyalty to the welfare state (essay two). The probability of mass
loyalty problems is further increased by the fact that the welfare
state becomes systematically 'overloaded' with demands which it
has directly sanctioned. Compared with 'liberal' capitalist state
forms charged with fewer functions, the welfare state has in some
measure raised expectations about what it *can* achieve. It visibly
assumes responsibility for a much wider gamut of functions – from
the management of human and physical resources to securing the

commodification process, weakening its scope, and compensating for its dysfunctions. As life increasingly becomes 'life by political design', these functions can no longer so easily be considered by electorates as inevitable or 'natural'. The claims of those who continue to advocate welfare state policies are subjected to direct 'reality-testing', especially when pressured by the decommodification, fiscal and planning contradictions mentioned above (essay nine). As a result, the potential and actual level of frustrations caused by policy failures tends to increase. Unable to effectively execute decisions for which they claim responsibility, welfare state administrators become victims of their own 'false promises'.

This process of demand creation and frustration tends to be reinforced, or so Offe claims, by the fact that the decommodifying activities of the welfare state seriously weaken the convincing power of norms which were formerly associated with capitalist exchange processes. The decline of the ideology of possessive individualism or the 'achievement principle' is of particular interest to Offe. He argues that, throughout early modern Europe and the New World, this ideology legitimated the spread of commodified relations of production and exchange guaranteed by formal law and the constitutional state. Through the prism of this ideology, the everyday life of (male) individuals was seen to be properly determined by the ethos of competitive achievement, the pressure of status-seeking, and the unlimited accumulation of property guaranteed by law. In the achieving society, the power, wealth and status of individuals were supposed to depend upon their performance within the commodified sphere of production and exchange. Offe suggests that, when compared to the heyday of liberal capitalism, the achievement ideology is much less convincing to the populations of welfare state countries (essay four). Contrary to certain schools of modernization theory, welfare capitalist systems do not effect continuous victories for the achievement principle. In some measure this is because the welfare state's provision of transfer payments and 'compensatory' subsidies (to the young, old, unemployed or disabled) has contributed to a rupturing of old assumptions about the direction relationship between the achievements of individuals and their remuneration for those achievements by 'the market'. In many zones of social life, 'work' and 'pay' are less closely interrelated, as individuals find themselves temporarily or permanently outside the sphere of the labour market. These individuals' former dependence upon the vicissitudes of markets is replaced by a sense of their growing dependence upon welfare state compensation. Offe suggests that the rationale of market exchange processes is further undermined by the direct intervention of state power into the economic subsystem. State policies which attempt to reproduce the commodity form (i.e., the profitable exchange of labour and capital) through decommodified means have the unintended effect of undermining both the institutionalized power *and* legitimacy of commodification processes. Within the state sector, for example, material conditions of life are determined only indirectly by the exchange relations which obtain in the competitive and oligopolistic sectors of the economy. While state-sector workers are dependent upon wages, it becomes evident to them that the state neither 'purchases' their labour power at an 'equilibrium price' nor 'sells' the products of their work. The welfare state's interventions into an economy which continues to be dominated by exchange values also facilitates the questioning of these exchange values by *other* social groups (essays seven, ten and twelve). Having considerably expanded the scope and power of decommodified institutions, welfare state administrators make themselves the possible focus of conflict over the social costs and utility of state-sector labour power, capital investment and scientific research and development within fields such as military planning, nuclear energy and health.

Alternatives to welfare state capitalism

Embedded within the problems of decommodification and fiscal and planning deficits mentioned above, these legitimation conflicts have in the contemporary period become an endemic feature of welfare state, capitalist societies. They have provoked a growing debate about the achievements and limits of the welfare state – a debate which is, in turn, bound up with struggles to develop *alternatives* to welfare state institutions. Offe remains convinced throughout these essays that these controversies and struggles will not easily lead to the replacement of the welfare state by fundamentally new arrangements. This state has become irreversible, in the precise sense that it performs functions essential for both the capitalist economy and the life chances of many social groups. In the face of whatever remains of the blind optimism about the future of the welfare state, Offe nevertheless seeks to theoretically determine its *limits*. He is concerned, in other words, to indicate and clarify not only what the welfare state has achieved but also what it *cannot* achieve. He therefore insists that the present contradictions of the welfare state are not merely 'dilemmas', if by the latter we mean problems which could be 'solved' or 'managed' by improved strategies of choice or temporary policy reforms. To be sure, these contradictions do not lead to the automatic, blind and irreversible collapse of welfare state capitalism. In his view, the contradictions of the contemporary welfare state are better understood as responsible for generating destabilizing situations or crisis tendencies, the deepening or overcoming of which continuously depends upon social struggles and political manoeuvrings.

The very great importance of these present-day struggles generated by the contradictions of the welfare state is registered in several of the essays in this volume. It is significant that in his more recent writings (for example, essays six and eight), Offe considerably de-emphasizes or even abandons his earlier reliance upon systems-theoretical categories. The limits and future viability of welfare state policies are no longer analysed as the outcome of the contradictory interplay of anonymous societal structures and subsystems. Instead, *state* policies are viewed as dependent upon the existing matrix of *social* power, which in turn is seen to be constantly subject to transformations by the activity of *social* power groups and movements. Welfare state institutions are, thus, viewed as both the medium *and* outcome of struggles over the distribution of power within the realms of society and the state.

At the most general level, Offe discusses three different forms of contemporary resistance to the welfare state. One obviously important source of this resistance is the so-called New Right. Supported by sections of large capital and the traditional middle classes, the goal of this *laissez-faire* coalition is the recommodification of social life. It seeks to *decrease* the scope and importance of decommodified political and administrative power by resuscitating 'market forces'. Those sectors of the economic subsystem unable to survive within the commodity form, it is argued, should also be allowed to fall victim to 'market pressures' and, at the same time, urged to 'modernize' by transforming themselves into marketable commodities.

Offe strongly doubts the viability of this *laissez-faire* strategy for depoliticizing the accumulation process and recommodifying the functions of the welfare state. It should be noted that his arguments neglect the considerable degree of success the New Right has had in *strengthening* the power of the state and popularizing the ideology of the 'free' – patriotic, lean, familial – society. Offe also fails to consider the possibility of an irreversible weakening of trade union power by the *laissez-faire* strategy of generating high rates of so-called 'natural' unemployment. He instead points out that the policies of the New Right are not universally favoured by big business, which frequently depends for its survival upon state contracts, special transfer payments and subsidies. Moreover, he claims that the policies of the New Right opposition to the welfare state are most strongly favoured by precisely that power group – the old middle class of farmers, shopkeepers and others – whose social base is at present very much in decline. Above all, Offe reaffirms his thesis that the frontiers of the welfare state cannot easily be 'rolled back' in the face of the self-crippling tendencies of the capitalist economic system. While the timing, scope and volume of state policies can be altered, welfare capitalist societies cannot be remodelled into 'pure market societies' (essay three). Privately-controlled capitalist economies could not continue to function successfully (or even at all) without the extensive state provision of 'public goods' such as housing, health services and education. These state policies are an indispensable condition of an economy which for instance concentrates labour power in conurbations, weakens the independence of households and persistently 'disorganizes' social life through its investment strategies. The New Right defence of 'reprivatization' is therefore impossible, because it is self-contradictory. According to Offe, it fails to recognize that capitalism is both endangered *and* made possible by welfare state interventions.

Given the probable failure of strategies of *large-scale* recommodification, a greater reliance upon state-supervised, 'corporatist' forms of policy-making and administration cannot be excluded as a second, and possibly complementary, response to the present contradictions of the welfare state. This strategy of corporatism, Offe contends, is concerned with reviving the commodification process and alleviating the fiscal and planning problems of the welfare state. It seeks to exclude 'excessively political' demands and to institute state-supervised and informal modes of bargaining between representatives of key interest groups such as labour and capital (essays eleven and twelve). Corporatist policies are designed to develop a consensus among power elites in order to readjust welfare state policy-making and administration to the requirements of the economic subsystem. Corporatist mechanisms rely upon arcane and highly inaccessible elite negotiations and increased political repression and surveillance, rather than upon autonomous public discussion and accountability. They are supposed to strengthen the forces of discipline and constraint, especially through measures (such as statutory incomes policies) designed to contain the wage and social consumption demands of trade unions.

Offe notes that the growth of corporatist or 'tripartite' forms of decision-making is encouraged by the relative decline of conventional liberal-democratic mechanisms (such as legislatures) which formerly functioned to articulate and secure agreement upon policy programmes. However, the strategy of restructuring the welfare state through greater reliance upon corporatist mechanisms is not without serious difficulties. Offe incisively points out, for example, that those corporatist mechanisms which are supposed to embody the principle of *paritätische Mitbestimmung* (the equal representation of capital and labour) typically disadvantage organized labour and other non-represented social interests. This is because the outer limits of what can become the object of 'realistic' bargaining and decision-making within a corporatist framework are strongly conditioned by the power of investment or non-investment of the representatives of capital. This power typically serves to define which issues or demands *can* be negotiated and which *must* be excluded as excessively controversial or 'unworkable'. Because of this 'class bias', which is frequently challenged as such by organized labour and other social groups, corporatist forms of policy-making tend to disequilibrium. They generate new patterns of conflict between organized labour, social movements, the state and capital.[16] These conflicts concern, for instance, the degree to which decisions reached through corporatist arrangements are equitable or *equally* binding. This tendency is strengthened by the permanent legitimacy problem of corporatist schemes of functional representation. These schemes are difficult to justify to the populations of welfare state countries. Apart from pragmatic necessity, it is unclear why *certain* groups or *particular* agendas or procedural rules are to be attributed a special status within the bargaining and decision-making process. This legitimation problem is only made more acute by the fact that corporatist schemes of functional representation and bargaining visibly erode the institutional boundaries between 'civil society' (the household, economy and social power groups) and the state. This increase of the *social* character of welfare state institutions contradicts the classical liberal-democratic notion of politics as the struggle for organized state power. Spheres of life once considered as 'natural' or 'pre-political' become the possible object of state policy and social conflict. Under pressure from these problems of parity and legitimation, corporatist solutions to the present contradictions of the welfare state seem to be neither equitable nor viable. According to Offe, corporatist mechanisms are most feasible when national traditions of opposition by capital and labour to the state are weak, when there are high levels of political repression and, finally, where a 'positive sum game' between capital and labour is made possible by uninterrupted economic growth. However, these conditions are rarely, if ever, found together.

These doubts about the viability of corporatist solutions prompt Offe to consider proposals for a third – democratic and socialist – alternative to the welfare state (essays ten, eleven and twelve). His stimulating discussions of democratic socialism are introduced through a question that is a mark of the socialist tradition: are there indications that the present self-paralysing tendencies of the welfare state are *also* constructive of a possible democratic socialist alternative to welfare state capitalism? Offe does not consider the *international* economic and political dimensions of this question. Once again, his account of the limits of the interventionist welfare state is too strongly bound to the single nation-state unit. Questions about the new international economic order and the perilous tensions within the nation-state system are inadequately considered. He does however suggest that an alliance of democratic-socialist forces is not altogether impossible under contemporary conditions. If such an alliance could gain the support of key sections of the trade union movement and the new middle classes, it might effectively reconstruct welfare state capitalism into an egalitarian 'welfare society', whose 'needs' would be autonomously determined through decentralized and publicly-controlled forms of social production and political organization.

Offe contends that this goal of a democratic and socialist welfare society is in some measure facilitated by the growth of new social movements, such as feminism, environmentalism and pacifism. Frequently engaging in direct forms of social action, these movements articulate and defend such 'post-material' values as gender identity, democratic rights and environmental safety. Significantly, their support does not derive from peripheral or marginal social strata but, rather, from groups whose co-operation is central to the overall management and functioning of welfare capitalist systems. The recent growth of these movements is seen by Offe as being not only a consequence of the general erosion of mass loyalty to welfare state capitalism. It is also the result of the relative displacement of political parties as an important focus of political consensus-building. This circumvention and loss of legitimacy of political parties is, of course, a complex development. In this volume, several important factors behind this development are analysed in some detail (essays eight and twelve). Offe considers the growing displacement of territorially-defined political institutions by functional (i.e., corporatist) forms of representation, as well as the de-activation of rank-and-file membership by the bureaucratization and professionalization of patterns of party leadership and recruitment. Consideration is also given to the transformation of governing parties into public relations agents for the particular government executive which they in fact only nominally 'control'. Finally, Offe points to the growth of the 'catch-all' party, whose overriding concern with 'winning a majority' is seen to produce a selective blindness towards controversial issues and particular demands, a loss of distinctive party identities, and a deepening sense among electorates that intra-party differences may be greater than differences between parties, or even that *all* parties 'fudge' the significance of *particular* issues.

These factors tend to greatly diminish the trust popularly accorded to political parties. In turn, this cynicism and distrust tends to promote the growth of autonomous social movements, which address various problems and issues (urban renewal, sexual domination, peace, environmental decay) that have been marginalized or 'screened out' by official party and state procedures of consensus-building. Offe reasons that the democratic socialist potential of these movements is enhanced by the fact that, under welfare state conditions, there is a marked increase in the social character of politics (essay eleven). As a consequence of its manifold interventions into the economic and socialization sub-systems, the scope of state power is spread wider and thinner. No longer institutionally 'separated' from its social environment, the political system becomes highly differentiated and, therefore, potentially more vulnerable to interest group disputes, the withdrawal of compliance or active resistance by organized labour and the new social movements.

A socialist civil society?

It can be argued that Offe's analysis of this 'withering away' of a coherent and strictly circumscribed apparatus of state power contains two very important implications for democratic socialist politics. On the negative side, it warns that *dirigiste* strategies of socialist transformation are not only undesirable – as the New Right ideologues emphasize – but also ineffective and unrealistic. His analysis provides the reminder that the political-administrative system has become so highly differentiated and complex that there is simply no single centre of state power which could be 'occupied' and used to radically transform the systems of socialization and economic life. More positively, Offe's discussion implies that the highly differentiated and disunified character of welfare state interventions renders non-statist strategies of socialist resistance and transformation more viable in the present period. It is not only that 'the welfare state' is sufficiently in one place to be 'seized'. In so far as this state penetrates all spheres of civil society, social resistance to its misformulated, inequitable and often repressive policies can and must also be everywhere. The 'parliamentary road' can no longer be seen as privileged, as occupying the centre stage of socialist politics. Especially on the peripheries of the welfare state – for instance at the level of the 'local state' – countervailing networks of democratic communication and mobilization are easier to develop and considerable advantage can be taken of the contradictions within welfare state policies. In these regions of civil society, decommodifying *state* institutions are accessible and highly vulnerable to the *social* initiatives of clients and workers. The expanding scope and power of these state institutions makes them more susceptible to redefinition and transformation by works councils, producer, health and housing co-operatives, refuges for battered women, neighbourhood organizations and other democratic, grass-roots institutions. No doubt, these spheres of democratic autonomy do not automatically secure more decentralized, horizontally-structured and egalitarian patterns of social life. It is also certain that vigorous political protection and legal recognition are necessary conditions of their survival and expansion. The recent emergence of these democratic initiatives nevertheless points to a paradoxical outcome of the welfare state settlement of the past four decades. This self-paralysing settlement not only becomes vulnerable to the reactionary crusades of the New Right. It also makes possible a new type of democratic socialism, which could effectively call into question the old uneasy compromise between capitalist production and administrative surveillance and control. In other words, welfare state policies of reform have the unintended effect of breaking their own spell. They encourage social struggles to develop new forms of mutual aid within a *socialist* civil society mobilized against the power of private capital and the interventionist, disciplinary state.

Notes and references

1 Offe's dissertation, a study of work organizations and the 'achievement principle', has been translated and published as *Industry and Inequality* (London 1976). A collection of his essays on trade unions, labour market policies, corporatism and the future of work will shortly appear as *Social Class and Public Policy* (London 1984).

2 Cf. John Rawls, *A Theory of Justice* (Oxford 1972); Robert Nozick, *Anarchy, State and Utopia* (New York 1974); Raymond Plant *et al.*, *Political Philosophy and Social Welfare* (London 1980).

3 These two types of descriptive approaches are represented in Maurice Bruce, *The Coming of the Welfare State* (London 1968), and Jürgen Kohl, 'Trends and problems in post-war public expenditure development in Western Europe and North America', in Peter Flora and Arnold J. Heidenheimer (eds.), *The Development of Welfare States in Europe and North America* (New Brunswick 1979).

4 See, for example, 'Praxisbezüge der Sozialwissenschaft als Krisenwissenschaft', in Christoph Hubig and W. von Rahden (eds.), *Konsequenzen kritischer Wissenschaftstheorie* (Berlin and New York 1978), pp. 234–51; 'Die kritische Funktion der Sozialwissenschaften', in Wissenschaftszentrum Berlin (ed.), *Interaktion von Wissenschaft und Politik* (Frankfurt 1977), pp. 321–9; and 'Sozialwissenschaften zwischen Auftragsforschung und sozialer Bewegung', in Ulrich Beck (ed.), *Soziologie und Praxis. Erfahrungen, Konflikte, Perspektiven* (Göttingen 1982), pp. 107–13.

5 This understanding is evident in the classic definitions provided by Asa Briggs, 'The welfare state in historical perspective', reprinted in C. Schottland (ed.), *The Welfare State* (New York 1977), and Richard Titmuss, *Essays on 'The Welfare State'* (London 1976), p. 42.

6 See, for example, John Fry, *Limits of the Welfare State* (Westmead 1979); Ulf Himmelstrand *et al.*, *Beyond Welfare Capitalism* (London

1981); Nicos Poulantzas, *State, Power, Socialism* (London 1978); and the essays on the German 'state derivation' approach in John Holloway and Sol Picciotto (eds.), *State and Capital. A Marxist Debate* (London 1978).

7   Jürgen Habermas, *Legitimation Crisis* (Boston 1975), Part 2.

8   Offe's thesis that state intervention has considerably weakened the sphere of commodified production and exchange is considered at greater length in John Keane, *Public Life and Late Capitalism. Essays Towards a Socialist Theory of Democracy* (Cambridge and New York 1984), essay 3.

9   Cf. the important study of Folker Fröbel *et al.*, *The New International Division of Labour* (Cambridge 1980).

10   This point generates a surprising amount of agreement among socialist and neo-liberal critics of the welfare state. See, for instance, Pierre Rosanvallon, *La Crise de L'Etat Providence* (Paris 1981); Joachim Hirsch, *Der Sicherheitstaat. Das 'Modell Deutschland', seine Krise und die neuen sozialen Bewegung* (Frankfurt 1980); David G. Green, *The Welfare State: For Rich or for Poor?* (London 1982); Frances Piven and Richard A. Cloward, *Regulating the Poor. The Functions of Public Welfare* (New York 1971). It can be noted here that whenever Offe discusses the problem of welfare state surveillance (see essay twelve) he tends also to underestimate its contingency. His conviction that certain forms of social administration are *irreversible* is reinforced by his reliance upon systems theory arguments. According to Offe, there is a genetic relationship between the complexity of social systems, their vulnerability to 'deviance' and increasing welfare state control. From this standpoint, 'complex' welfare capitalist societies are highly sensitive to the effects of 'deviant' social action, which it is therefore *necessary* to monitor and bureaucratically control.

11   This argument draws upon the earlier work of James O'Connor, *The Fiscal Crisis of the State* (New York 1973).

12   This point is developed (with Volker Ronge) in a study of the West German construction industry, 'Fiskalische Krise, Bauindustrie und die Grenzen staatlicher Ausgabenrationalisierung', *Leviathan*, 1, no. 2 (1973).

13   cf. Derek Fraser, *The Evolution of the British Welfare State* (London 1973). Offe is also critical of the view of orthodox systems theorists that, under the complex conditions of modernity, welfare state administration has a general competence to process information and decisions and steer other social subsystems. This view is proposed, for instance, in the earlier writings of Niklas Luhmann, *Politische Planung* (Opladen 1971), and *Demokratie und Verwaltung* (Berlin 1972).

14   Compare Offe's comments on the 'unplanned, nature-like' character of state policy-making in his introduction (with W.-D. Narr) to *Wohlfahrtstaat und Massenloyalität* (Cologne 1973); *Strukturprobleme des kapitalistischen Staates* (Frankfurt 1972), Chapter 4; and *Berufs-bildungsreform – Eine Fallstudie über Reformpolitik* (Frankfurt 1975), especially Chapters 3 and 6, where Offe discusses the systematic limits upon different forms of state planning, with particular reference to unsuccessful Social Democratic Party attempts to rationalize the provision of vocational training.

15   Jürgen Habermas' most recent restatement and elaboration of this subject appears in the two volumes of *Theorie des kommunikativen Handelns* (Frankfurt 1981).

16   cf. Offe's analysis of these unintended consequences of corporatism in 'Die Institutionalisierung des Verbandseinflusses – eine ordnungs-politische Zwickmühle', in Ulrich von Alemann and Rolf G. Heinze (eds.), *Verbände und Staat* (Opladen 1979), pp. 72–91; the introductory remarks to Rolf G. Heinze, *Verbändepolitik und Neokorpor-atismus'. Zur politischen Soziologie organisierter Interessen* (Opladen 1981), pp. 7–9; Wolf-Dieter Narr and Claus Offe, 'Was heißt hier Strukturpolitik? Neokorporatismus als Rettung aus der Krise?', *Technologie und Politik*, 6 (1976), pp. 5–26; 'The attribution of public status to interest groups: observations on the West German case', in Suzanne Berger (ed.), *Organizing Interests in Western Europe* (Cambridge 1981), pp. 123–58; and (with Helmut Wiesenthal) 'Two logics of collective action: theoretical notes on social class and organizational form', *Political Power and Social Theory*, Vol. 1 (1980), pp. 67–115.

1 'Crises of crisis management': elements of a political crisis theory*

The concept of crisis

While there have been numerous attempts in political science to increase the reliability of strategies of political-administrative intervention through the improvement of information, organizational, planning and legal techniques, there are hardly any studies which proceed from the opposite point of view. The question of why the capacity of late capitalist societies[1] for political regulation is so slight and their capacity for 'planned social change' so defective is either not asked or implicitly dismissed by conceiving the well-known limitations of state regulation as due to factors of a contingent nature which may in future be brought under control through improved administration and budgetary management.

This point of view, which dominates political science, and particularly its new branch of 'policy sciences', is justified neither by practical successes nor by theoretical reasons. The following contribution thus examines the interventionist, welfare state regulatory strategies of late capitalist societies not from the standpoint of how their effectiveness could be increased but rather from that of why their effectiveness is – in spite of all attempts at improvement – so *limited*. The object of this study is to theoretically comprehend the limits of the 'policy-making capacity' of the capitalist state, as well as to establish these limits through a discussion of specific examples.

This kind of theoretical approach, which amounts to a critique (in the sense of the determination of the limits) of the regulatory capacity of the capitalist state, is also a legitimate continuation of

* The following essay summarizes the theoretical approaches which guided a research project on the 'limits of administrative conflict management and control', conducted during 1971–2 at the Max-Planck-Institut, Starnberg. It originally appeared in Martin Jänicke (ed.), *Herrschaft und Krise* (Opladen 1973), pp. 197–223. An earlier translation was published in *International Journal of Politics*, **6** no. 3 (Fall 1976), pp. 29–67.

the kinds of questions asked by the Marxian critique of political economy. Today its subject has undergone a peculiar change. For Marx, the point was to examine the 'laws of motion' of capital in order to prove that capitalism as a social formation was – contrary to the usual belief in harmony of vulgar economics – in fact a 'dynamic', historical and transitory social formation. Today, by contrast, the tantalizing and baffling riddle (in a political as well as a theoretical sense) is why capitalist systems have so far been able to survive – in spite of all existing contradictions and conflicts – even though an intact bourgeois ideology that could deny these contradictions and construct the image of a harmonious order no longer exists. The usual (or, more precisely, temporary) answers to this riddle either take the form of references to the postponement of the point in time at which the internal contradictions of the system 'ripen' and develop their transformative power or, conversely, of making the state responsible for the achievement of a permanent stabilization. However, both responses are defective. They abstract from their appropriate historical contexts and erroneously ascribe absolute validity to either a traditional concept of crisis or its opposite, the 'panacea' of administrative intervention and regulation. A theoretically useful and practically relevant way out of this dilemma may lie in the attempt to see neither 'crises' nor 'crisis management' but rather 'crises of crisis management' as a constant – in the attempt, in other words, to systematically anticipate and analyse the deficiencies and limitations of the stabilizing activity of the state.

In a preliminary way, crises can be defined as processes in which the structure of a system is called into question. This formulation immediately prompts the following question: what are the analytical conditions for structures being 'called into question'? It is possible to answer this question in two different ways.

Crises endanger the identity of a system. According to a first approach, identity can be defined in relation to the total range of events possible in a system. Seen from this first point of view, the system would be endangered whenever events occur that lie 'outside' the boundaries determined by the system. To conceive a 'crisis' as an event foreign to the system or destructive of that system is to rely upon a *sporadic crisis concept*. The point of departure of a sporadic crisis concept is the notion that crises are particularly acute, catastrophic, surprising and unforeseeable events which, consequently, necessitate a 'decision-making process under the pressure of time' (K. W. Deutsch). The crisis is thus seen as an event or a chain of events confined to one point in time or a short period of time. This makes it difficult to describe the *tendency towards crisis* or *crisis-proneness* of a social system. This type of crisis concept fails to systematically link events with the structures of the system, in the sense that the crisis event or the defencelessness against it is not seen as a characteristic quality of the system.

A sporadic crisis concept is at best suitable for the analysis of well-demarcated *subsystems*: for instance, a business enterprise goes bankrupt because it is confronted by its environment (banks, customers, competitors, etc.) with data and events incompatible with its continued existence. In analyses of society as a whole, however, any conceptual strategy which conceives of crises as 'events that are neither anticipated nor provided for' encounters difficult problems. Logical distinctions between, on the one hand, events provided for and those which are not and, on the other, between events compatible with the system and those which are not can hardly be operationalized. These difficulties indicate the need for an alternative concept of crisis.

The alternative approach conceives crises not at the level of events but rather at the superordinate level of *mechanisms that generate 'events'*. According to this second definition, crises are processes that violate the 'grammar' of social processes. Such a definition favours a *processual* concept of crisis. Crises are developmental tendencies that can be confronted with *'counteracting tendencies'*, which means that the outcome of crises is quite unpredictable. Moreover, this processual crisis concept has the advantage of making it possible to relate the crisis-prone developmental tendencies of a system to the characteristics of the system. In contrast to the first type of crisis concept, such developmental tendencies need not be seen as catastrophic events having a contingent origin.

The price that must be paid for the greater precision of this second approach to the concept of crisis is the difficulty it encounters in identifying and defining the boundaries of such event-producing mechanisms. Some guidelines might be drawn from Dahl and Lindblom,[2] who distinguish exchange, political choice, bureaucracy, and bargaining processes as four ways social events are produced in industrial societies. If one disregards the fourth type as a problematic intermediate case,[3] the remaining three organizational principles can be reconciled with a typology developed by Etzioni[4] for the classification of formal organizations. This typology differentiates social processes according to whether they are based on *normative structures, exchange relationships* or *coercive relationships*.

Now, capitalist societies are defined by the fact that in them – on the basis of an unequal distribution of property resulting from precapitalist 'primitive accumulation' – the organizational principle of the exchange (of equivalents) is *universal*. This principle of exchange, which also includes the commodification of labour power, becomes *dominant* because it is freed from normative and political-coercive restraints. To be sure, a society organized by means of exchange relationships can never be organized *solely* through exchange relations but, rather, requires 'flanking sub-systems': even in a purely competitive-capitalist social system, individuals must be socialized in normative structures, while the established rules of social intercourse must be sanctioned by sovereign power. *A society based on market exchange cannot function without the family system and the legal system.*

If the dominant organizational principle of the social processes of every capitalist society is that of exchange, a theory of the crises of capitalist society can identify those processes which challenge the dominance of this central principle. This, in turn, can be done in two ways.

1   The theory of historical materialism attempts to show that processes organized and formed through exchange lead to results that cannot be dealt with by the exchange process itself. *Economic crisis theories* in a narrow sense, such as the theorem of the historical tendency of the rate of profit to fall, reconstruct the processes of self-negation of the exchange principle that potentially result in the revolutionary transformation of the entire ideological and political 'superstructure'.

2   As an alternative to this approach, a theory of the *system crises* of capitalist societies would examine crisis-prone developments not in the exchange sphere itself (i.e., in the form of an *economic* crisis theory); rather, it would concentrate on the *relationship* between the three fundamental organizational principles of society as a whole. Not the self-negation of the exchange principle but its restriction and questioning by the other two organizational principles would serve as the criterion of crisis processes.

In order to consolidate this second possibility, a distinction may be made between two different kinds of relationship that can exist between the three organizational principles. This distinction reflects the manner in which the normative and political-coercive subsystems are subordinated to the dominant organizational principle of exchange in capitalist societies.

One kind of relationship is that of *positive subordination*. By this I mean a relationship between the economy and the normative and political-administrative systems in which the latter are structured in such a way that they *positively contribute* to, and create the preconditions for, the functioning of the dominant organizational principle and the sphere of the economy determined by it. The distinctive feature of this type of positive subordination is the *adjustment of the content* of the normative and political subsystems so that they *conform* to economic processes. This form of subordination takes place through the norms and ideologies that bring individuals into harmony with the functions within the framework of the economic system, or through a political-administrative system that co-ordinates state policies and the requirements of the economic system.

The *negative subordination* of both the subsystems outside the exchange sphere must be distinguished from the first type of subordination. In this second case, the ideological and state power systems are related to the capitalist economic system in such a way that they are *limited* by, and *insulated* from this economic system without, however, being able to substantively contribute to its ability to function. Successful negative subordination consists of the protection of the sphere regulated by exchange against overlaps and interferences, which are a possible consequence of the development of the normative and political subsystems. The way in which such overlaps result from capitalist development will be discussed below. The aim here is merely to contrast two types of subordination. The production of complementary functions is what matters in positive subordination. In contrast, in negative subordination the dominance of the economic system over the two subsystems depends on whether – given the possibility of the partial functional irrelevance of these two subsystems for the economic system – the boundaries between the respective systems can be stabilized, so that the economic system is able to *prevent* the alternative organizational principles of the normative and state power systems from interfering with its own domain of the production and distribution of goods. In accordance with these considerations, one would have to characterize processes as crisis-prone if they made the demarcation of the economic system from the other two systems more difficult.

The growth of non-market organizations

In order to develop these quite formal attempts at conceptualization with a few material hypotheses, I would like to describe in
greater detail the process of the formation and expansion of 'extra-
territorial', or non-market areas of the capitalist social structure – a
social structure regulated by exchange relationships. In terms of the
structural type of positive subordination discussed above, capitalism
can be described as a social structure which – apart from 'residual'
feudal elements – is entirely determined by the dominant structural
principle of exchange relationships. We can also express this circumstance in a different way: in such a structure, all elements are
'necessary' from the standpoint of the creation of surplus value.
However, closer examination immediately indicates that this
concept of necessity mixes together two elements that must be
distinguished from each other if one wants to avoid hypostatizing
the concept of necessity.

First, the relationship between the economic system and the
normative or political systems can be necessary in the sense that the
structures of the latter are genetically dependent on the economic
system. Necessity here means a genetic relationship of determination. The concept of necessity can also acquire a completely
different meaning, namely, that the ideological and political subsystems are necessary for the reproduction of the economic system.
One can speak of positive subordination in the above sense only if
both elements of the concept of necessity coincide; in other words,
only if the conditions of the ideological and political systems are not
only *produced* in a capitalist society but are also *required* for the
reproduction of a capitalist economy.

On the other hand, the problems associated with negative subordination – the interference of the logics of subsystems and their
insulation from each other – arise only when the genetic and
functional aspects of 'necessity' no longer coincide. This non-
coincidence is characterized by the 'necessary' production of
phenomena and structures which are nevertheless not 'required' by
the capitalist economic structure that produces them. The empirical
thesis I would like to tentatively advance below is the following: the
movement of capital systematically, cumulatively and irreversibly
produces social phenomena and structural elements which are
functionally irrelevant and of no value for the continuation of
capitalist development. While this thesis requires much more

empirical evidence, I contend that the nonintegrable by-products of capitalist development are systematically increasing, and that these by-products are having their effects only as impediments, threats, and as 'ballast', without any longer usefully contributing to the process of the creation of surplus value.

The difference between this developmental pattern and the early capitalist pattern of development is obvious. The development of early capitalist systems was defined by the creation of the conditions for universal capitalist growth: labour power was freed from its pre-capitalist agrarian bonds, mobilized and made available for absorption by capitalist industry; the transportation and communications network was rationalized by the evolution of nation states and territories and adapted to meet the requirements of the capitalist socialization of production; the same was true of the legal and fiscal systems, customs and international economic relations, science and technology, the family and urban development, and so on. While this is evident, many of the social results and structural transformations of the developed capitalist economies are in a general sense destined to play only a subordinate and unimportant – in any case ambivalent – role as functional prerequisites of the economic process.

This thesis could be exemplified in detail with respect to the crisis of the theory of imperialism. That the conditions of military oppression and intervention, of induced impoverishment and forced underdevelopment which characterize the contemporary Third World are a direct *result* of the strategies of the developed imperialistic nations seems to be as certain as the fact that the *functional* explanation of this set of circumstances has become questionable and implausible. The American war in Indo-China and, in general, the dependence of the countries of the Third World on the industrialized capitalist nations hardly conforms to a theoretical schema that attempts to interpret the imperialistic strategies as *means* for both the fulfilment of the present needs of the system and the creation of necessary pre-conditions for the further existence of the imperialist countries. The purpose of these strategies is not to create or expand the necessary economic pre-conditions for the continued existence of capitalist economies by opening up raw materials, labour, investment and export markets;[5] rather, their purpose is to *obstruct* processes of emancipation that are seen to threaten capitalist hegemony.

The course of development of capitalist industrial society seems to cumulatively produce phenomena and structural elements that are not determined by the interest of individual capital units in the creation of surplus value, and that can be linked to the 'interest of capital as a whole' only in a highly ambivalent way. These phenomena and structures contain the seeds of non-capitalist organizational forms, and for this reason are of interest to capital primarily from the *negative* standpoint of how their independence can be restrained. Consequently, it is not the offensive opening up of sources of value and conditions for the creation of surplus value but, rather, the defensive exclusion, prevention and avoidance of 'extra-territorial' or non-market structures that is characteristic of the 'system problems' of capitalist development today.[6] The development of the internal social structure of the capitalist countries is also characterized by the appearance of phenomena which are functionally irrelevant or useless for capitalist growth. In order to maintain the stability of the system, priority must be given to minimizing the possible disruptive effects of these phenomena on the dominant system of surplus value creation.

This structural transformation of capitalist development – from a type of development that produces the indispensible conditions for its own continuation to one that necessarily behaves *defensively* towards its own outcomes – can be analysed more precisely by investigating the organization of social labour power. In certain phases of early capitalist development ever greater portions of social labour were rendered as 'free wage-labour' and thereby made into the raw material of industrial exploitation. Today, however, a different development is taking place in which an ever smaller portion of labour time and 'life time' is directly subsumed under the capital relation. In order to illustrate this developmental tendency – which could also be characterized as a relative decline in the organizing potential of the wage-labour–capital relationship *vis-à-vis* total social labour power – the following argument draws upon a sector model that represents the relative absorption of the total available labour time and of 'life time' in the various sectors of the capitalist system (see Figure 1). The model comprises the monopoly sector (M), the competitive sector (C), the state sector (S), and a sector of 'residual' labour power (R).

The *monopoly* sector is characterized by a high degree of organization of the retail and capital markets. Price competition plays – at least in national markets – a subordinate role. The organic composition of capital is high, i.e., labour costs account for a relatively small

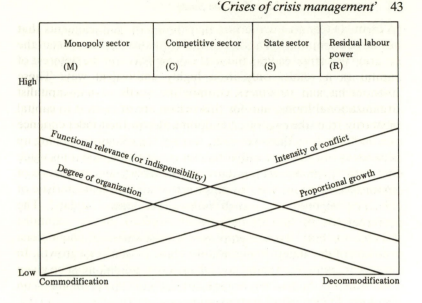

	Monopoly sector (M)	Competitive sector (C)	State sector (S)	Residual labour power (R)

Figure 1   *Four sector model of the capitalist system*

share of the total costs. As a rule, the labour power within this sector is represented by strong trade unions with a high degree of organization. The fact that wage levels in the monopoly sector are relatively high is the combined result of this sector's structural ability to pass on higher labour costs through price increases, the degree of trade union organization, and the small share of its total costs accounted for by labour costs.

Within the *competitive* sector price competition plays a significantly greater role. Labour power is organized to a lesser extent in trade unions, and the likelihood of companies yielding to wage demands is therefore smaller. The competitive sector is dependent on the monopoly sector; this relationship of dependency is determined not by competition but rather by administrative power relationships. Only superficially can this relationship be described as one between market partners enjoying equal rights, because the room for manoeuvre of small- and medium-sized businesses is determined, both qualitatively and quantitatively, by the degree to which they are able to function as suppliers and distributors for the large corporations, for whose patronage they can only compete. The characteristic feature of such a 'dual' economic structure

(Averitt, O'Connor) is the fact that the small- and medium-sized businesses operating on a competitive-capitalist basis are limited to an area the large capital blocs let them have for technical and organizational reasons. Accordingly, the cost structure and profitability of firms in the competitive sector are predetermined by the administratively enforced decisions of the banks and big capital. Moreover, the strategic variable upon which the economic survival of small- and medium-sized businesses (including agriculture) depends is not the innovative behaviour of the 'creative business enterprise' (Schumpeter); rather, it is the mobilization of *political-administrative protection*. In this sector, an adequate economic existence depends upon such non-market means as subsidies, preferential tariffs and tax measures.

Thus, for both the self-employed businessmen and the entrepreneurs of the 'independent' middle class, as well as for the wage-earners working for them, not *all* material conditions of life are determined by bodies and organizations defined by *exchange* relationships. In fact, in this sector the conditions of production and the exchange of labour power are – to an increasing extent – determined through direct economic and political *power* relationships (i.e., relationships which are no longer exchange relationships).

For that portion of social labour power organized in *state bureaucracies and institutions*, either as civil servants or as salaried employees, it is obvious that sovereign political organizational principles predominate over those of exchange. In this sector, labour power still belongs to the 'wage-dependent' category. However, the payment of civil servants' salaries differs qualitatively from the payment of wages in private industry because of the fact that, in the case of civil servants, an 'equilibrium price' between partners in an exchange transaction is not arrived at. The state does not 'buy' the labour performed by its civil servants and salaried employees, just as it does not 'sell' the products of this labour. The mass of funds from which salaries are paid constitutes 'revenue' and not capital, and it is only an 'external' consideration (namely, that the state must compete with the private economy for labour power) that produces a tendency towards the equalization of public and private wage rates. This indirect dependence of the state upon the private economy cannot, however, disguise the fact that the payment of state personnel with public funds is decided through sovereign power budgets (and not through decisions about the investment of variable capital). The regulation of the relationship between the state and the public 'servant' through labour legislation is also in accordance with the fact that 'obligations of loyalty' and restrictions upon labour's right to strike are the counterpart of the special wage, employment and social security status often enjoyed by state employees. The limited degree to which labour performed in the state sector can be mechanized, the correspondingly high intensity of labour, as well as the impossibility of calculating the value of this labour in terms of 'productivity' or market prices also rule out wage determination through exchange as a practical possibility in the state sector. In this sector, in short, the mode of allocating material resources is only indirectly determined by the exchange relation.

Finally, in the sector of *'residual' labour power*, labour power does not – even in a formal sense – receive its material basis of existence as compensation for some sort of work performed; its existence is maintained through official allocations of financial and material resources and life chances. In the monopoly sector, labour power is *sold* in the strict sense of the word; in the competitive sector it is in fact sold, albeit at prices determined by power relationships and political-administrative measures; while in the public sector labour power is remunerated under conditions only indirectly dependent on the market. In the realm of 'residual' labour power life is virtually 'decommodified': transfer payments to unemployed persons, invalids and old-age pensioners, the living conditions of school pupils, college students, drafted servicemen, full-time housewives and the occupants of prisons, hospitals and other 'total institutions' are determined directly by political or institutional means. Here, the market-mediated relationship of correspondence between work performed and remuneration plays no role as a criterion of equivalence and equity.

The four sector model sketched above can thus be interpreted as a way of classifying sectors according to their relative 'degree of commodification'. In order to measure the qualitative (and changing historical) relationships between these sectors, it is necessary to specify not the numbers of persons who are members of each sector but, rather, the proportion of the total available social labour time or 'life time' accounted for by each sector. Thus it is a matter of arriving at a 'two-dimensional' quantity by multiplying the number of individuals by the number of units of time during which their labour power is organized in one of the sectors. This procedure has the additional advantage of making it possible to incorporate into the calculation of the quantitative ratios those portions of 'free time' (for example, time spent on travelling to and from work, and on leisure, vacation and further education) structured not by individual expenditures of earned income but, rather, by administratively determined programmes which take place independently of commodity exchange.

Late capitalism: some hypotheses

This scale of the 'degree of commodification' only becomes significant if it can be shown that there is a relationship between it and other analytically informative variables. In the accompanying model (Figure 1), four such possible relationships – which depend on the variables of 'proportional growth', 'degree of organization', 'functional relevance' and 'intensity of conflict' – are described. I intend to briefly explain the four hypotheses that illustrate these relationships. I will set aside the serious difficulties associated with the operationalization and empirical measurement of these hypotheses and, instead, advance the proposition that the four relationships in question are steadily becoming more and more prevalent throughout the developed capitalist industrial world.

The hypotheses are as follows:

1   In all developed industrial capitalist societies, *sectoral growth rates* (measured in terms of their share of the total fund of available social labour, discussed above) increase as one moves from sector M to sector R. There are several reasons for this: the stagnation or perhaps even absolute decline of the share of labour time absorbed in sector M; the relative growth of service and distribution functions organized by private enterprise (C); the even greater growth of state-organized services and infrastructures (S); finally, sector R grows most rapidly because it includes the institutional training of labour power (and, thus, increases in the number of pupils and the length of attendance within the school system), as well as the material provision of labour power either temporarily or permanently incapable (for physical, psychic, institutional or economic reasons) of being absorbed elsewhere.

2   The *functional relevance* of each of the sectors (measured in terms of the threats to the further existence of the whole system which would result from dysfunctions within that sector) decreases as one moves from M to R. The prosperity of the system as a whole

depends quite substantially on the contributions to growth, the potential for innovation, and the market strategies of sector M. As a result, disturbances within this sector have direct and far-reaching consequences for all of the other sectors. The converse is not equally valid: the dysfunctioning or even revolutionary transformation of schools and universities would not, for a relatively long time, endanger the monopoly capital blocs.

3   The *degree of organization* of class and interest groups (expressed as the ratio between actual and potential membership) decreases as one moves from sector M to sector R. The trade unions in sector M – not to mention the business associations of the corresponding large corporations – are in a position to organize a greater proportion of their potential membership than is possible at the other end of the scale. This means that the economic and organizational power and resources at the disposal of various class and interest groups are not mutually counterbalancing (as has been claimed by Strachey, Galbraith and others). It rather means that – within the framework of the given organizational paradigms of the political system of capitalist societies – these resources and powers accumulate in the positive as well as the negative sense.

4   The manifestation of *militant conflicts* (measured in terms of the utilization of extra-legal means and/or the articulation of non-integrable objectives) is greater in R than in M. If one also considers the ambivalent potential of populist and Poujadist middle-class movements, as well as the political strike movements among French and American public employees, militant conflict most probably increases through the intermediate sectors as well. This comparative statement does not indicate anything about the significance which should be attributed to the militant conflicts (and their strategies) fought out in sector M. It only suggests that the conflicts fought out in this sector have the greatest potential for disrupting the whole system, and that this sector therefore possesses the most effective safeguards against endogenously produced conflicts. The examples of the militant Italian, French (May 1968) and American strikes in large-scale manufacturing plants seem to confirm this assumption. These strikes typically omitted the 'endogenous', economistic phase of the development of classic strikes by drawing upon 'external' impulses, which industrial workers had applied to their own job situations: either the struggles of student and intellectual groups and/or those of the subproletarian strata (Italy, USA) provided models and stimuli (May–June 1968), or the

structure of domination within the plant was challenged by suddenly and abruptly appealing to 'anti-authoritarian' motives. In any case, strikes exhibiting these patterns of development most probably outnumber conflicts in which strikes for higher wages 'organically' outgrow their original goals and become more and more politicized.

On the basis of these brief reflections, I draw the paradoxical conclusion that in late capitalist societies the processes of exchange-regulated capitalist accumulation are simultaneously dominant *and* 'recessive'. Although exchange processes are decisive for the stability of the system as a whole, they have become increasingly obsolete as their potential to organize social life has been restricted to a small core area. This leads to the creation of a new problem for the system of *late* capitalist societies: the problem of preventing the regulatory processes of *administrative power* (which are 'foreign to capital' and yet upon whose permanent expansion the monopolistic sphere of the economy is dependent) from becoming autonomous and controlling private exchange relationships, either through paralysing them or subverting them in revolutionary ways. The increasing utilization of the regulatory medium of non-market, state power cumulatively produces weak points that facilitate intrusions into the system by non-capitalist structures. The closing of these vulnerable points through mechanisms of 'negative subordination' consequently becomes the main problem of late capitalist social systems.[7]

The distinction between positive and negative subordination, or between the substantive subsumption and formal exclusion of non-exchange principles of organization can now be utilized for a phase model of capitalist development. At the most abstract level, the dynamic pattern of development described by this phase model contains four stages.

1   The dominance of the sphere of exchange triggers *processes of socialization* (in the Marxian sense of *Vergesellschaftung*, the 'increasingly social' character of privately controlled production relations), that is, a growing division and differentiation of labour and other functions as well as a growing interdependence[8] between the elements of the social system. Differentiation and interdependence are resultant problems that can no longer be dealt with adequately by the dynamics of market processes. The process of 'socialization', which is pushed forward by the dominant economic

subsystem, is determined by three criteria. First, socialization is triggered by market exchanges between the owners of commodities; second, it creates social conditions that threaten to obstruct this exchange; third, these conditions cannot be compensated through exchange processes themselves. This tendency is characterized by historical materialism as the contradiction between private appropriation and socialized production.

2   As means which deal with the problems generated by capitalist exchange processes, the 'flanking subsystems' (normative structures and state power) become increasingly important. In order for them to be able to compensate for these problems, it becomes functionally necessary for these subsystems to partially emancipate themselves from the relationship of positive subordination. The more that steering problems result from the failure of the exchange mechanism to integrate the process of socialization, the greater is the degree of independence or relative autonomy required by the political-administrative centre if it is to repair, or compensate for, these problems.

This relationship results from the 'anarchic', competitively-regulated movement of capital as a whole. Since 'capital as a whole' exists only in an ideal sense, i.e., is incapable of articulating and perceiving a common and unified class interest, it requires special guidance and supervision by a fully differentiated political-administrative system. Only a fully harmonious economic system that did *not* trigger self-destructive processes of socialization could tolerate the complete positive subordination of the normative-ideological and political systems to itself. As soon as the exchange process requires compensatory regulation, a process of autonomization, which dissolves the positive relationship of subordination, becomes indispensible. To the extent that the process of market exchange between commodity owners is forced to ensure its survival by subjecting itself to state control, the former relationship of subordination must be loosened, and the regulatory medium of state power must be utilized and conceded. In general, the capitalist state has the responsibility of compensating for the processes of socialization triggered by capital in such a way that neither a self-obstruction of market-regulated accumulation nor an abolition of the relationships of private appropriation of socialized production results. The state protects the capital relation from the social conditions it produces without being able to alter the status of this relationship as the dominant relationship. To do otherwise would sanction such mechanisms as the 'investment strike' which would make the therapy more harmful than the illness it was designed to cure. This precarious double function of the capitalist state continuously demands a combination of intervention and abstention from intervention, of 'planning' and 'freedom' – in short, it demands an 'opportunism' (Luhmann) whose adherence to its own principles is absolutely unswerving.

State power subject to such contradictory demands can determine its own strategies neither through a general consensus of citizens nor through technocratic calculation: its opportunistic actions can neither be willed nor calculated. However, this interventionist power does not draw quietly or exclusively on its own resources; it is constantly in danger of succumbing to the competitively-regulated movement of individual capital units. Consequently, it must procure for itself a basis for overall legitimation. Thus, because of the autonomization of the political-administrative system, the normative system must also break free from the relationship of positive subordination and become variable so that it can in turn satisfy the need of the political-administrative system for legitimation.

3   The autonomization of non-market-regulated ('extra-territorial') subsystems and regulatory principles induced by the failure of the exchange principle as an organizing principle for the whole society creates *problems of demarcation* (described above through the concept of negative subordination). The maintenance of the rules governing the creation of surplus value and the retention of the exchange principle as the dominant organizing principle of society necessitate the establishment and growth of subsidiary regulatory principles. These principles must then be prevented from intruding into the domain of private production. This problem of demarcation is determined by the contradictory nature of capitalist 'socialization'. In order to be able to maintain its dominant position, the sphere of exchange needs to be safeguarded through external regulatory principles whose expansion – especially in cases of 'overregulation' or an 'overdose of therapy' – threatens the survival of this sphere. Hence, corporatist tendencies towards *reprivatization* continuously counteract state-capitalist tendencies toward 'global regulation'. In view of this contradictory problem of demarcation, all processes are crisis-prone[9] which call into question and impede a balance between mechanisms of positive subordination (i.e., the totality of positive contributions coming from non-

market subsystems) and negative subordination (which prevent non-market processes from encroaching on the dominant principle of exchange and of surplus value creation).

4 In principle, economic crisis theories are inadequate for the analysis of these crisis-prone processes because they only examine 'first order crises' – in other words, crises that can be described as a cumulative self-obstruction of the process of surplus value creation by means of the effects triggered by this process. On the other hand, the crisis tendencies related to the problem of demarcation (discussed above) take the form of 'second order crises' which are connected with the utilization of regulatory principles external to both capital and the market. In the current phase of capitalist development, second order crises are more relevant than those of the first order, although they are, of course, produced by the latter. This supposition is based on the hypothesis (sketched above) concerning the general pattern of capitalist development: the more the capitalist economy is forced to utilize 'external regulatory mechanisms', the more it is faced with the difficult problem of surviving against the inner dynamics of these encroaching mechanisms.

Problems of the capitalist state

If this problem henceforth serves as the frame of reference for our analysis, it becomes both possible and meaningful to define more precisely the concept of the 'capitalist state'. The capitalist state can no longer be characterized as an *instrument* of 'the' interest of capital (an interest which is neither homogeneous nor 'generally understood'); rather, this state is characterized by constitutional and organizational structures whose specific selectivity is designed to reconcile and harmonize the 'privately regulated' capitalist economy with the processes of socialization this economy triggers. The more actual and problematic this attempt becomes, the greater the legitimacy of a theoretical perspective that seeks to conceptualize the *objectivity* of capitalist development not at the level of the inherent crisis cycles of the economy but, rather, at the level of those formal structures and 'conversion processes' with which the sociology of organization and administration are concerned. This important connection between political-sociological categories and the categories of the sociology of organization has already been emphasized by Selznick and others in many fruitful studies of the organizational pathologies of the political-administrative system.

While this connection also helps overcome the uncertainties and immense difficulties associated with the Marxian theory of value, it is not merely one of convenience. It is a consequence of assumptions about second order crises, whose emergence is necessary and irreversible, and whose significance can be determined only with the help of such political-sociological-organizational categories. This crisis potential (as well as its 'counteracting tendencies') must be analysed in relation to the structural problem of 'negative subordination', i.e., in relation to the problem of whether the political-administrative problem can politically regulate the economic system without politicizing its substance and thus negating its identity as a capitalist economic system based on private production and appropriation.

The success or failure of the attempt to balance contradictory imperatives depends upon the organizational linking or mutual insulation of three 'subsystems' (Figure 2). Depending on the specific regulatory media involved, three subsystems can be distinguished: the economic system, the political-administrative system, and the normative (legitimation) system. The economic system depends on continuous state intervention for the elimination

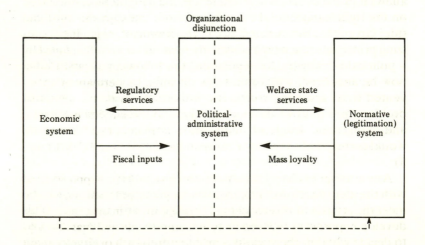

Figure 2   *Three subsystems and their interrelationship*

of its internal malfunctions; for its part, the economic system transfers – by means of taxation – portions of the value produced in it to the political-administrative system. The political-administrative system is linked to the normative system by the expectations, demands and claims ('specific demands', according to Easton) with which it is confronted and to which it reacts through welfare state and organizational services. On the other hand, the autonomy and capacity of the political-administrative system to act is dependent on 'mass loyalty' ('diffuse support'). These functional legitimation processes are determined by the political system itself, namely, by its welfare state, ideological (Poulantzas, Miliband) and repressive functions, as well as by autonomous, 'pre-political' changes in the system of norms, ideologies and class consciousness. The problem facing the political-administrative system is not merely that of maintaining a specifically 'positive balance' between essential regulatory services and fiscal inputs (left side of the diagram) or between mass loyalty and welfare state or repressive policies (the right side). It also consists in dealing with these two problem complexes (the avoidance of economic malfunctions and political conflicts) in such a way that one type of problem is not solved by aggravating the other: malfunctions must not be allowed to turn into conflicts, and vice versa. In order to solve this problem, the political-administrative system must undergo an internal 'disjunction' that allows it to achieve a relative insulation of the problems represented on the right-hand side of the diagram from those on the left-hand side. Given that the maintenance of the dominant, capitalist organizing principle of exchange constantly *requires* – and is *challenged* by – political-administrative regulation, the following question must now be answered: why cannot this dilemma be permanently prevented from assuming true crisis proportions so that a relatively problem-free path of development lying between the 'necessary' and 'dangerous' levels of intervention is maintained? This path would correspond to the field between the lines AB and CD (Figure 3).

Any attempt to clarify the concept of crisis must be supplemented with the identification of empirical phenomena and processes which meet the criteria of this concept. There is a need, in other words, to develop hypotheses that can be tested empirically and that allow us to decide whether there exists a problem-free path of development for the processes of state regulation. In order to generate such hypotheses, we will use a co-ordinate system whose x-axis indicates

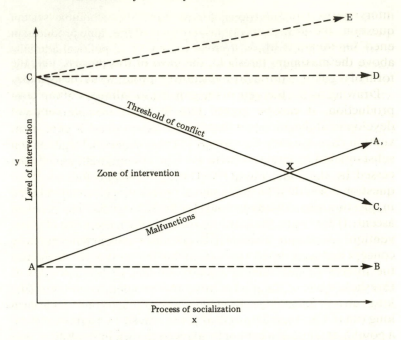

Figure 3   *Thresholds of state intervention*

a process of historical development and whose y-axis indicates the level of state intervention, i.e., the number and scope of regulatory services performed by non-market bodies. For each and every phase of development (i.e., for every point along the x-axis) there is a minimum and a maximum level of intervention.

The *minimum* level of intervention is defined by the 'inventory' of problems produced by the economic system. These problems potentially endanger its existence, but cannot be 'processed' and solved by this economic system. At the same time, a *maximum* level exists for every point on the x-axis; beyond this point, regulatory services and initiatives cease to compensate for the defects of the market-regulated process of creating surplus value, by in fact over-compensating, and thereby challenging the identity of the system regulated by exchange principles. In other words, beyond this maximum point interventions stimulate interpretations of needs which are both antagonistic to the system and which potentially subject the exchange system not merely to subsidiary political control but to actual political control. In the case of a level of intervention lying below the specific minimum threshold in question, the *process* of capitalist reproduction would be threatened. On the other hand, in the case of a level of intervention lying above the maximum threshold, the *form* of this process, i.e., the form of regulation through production for profit, would be violated.

Drawing on the theorem of the growing socialization of capitalist production, it can be argued that in the course of capitalist development the minimum threshold of the required level of intervention rises in a long-term sense (line AA). This argument is well substantiated by empirical evidence (the rising share of GNP processed by the state, etc.). However, the important (and open) question is whether the development of the specific maximum level in question also exhibits an equal (or perhaps even greater) rate of ascent. If this were the case, one could expect the 'zone of intervention' to remain constant (CD), or to expand, and the crisis concept deduced above would remain empirically unverified. Now the interesting hypothetical case is the one in which the upper threshold value of the level of intervention remains constant in the long run or – and this would be the toughest hypothesis – falls in the long run (CC). According to this hypothesis, there would have to be a point X at which the minimum and maximum thresholds intersect. This point would have to be interpreted as one at which the interventions necessary for the material reproduction of capitalist society are, at the same time, the kind which stimulate interpretations of needs which negate the capitalist form of social reproduction as such. This 'vanishing point' is however useful only for purposes of illustration. As stated at the beginning, I do not wish to use the concept of crisis to produce statements about 'events' which are external to, or which 'break into' the system. Rather, my aim is to identify laws of motion that can be represented as an inverse development of the minimum and maximum thresholds of the level of intervention in the process of capitalist socialization.[10] It is possible to identify five hypotheses that describe the interaction between those interventions necessary for preventing malfunctions and those which relate to conflicts (maximum threshold):

1 Lowi's formula, 'policies determine politics', can be interpreted as a lowering of the maximum threshold in reaction to a raising of the minimum threshold: the more numerous and visible the regulatory activities of the political-administrative system, the more intense the conflicts constituted by policies. The commitment of the

'process of policy formation' to giving preferential treatment to the functional problems of the capitalist economy – a commitment guaranteed by objective, political-organizational channels and mechanisms – implies material, social and temporal 'biases', i.e., privilege-granting rules whose effects in turn play an essential role in 'delegitimating' political conflicts. The analysis of these biases depends not only on empirical verifications of the connection between the limited 'potential for considering problems' and its resultant conflicts; it also requires detailed genetic accounts of the production of political conflicts by the bias-structure of policies.

2   The second hypothesis refers to the 'overburdening' of policy-making capacity by political conflict. As a way of pacifying and isolating centres of conflict the political system adopts strategies which either underregulate or overregulate (and therefore endanger) the system. In this case, the above-mentioned relationship between policies and politics is subject to obstructive repercussions.

3   The use of fiscal resources (for example, subsidies and transfer payments) can remedy as well as exacerbate problems at the level of malfunctions.

4   The use of legitimation resources can likewise be described by means of a double-sided hypothesis: a distinction must be made between the positive and negative results of their utilization.

5   As a regulatory resource, administrative rationality relates to the problem of disjunction, i.e., to the possibility or impossibility of separating and insulating developments of the minimum or maximum threshold.

The last three hypotheses are versions of the argument in support of the thesis of the self-obstruction of regulatory resources, which will now be explained. The 'environment' of the political-administrative system comprises the *economic* subsystem, which is determined by the developmental processes of the capitalist economy, and the *normative* or *legitimation* subsystem, which is determined by the dynamics of conflict and consensus processes. It is not necessary here to secure the concept of an 'organized system of action' against misunderstandings by referring to theories of action and decision-making. Rather, the concept of *regulatory resources* must at this point be examined more closely. The hypothesis that all three of the resources discussed below are subject to a process of cumulative self-obstruction will also be defended and illustrated. Finally, I shall try to characterize more precisely those deficit phenomena which result from the relative failure of regulatory resources in an environment that is characterized by self-contradictory processes of capitalist socialization.

The three resources, mentioned in Figure 2, include: the fiscal means of the political-administrative system, administrative rationality, and mass loyalty.

Fiscal resources

The socialization of production organized by the state apparatus depends upon the conversion of large and generally increasing portions of the gross national product into 'revenue' by withdrawing it from the process of surplus-value creation. This is accomplished through direct and indirect taxation, tariffs and state borrowing. Facing this conversion process on the side of expenditures are a great number of economically relevant functions of the state, which can be divided into:

1   activities that create the *pre-conditions* for capitalist production (for example, the socialization of private costs through infrastructure investments, the mobilization of capital);
2   the absorption of the side effects and costs of capitalist production;
3   the absorption of surplus capital (as defined by Baran and Sweezy) and the organization of surplus labour power through transfer payments or 'institutions'.

The crisis-prone deficits of this regulatory resource can – in agreement with James O'Connor – be conceptualized in the following way. Budgetary decisions concerning revenues and expenditures have the double function of creating the conditions for maintaining the accumulation process as well as partially hampering this accumulation process by diverting value from the sphere of production and utilizing it 'unproductively' in the capitalist sense. There can be discrepancies between these two functions – discrepancies that appear to be of a systematic nature. Apart from the numerous and complex reallocation processes which are evidently the result of budgetary strategies, and aside from the consequences these reallocations have for the problem of mass loyalty, the following types of discrepancies can already be discerned in the areas of economic regulation and programming:

1   It is possible that the state-funded infrastructural investments required to guarantee the viability of national capital at the international level grow to an extent which is incompatible with the short-term stabilization of economic growth. (This can be explained with reference to the anarchy thesis: capital is itself incapable of perceiving and realizing its long-term and collective conditions of existence.)

2   Another discrepancy is manifested in the inability of the state to achieve a synchronization of decisions in the areas of economic policy and fiscal planning.

3   Finally, the universal subsidization and regulation of economic processes via the state budget has a contradictory effect: while these subsidies become irreversible, their contribution to stabilization decreases through time.

The liberal assumption that social policy is a temporary 'aid to self-help' is no longer valid today. Similar views in the areas of economic policy and structural policy are equally unconvincing, for stabilization policy organized via state budgets produces ever more far-reaching demands and claims. This contradictory process can be seen as analogous to that of physiological addiction: the addict requires ever larger drug doses at the same time as the potential withdrawal phenomena that would follow a reduction of these doses become more and more crucial.

Administrative rationality

Administrative rationality, the second category of regulatory resources, is the ability or inability of the political-administrative system to achieve a stabilization of its internal 'disjunctions'. There are five preconditions for a 'system policy' that is 'rational' in this sense:

1   'Distance': the political-administrative system must be sufficiently isolated from its environment – the economic system and the process in which political demands and support is formed – in order to be *relatively* independent of its functional requirements or specific political demands.

2   In addition to this external differentiation, the political-administrative system must exhibit an internal differentiation which prevents interference between those institutions responsible for its legitimation and steering functions.

3   In spite of this necessary, two-sided differentiation, the political system requires co-ordination which prevents its various agencies and departments from acting in mutually contradictory ways; particular policies must not be allowed to cancel each other out.

4   The political system must have at its disposal sufficient information about the processes that take place in its environment, and which are relevant both for safeguarding the system and for avoiding conflicts.

5   Finally, the state must exhibit a forecasting capacity whose chronological range is congruent with its own 'planning horizon'.

All these conditions seem to be systematically undermined by the expansion of state functions. The *external differentiation* (or distance) requirement is impeded by the fact that the administration is compelled to enter into a symbiotic relationship of dependency with specific groups in order to be able to implement its policies at all. As a result, the distance required at the level of the formulation of policies is forfeited at the level of their implementation. The need for *internal differentiation* is – given the expansion of state functions – limited by the fact that the uncoupling of the administrative system from the political system is continuously blocked by the administration's need for support, or by the governing political parties' strategies for retaining power. It is obvious that *co-ordination problems* are multiplied by the expansion of the scope of state activity. Scharpf's suggestion that mutual non-interference could be guaranteed by delimiting only certain spheres of life as political is implausible because it would, in practice, merely amount to the selective non-consideration of already existing relations of interdependence. While the *capacity for processing information* can, in a purely technical sense, be readily increased, the reliability of information is reduced by the unpredictable strategic counter-reactions of co-participants within the environment of the state administration. Finally, these strategic counterreactions seem to produce a wide gap between the expanding chronological 'planning horizons' and the *actual forecasting capacity* of the state. These considerations can be summed up in the following hypothesis: the substantive, temporal and social expansion of administrative action is necessarily accompanied by an internal irrationalization of the organizational structure of the state administration.

Mass loyalty

The third regulatory resource, mass loyalty, can be described as the ability of the administrative system to win genuine acceptance for its structures, processes and actual policy outcomes. This ability is ultimately dependent on the cultural norms, symbols and self-understandings that the political system is capable of mobilizing. Of the mechanisms which can be assumed to *reduce* this ability, the following are important:

1   The political-administrative system must not only factually but also avowedly and programmatically assume the task of regulating and guiding the living conditions and actual life chances of the mass of the population in accordance with accepted and acknowledged norms and expectations. This necessity leads to pretensions and to the assumption of responsibilities whose non-fulfilment is much more clearly visible and attributable than was the case in phases of social development in which the state actually assumed tasks of regulation and stabilization that were not in fact part of an avowed programme.

Thus, it is not the reduced level of success but the increased level of pretension of, say, social democratic social policy which subjects this policy to a permanent 'reality test' at the hands of the voting public. Accordingly, the level of articulated disappointments and public 'suits' rises.

2   In developed capitalist societies, it is to be expected that pre-industrial and primary group norms and symbols will be increasingly eroded. For this reason, the recourse to such norms and symbols for the purpose of political socialization and integration is (in post-fascist societies) less probable, or at least less successful. The reservoir of integrative symbolism evaporates. The extent to which it can be replenished by a growth- and prosperity-oriented 'substitute programme' seems to be limited by some of the following considerations.

3   Drawing upon the thesis of the tendency of capitalist societies towards anomie (Brückner), it can be expected that the formal inconsistencies between simultaneously held expectations and norms will lead to the destabilization of the political culture. While one would have to refer to studies of political socialization and political culture (for example, those of Free and Cantril), it appears that the coexistence of the Protestant ethic and hedonism, of individualism and norms of solidarity, and of acquired and ascribed

criteria can no longer be accommodated within the boundaries of social identity.

4   One further consideration, which is emphasized particularly by conservative authors, concerns the 'commercialization of the production of meaning'. The decisive structural element of norms is their possession of counterfactual validity. This is suspended by the process of commercialization. The validity of symbols and of their corresponding life-styles comes to depend on their actual ability to establish themselves in markets. As a result, it might also be expected that politically integrative symbols become superficial and subject to constant recall.

5   Finally, the growing 'decommodification', i.e., the with-drawal and uncoupling of an increasing number of social areas and social groups (surplus labour power) from market relations, might be expected to affect the discipline of the population by the com-modity form of industrial labour. The socializing effects of exchange relations and capitalist structures of domination undergo a relative decline in importance.

Towards a political crisis theory

While the hypothesis that state regulation has a self-obstructing character clearly requires more empirical evidence to be plausible, it does provide a conceptual framework for a *political* crisis theory. This theory enlarges the field of vision of traditional economic crisis theories in so far as it no longer traces the origins of crises exclu-sively to the dynamics of the sphere of production. Instead, it explains crises with reference to the inability of the political system to prevent and compensate for economic crises. In summary form, this inability results from the self-contradictory imperatives of state policy: while it must organize the dysfunctional social consequences of private production, state policy is not supposed to infringe on the primacy of private production. If state policy is to be adequate, however, it is forced to rely on means which either violate the dominant capital relation or undermine the functional require-ments – the legitimacy and administrative competence – of state regulation itself.

Notes and references

1   For the definition of this concept, see the introduction to W.-D. Narr and Claus Offe, *Wohlfahrtsstaat und Massenloyalität* (Cologne 1975).

2   Robert Dahl and Charles E. Lindblom, *Politics, Economics and Welfare: Planning and Politico-Economic Systems Resolved into Basic Social Processes* (New York 1971); see also, J. Stohler, 'Wirtschaftswachstum und Wohlfahrtsstaat', *Zeitschrift für Nationalökonomie*, **24** no. 4 (1964).

3   The type of activity encountered in bargaining processes contains normative, exchange-based and hierarchical elements. Because it lies on a different logical level, it can be neglected here – and not because of any wish to ignore its significance as a heterogeneous type. The question of whether this triad of social regulatory media is complete could be answered negatively by referring to the category of 'knowledge' or 'truth'; as is well known, this category plays a central role not only in the works of the theorists of 'post-industrial society' (Bell, Etzioni, Touraine), but also in sociological systems theory such as that of Luhmann. Here, however, instead of granting this category a measure of analytical autonomy, I prefer to deal with 'knowledge' as an element within the self-objectification or self-programming process through which social systems generate a 'practical contingency' over themselves.

4   A. Etzioni, *A Comparative Analysis of Complex Organizations* (New York 1961), pp. 23–40.

5   See the elaboration of this thesis in S. M. Miller *et al.*, 'Neo-imperialism critique: do the rich nations need the poor?', *New York University, Center for International Studies Policy Papers*, **4** no. 5 (1971).

6   This can be illustrated by a thought experiment: if a strangely selective natural catastrophe were to suddenly strike and physically destroy India, Indo-china, large parts of Latin America and Africa – and even if such a catastrophe were also to extend to the ghettoes of the large American cities and the poverty areas of the USA itself (or comparable areas of Europe, for example, Naples and southern Italy) – American imperialism would be confronted with medium-sized and intermediate-range problems of adaptation and adjustment. (Obviously, the same was not true of colonialism in its classic form.) This fact alone makes conceivable policies of unrestrained genocide, such as those pursued by the USA in Indo-China.

7   This conclusion is suggested by the following question: since the Second World War, which groups and social strata have been the

principal objects and victims of the coercive apparatus of the state and its *domestic* protection and defence functions? Certainly neither the organized working class nor the trade unions (whose 'disciplining' functions often resemble those of the police). The industrial working class as such has not been the object of the majority of acts of direct repression, and even the radical workers' parties have certainly not been the focal point of such repressive measures. Rather, the more groups are irrelevant for the maintenance or expansion of the material production process, the more systematically and frequently have they been the object of direct repression (cf. the student revolts and other institutional rebellions, the combating and control of ghetto resistance, and citizens' action groups who deviate from the 'rules of the game'). As is also shown by the 'incidence profile' of acts of state repression, the problem of preserving the system is a problem of warding off non-integrable elements on the periphery of the capitalist social structure.

8   This concept of 'interdependence' is itself in need of elucidation. It is normally taken to mean that the execution of every action, including the labour process, is not self-sufficient, but rather presupposes the execution of other (superordinate, co-ordinate or subordinate) actions. It follows that the disruption of the execution of one action produces a chain of resultant disruptions whose range increases as the amount of interdependence within the system increases: the system becomes more fragile and susceptible to disruption. These implications of the concept of interdependence are common to organic, mechanical and social systems. However, a social-scientific concept of interdependence must take into consideration the fact that social systems can make their own interdependence the subject of further development and full differentiation through the development of 'reflexive mechanisms' (Luhmann). Through such mechanisms, they acquire the ability to control their own susceptibility to internal disruption. This control is achieved, for example, through the temporary suspension of certain relations of interdependence, and the utilization of functional equivalents for a precarious function. This dimension of the concept of interdependence is applicable only to social systems, and it is important only in so far as social systems acquire a 'practical contingency' over themselves; in other words, they must possess elements sufficiently *autonomous* to be able to exercise control over other elements (and their mutual disruption). These formal considerations have an interesting consequence for the relationship between interdependence and autonomy: the larger the network of relations of interdependence

which is developed in the process of capitalist socialization, and the more susceptible to disruption the system formed by these relations consequently becomes, the greater the need for autonomous elements which manipulate and reflexively control the amount of disruption within the system.

9   At this point the type of crisis concept being utilized here should be recalled. The capitalist state, which can neither let the dominant economic system take care of itself nor seriously restrict or impinge on that system, exhibits a tendency to stray from the 'path of balance' defined by those contradictory conditions. This *tendency* is indicative of, and conducive to, crisis. The same logical configuration of simultaneously valid but contradictory functional imperatives serves as the basis of the theory of the historical tendency of the rate of profit to fall (i.e., individual units of capital can only accumulate by increasing their organic composition – but this is precisely what they must avoid doing in the interest of maintaining their rates of profit and thus their accumulation). In both cases, the use of this crisis concept does not prejudge questions about either the availability and effectiveness of 'counteracting tendencies' or the If and When of 'the breakdown'. Of course, just as little can be said conclusively about the quality of the social results of this crisis tendency; for instance, whether it will result in the establishment of a socialist society or in a continuing process of historically unproductive decay. This depends upon political practice which, although it can draw upon knowledge of crisis tendencies, cannot hide – lying in wait, as it were – behind knowledge of the certainty of the collapse of the system.

10   There is an obvious connection between, on the one hand, the inverse development of the thresholds determining the minimum and maximum possible levels of state intervention and, on the other, the crisis concept explained above: capital utilizes state organizations and regulations whose own inner dynamics – which are of course dependent on legitimation – cumulatively exacerbate the demarcation problem of 'negative subordination'.

2 'Ungovernability': the renaissance of conservative theories of crisis*

A number of structural similarities exist between neo-conservative theories of the 'ungovernability' of the state and society and the socialist critique of late-capitalist social formations.[1] For obvious reasons these similarities are not emphasized by either side. Such parallels become clearer when we compare the theoretical and practical constellations that determined the debate in 1968 with those ten years later. The comparison indicates that in both macrosociology and political science, theories of crisis have undergone a radical change in their socio-political 'base' or 'clientele'.

In 1968–9 *Leftists* were the ones who advanced the theoretical arguments and held the practical conviction that 'things cannot go on like this'. They assumed that class contradictions, in however modified a form, and the ensuing struggles must result in the dissolution of the basic structure of capitalism, together with its corresponding political constitution and cultural–ideological system. In a perhaps overly enthusiastic 'dismantling' of the corresponding basic assumptions, Koch and Narr have shown that the Left today lacks a solid foundation in crisis theory, something they claim can be found at most in the efforts of a few manipulators of scholastic concepts.[2] At the same time, the theoretical positions employed to defend the existing order, which was so strenuously affirmed in 1968, have been almost totally silenced. Today bourgeois consciousness is everywhere engaged in doomsday ruminations over its fate. The limits of growth and of the welfare state, the world economic, financial and environmental crisis – including the crisis of legitimation or 'the crisis of the authority of the state' – have become standard topics, presented in every conservative or liberal newspaper to characterize the national and international condition of society. The conviction that 'things cannot go on like this' today

* This essay first appeared in Jürgen Habermas (ed.), *Stichworte zur 'Geistigen Situation der Zeit'* (Frankfurt 1979), pp. 294–318.

inspires *conservatives*, while the crisis theories stemming from the critique of political economy have themselves become questionable, or at the very least are no longer capable of yielding the optimistic political conclusions that once constituted their very essence. Certain members of the Left, unable to rely on their theoretical certainties, are now displaying the withdrawal symptoms of a 'new irrationalism'. By contrast, it appears that theoretical and practical points are being scored by those who have for a long time considered political modernization in the direction of social democracy as a road to crisis.

Not only has the neo-conservative crisis literature almost completely removed the remnants of its Leftist counterpart from the sphere of public attention; it has also skilfully redefined and adapted for its own purposes certain positions and approaches that derive from the tradition of a critical theory of advanced capitalism (from theories of the fiscal crisis of the state, legitimation problems, conflicts associated with structural disparities and with peripheral social groups, ecological crises). But what is most remarkable is that this literature, or at least a large part of it, identifies crisis causes that are directly or indirectly connected with the continuing explosiveness of *class conflicts* or their inadequate institutionalization; that is, with the problem of the economic base. Sociologists and political scientists during the 1950s and 1960s sought to deny this problem, because they believed that it had found its definite solution in the 'modern' political economy. Much of this neo-conservative literature reads like a series of case studies confirming the Marxist thesis that bourgeois democracy and the capitalist mode of production stand in a precarious and immanently indissoluble relation of tension. The difference consists only in the fact that the neo-conservative theorists of crisis see the source of crisis and what they wish to eliminate not in conditions of capitalist *wage-labour* but, rather, in the institutionalized arrangements of welfare state mass democracy. 'That which Marxists erroneously ascribe to the capitalist economy,' writes Huntington, 'is in reality a result of the democratic political process'.[3]

I shall begin by addressing the political aspects of the crisis theory, which has shifted its base to the conservative camp, and will then turn to a presentation and critique of its analytic content. By way of conclusion, I shall return to the relationship between crisis and capitalist development.

The 'overburdened' state

The political aspects of the crisis theory result, first, from the diagnosis of the problem of ungovernability, that is, its conceptual links with specific pragmatic premises; second, from the prognosis, or the prediction regarding the probable course and the individual symptoms of the crisis; and third, from the recommended therapy. Neo-conservatives, it should be noted, often employ a medical-biological metaphor in presenting their crisis theory; this has the effect, of course, of modelling the structural problems of society on the patient–doctor relationship and its connotations of authoritative expertise.

Let us begin by looking at the diagnosis. It details the immediate danger of a chronic or even acute failure of the state. This has two components: first, the overload of expectations to which state power is exposed under conditions of party competition, pluralism of associations, and relatively free mass media. This results in a constantly growing burden of expectations, obligations and responsibilities with which government is confronted and which it cannot escape. But why is government unable to fulfil them? This question is related to the other component of the diagnosis: the intervention and steering capacities of the state apparatus are in principle too limited to be able to process effectively the burden of these demands and expectations.

The first component of this diagnosis refers quite plainly to an 'overstretching' of claims to welfare-state services and democratic participation – an inappropriate politicization of themes and conflicts, whereby expression is given to 'the unbridled and mindless covetousness of the citizens'.[4] The second component of the diagnosis is related to the economic and political guarantees of freedom: an effective processing of the avalanche of claims would be conceivable only with the annulment of some of the constitutional guarantees whose continued existence ties the hands of state power. 'Whoever says A must also say B; whoever desires indivisible state responsibility must also be prepared to sacrifice many enjoyed freedoms.'[5] Such formulations of the problem recall, down to the last detail, certain determinations of the political crisis network found in the Marxist tradition. From this latter viewpoint, the concept of 'liberal democracy' presents a deceptive unity of elements that in fact are not amenable to combination, indicating instead ruptures that are at most temporarily obscured under conditions of prosperity.[6] Unlike the 'false apocalypse of the bourgeoisie' (J. Schumacher), which in the 1920s accounted for the popularity of, say, Spengler's *Decline of the West*, the new crisis scenarios of the conservatives have proven resistant to the Marxist critique of ideology and to the suspicion of being mere propaganda and mystification. This is due not only to their clearly improved theoretical quality, but also to the fact that they retain – albeit for opposing political purposes – a central component of the political-economic crisis argument that the theoretical Left had long held to constitute its own theoretical superiority.[7]

Crisis symptoms are expressed, so the conservative analysis continues, in the frustrations caused by the disparity between the volume of claims and the government's steering capacity. This leads to a noticeable loss of confidence between party organizations on the one hand and their voters and members on the other, which results from the fact that the parties must almost necessarily frustrate the expectations they generate in obtaining a governing majority.[8] The promises of a given party platform remain *unfulfilled*, whereas the 'blunt' methods (such as wage and price controls, increased taxation, additional regulation), whose use the party had previously renounced explicitly, must none the less be put into operation.[9]

The disappointments accumulated in this manner may release their explosive force in one of two directions. Either they lead to a polarization within the party system, to a re-ideologizing and 'fundamentalizing' of the praxis of a particular opposition, which then seeks to avoid the predicament of the tension between expectations and performance capacity through 'principled' alternative programmes; or, where such a polarization process does not occur, there is the likelihood of a decrease in the canalization capacity of political parties, in their ability to articulate the electoral will and, conversely, to contribute to its formation. In this case it is further to be expected that the established parties will be opposed by political movements, for whom the goal of parliamentary struggle and the possible exercise of governmental power is not of primary significance. Both alternatives – polarization within the party system and polarization between the party system and social movements operating in a non-parliamentary fashion – must lead to a further exacerbation of the basic situation. The level and volume of articulated demands increase, just as the action capacities of the besieged state decrease. Thus, in essence, the prognosis implies that the basic

discrepancy between claim level and performance capacity un-
leashes a dynamic ensuring that this discrepancy is reproduced in
intensified form: an ungovernable system always becomes more
ungovernable. One cannot assume the existence of built-in mechanisms or, as in economic cycles, so-called self-healing forces that will
reverse the trend (for the opposite view see Huntington).[10] Rather,
at some unknown but possibly not too distant point in time, extensive breakdowns and even a disintegration of organized state power
will occur.

This course of development is to be prevented by a therapy whose
two variants correspond to the two components of the diagnosis.
The therapy can either seek to diminish the overloading of the
system with claims, expectations and responsibilities, or it can
attempt to enhance its steering and performance capacity.

Let us begin by examining the first variant, claim reduction. If I
am not mistaken, three forms of implementation are at issue here.
They are of particular interest in the Federal Republic because they
still seem to be mostly at the 'testing' and development stages
(although they are not clearly connected with the aforementioned
arguments of crisis theory). In classifying these strategies I am
making use of Luhmann's assumption, according to which there are
in principle four societal media through which social claims and
expectations can be processed:

1 political power relations;
2 monetary, exchange and market relations;
3 cultural norms or socialization relations;
4 the medium of 'truth' or knowledge.

It follows that if, as the crisis hypothesis of 'ungovernability'
suggests, the *political* medium of processing demands is to be unburdened, then each of the other three media must be considered as
the object of a possible strategy.

The proposal to redirect claims that lie beyond the 'boundaries of
the welfare state' towards monetary exchange relations, that is,
markets, is on everyone's lips today. The watchwords are the
'privatization' or the 'deregulation' of public services and their
transference to competitive private enterprise. Examples of this
proposal include the conversion of public services from the support
of 'objects' to that of needy 'clients', as in transportation policy or,
more generally, the introduction of cost-covering fees for residual
public services. Other key phrases include the West German

Council of Economic Advisers' 'minimum wage unemployment' or even Friedman's 'natural unemployment' – i.e., diagnoses of employment problems that recommend the re-establishment of a functioning market mechanism to dispose of such problems. This list of examples of reprivatization also includes liberal proposals for industrial policy. In essence, this liberal policy aims at, or limits itself to, demolishing protectionist enclaves that shelter individual sectors of the economy from the innovation-promoting fresh air of national and international competition. Generally it is a question of strengthening the workings of the mechanisms of 'exit' against those of 'voice' (Hirschman) – specifically, of dismantling the mechanisms of welfare state security, as well as the political and economic power positions occupied by the trade unions in their struggle to establish and defend these mechanisms.[11] It is expected that the solution to the problem of ungovernability will come from a restoration of the mechanisms of competition, which are supposed to arrest both inflation in the narrow sense and political demand inflation in the broader sense. In this connection mention must also be made of the projects that in the Federal Republic are associated with the slogan 'the new social question'; while initially directed to a 're-examination' of the social welfare functions of the state, these projects in fact amount to the reduction of these welfare functions.

By contrast, the second strategy, which of course can be combined with this first strategy of claim reduction, goes deeper. It is directed to the institutions of social control, to the agencies that regulate the formation and preservation of social norms as well as cultural and political value orientations. This second strategy seeks to promote values like self-restraint, discipline and community spirit, to fortify national and historical consciousness, and to contain the post-acquisitive values elaborated in the progressive doctrines of educators and school reformers. This last aim is to be accomplished with an alternative pedagogy that confronts questionable socio-political circumstances with the slogan 'Dare to Teach!' (*Mut zur Erziehung*), and which proceeds pedagogically from the maxim 'That's just the way things are' (F. K. Fromme). Operating in the realm of socialization, these strategies employ a wide range of tactics – from praise for the 'earnestness' of vocational training on the shop floor to attacks on broadcasting freedom, from the strengthening of parental rights in schools to the political disciplining of social studies teachers. What is important to emphasize is that in these strategies, 'deviant' interests, claims and socio-political orientations are to be brought under control at their point of origin, whereas the first strategy (of claim reduction) is concerned with transferring the modalities of their fulfilment into extra-political 'market' domains.

Third, and finally, those claims and demands upon the political-administrative system that can neither be prevented at their source nor shunted into other domains can be checked through the installation of filter mechanisms that decide which claims merit being heard – whether certain claims should even be taken seriously as political inputs, or whether they should be dismissed as unrealistic or inadmissible. These filter mechanisms perform the function of rendering cognitive judgements, which themselves stand above the specific claimants and the institutions of a democratic process of will formation, and are not to be attributed to them. In the Federal Republic, the Federal Constitutional Court performs the role of an institution that, independent of, and beyond the influence of, intra-group conflict, renders judgements regarding the common good.[12] The striking functional gains made by the Court in recent years can be interpreted almost entirely as the functional aspect of a resistance to claims; the same is true for other authorities, such as the West German Council of Economic Advisers and other scientific advisory bodies. Within political science and political philosophy increased attention has also been accorded the notion of an authority that stands above parties, counsels moderation, and claims a privileged access to knowledge of the common good.[13] Its promoters are active journalistically as well, either in defending the state against an overburdening of claims by social groups or in discrediting those claims.

I shall reconsider the question of whether and under what conditions these three claim-reducing strategies are realistic after I present the other main variant of the therapy that follows from the ungovernability diagnosis. This encompasses all strategies that, in the conflict between steering capacity and its overburdening by claims, concentrate not on the reduction and warding off of demands but, on the contrary, on an increase in the state's steering capacity. With regard to this second therapy, I should like to distinguish between an administrative and a political version.

The *administrative* strategy for the improvement of governmental steering and performance capacities – as stated in, say, the first draft of the Social Democratic Party's *Orientierungsrahmen '85* (a long-term policy document accepted by the SPD in 1972) – provides for an increase in the state's share in the gross national product. It seeks to expand quantitatively and fiscally the room for manoeuvre the state has at its disposal. Likewise the regulatory capacity of the government is to be improved qualitatively and organizationally, in order to achieve a higher degree of efficiency and effectiveness in political and administrative actions. At this level are to be found jurisdictional and functional reforms, an increased use of social indicators, the techniques of programme budgeting and of cost-benefit analysis, and especially the concepts developed by Scharpf for improving the representation and consideration of the actually operative relations of interdependency in the process of policy formulation.[14] This strategy of administrative modernization is based on the principle of expanding the state's horizon for conceptualizing and acting – in both an objective sense, through a consideration of actual interdependencies, and a temporal sense, according to the principle of active-reformative, long-range planning and problem anticipation.

Reflection and experience demonstrate rather quickly that this kind of expansion of horizons is possible only if the consensual basis or the ability of the political-administrative system to absorb conflict can also be expanded. In other words, interdependencies can be adequately considered and long-term policies adequately conceptualized only if the requisite basis of trust and confidence is successfully consolidated. The objective and temporal expansion of the performance capacity of governmental policy can succeed only if this corresponds to an expansion of the social alliances and mechanisms of integration on which it is to be based. Thus 'consensus' becomes the decisive bottleneck.[15] Consequently, Scharpf recently emphasized (albeit in a manner requiring fuller explanation) the need for 'new interpretations of reality that more properly correspond to the changed situation'.[16]

The *political* version of the increased-performance strategy draws the consequences from this insight, most clearly in those political systems dominated by strong social democratic and labour parties. The arrangements that underlie Swedish economic and labour market policy, the Austrian 'social partnership', the German 'concerted action', the National Economic Development Council used in Great Britain by Labour and Conservative governments alike, and the 'social contract' between governments and trade unions – all these are examples of the attempts – intensified in the 1960s and 1970s – to enhance the performance capacity and steering effectiveness of state actions. This was attempted not only through intra-administrative forms of co-ordination, but also through an institutionalization of alliances and consultative mechanisms among government, trade unions, employers' associations, organizations of managerial personnel and even consumer groups.[17]

Yet such consultative mechanisms, which under the title 'liberal corporatism' have recently generated lively interest in political science, are highly unstable constructions. This is evident in two respects. First, they represent extra-parliamentary forms of political representation and, to this extent, are in competition with the 'proper' channels of political will-formation. This relationship of competition remains ambiguous in terms of constitutional law. Second, it is altogether unclear in which relationship and about which questions groups are entitled or even obligated to negotiate. Nor is it any clearer what binding force the results thus achieved could have on either the government or the participating members.[18] The solution to these difficulties lies, paradoxically, in a type of organized formlessness: strict shielding from publicity, informal discussions, personal agreements, cultivation of an attitude of concern. These are the preferred means of attaining a para-constitutional co-operation on which every effort to enhance the performance and steering capacity of state policies depends.[19] Decisive for the creation of such alliances is the question of whether the organized interests affected by state policy are prepared to renounce their power to obstruct (which they possess in great measure), despite the fact that the interdependencies resulting from any given state policy become more and more extensive.

Given this brief summary, the highly descriptive value of the ungovernability thesis should be obvious. In my opinion the two components of the diagnosis fully and correctly circumscribe the functional problems that now confront the capitalist welfare and interventionist state. The prognosis appears to be confirmed by a wealth of symptoms, manifested in the development of both the party system and the social movements of these countries, particularly the Federal Republic. And the five therapeutic approaches (reliance on markets, social control, expertise, administrative rationalization, and liberal-corporatist arrangements) appear to comprise almost fully the reorganization strategies being practised, particularly in north-west European political systems, through explicit or implicit references to the ungovernability thesis.

The explanation and control of crisis

Marxists also affirm the partial validity of the conservative crisis theory. A policy statement of the German Communist Party (DKP) asserts that 'the capacity of governments to function has once again been called into question'.[20] Just as conservatives adapt certain Leftist theorems, so their analyses are in turn appropriated in Marxist and socialist theory. (See the characteristic position adopted by Wolfe with regard to Huntington's *The United States*: 'One need not agree with the Trilateral Commission's conclusions to be sympathetic to the analysis'.)[21] In view of such unanimity we must ask whether the theoretical differences separating the liberal-conservative and materialist approaches in the social sciences have actually evaporated and whether the differences result less from the analysis itself than from the normative criteria and political aims with which the analysis is associated. In other words, in a situation where everyone is convinced of the facts of crisis and where general agreement exists regarding its symptoms and course of development, one is faced with the question of the specific political-theoretical role of crisis theories. The accused, who is indicted by the conventional crisis theories of the historical-materialist tradition, surprises the accuser not only by confessing without reserve but also by asking for sanctions that were by no means sought by the accuser. Thus it must be asked if the heirs of the Leftist crisis theory are still able to offer insights and points that will not immediately be stolen by adversaries who bend them to fit their own ideology.

If one wishes to speak seriously of a crisis *theory*, then answers must be provided – beyond current scenarios and the pragmatic search for therapies – for at least two questions thus far unmentioned. First, what is the causal mechanism that in societies of advanced capitalist welfare states always produces the re-emergence of a discrepancy between expectations and the political-administrative steering capacity? To continue with the medical metaphor, what is the etiology of the ungovernability phenomenon? Second, and analogously, what justifies the expectation that the individual remedying strategies I have distinguished would be appropriate, either alone or in some combination, for bringing the problem under control? Can the therapy be justified as a causal therapy? The answers to these two questions will ultimately indicate whether the ungovernability thesis is a scientific social theory that must be taken seriously, or whether it is rather a crisis ideology conceived out of pragmatic considerations.

We can begin by looking at the various hypotheses and approaches that attempt to explain the origin of the problem. They can again be subdivided into those that are directed to an explanation of the growing pressures of expectation, and those directed to the (relatively) decreasing steering capacity of the state.

According to a social-psychological theory of Maslow the level and type of desires and demands directed to the political-administrative system express a developmental pattern in which each achieved level of need satisfaction allows for the actualization of a qualitatively new category of needs. The empirical investigations conducted by Inglehart into the change of values in West European social systems can be interpreted within the framework of this social-psychological theory: material needs, those directed to the economic and military securing of social life, will permit, as soon as they are nearly satisfied, a different category of needs to step into the foreground – namely, post-acquisitive needs, such as those for an actualization of universal moral, political and aesthetic values.[22] An independent logic or an independent meaning in the development of world views and moral systems has also been espoused by Habermas, whose theory of motivation crisis lays particular emphasis on the irreversibility of an achieved level of moral consciousness.[23]

Various approaches in the discipline of the sociology of culture – which are best understood as versions of the secularization thesis – refer, by contrast, to a process of deinstitutionalization. Scientific rationality and the welfare state are seen to destroy the agencies of social control and the bearers of traditional values. This development results in the dissemination of a political-moral and aesthetic hedonism whose satisfaction in turn engenders a further extension of the welfare state.[24] The agencies of the welfare state therefore produce, through paradoxical and latent functions, the very problems they are manifestly concerned with removing.[25] Thus Klages observes a 'systemic crisis of a fundamental nature' in the fact that there is 'a wide gap between the self-confidence, the societal understanding and the "objective" achievements of ruling political elites on the one hand, and the social-psychological realities of the subjective state of mind of individuals in welfare-state democracies on the other'.[26] In a narrower sense theories in the discipline of political science lay particular emphasis on the

claim-inflating effect of party competition: through their programmes, political parties stimulate citizens' demands and expectations that subsequently prove unrealistic, thus causing a spiral of
constantly re-induced forms of 'relative deprivation'.[27] It has also
been asserted that the international transfer of the norms underlying such demands and the effects of the competition among
systems will result in a steady and uncorrectable overburdening of
the state apparatus. Recently a role has been played by a hypothesis
developed in the sociology of organizations, according to which the
officers of large organizations like trade unions, in order to maintain
their organization's internal cohesiveness and to secure themselves
vis-à-vis competing organizations, are structurally forced to
advance particularly drastic demands. This is especially the case in
the discussion of organized interests (and the desirability of their
taming through legal regulation and restriction).[28] Thus, for
instance, Margaret Thatcher recently expressed the view that in
reality the conflict is not between trade unions and the state but,
rather, among union leaders who themselves compete for higher
wages because of organizational pressures. An additional factor in
the crisis-engendering increase of demands is said to be evident in
the specific interests of the officials who administer the welfare
state. It is argued that, while supposedly concerned with the welfare
of the citizenry, these officials are in fact pursuing their own egoistic
claims to power and patronage. (Schelsky even ascribes to them the
character of a class.)[29]

Finally, proponents of systems-theoretical and welfare economics
models offer the explanation that under conditions of high societal
complexity – which, owing to high informational costs, cannot be
adequately conveyed either to the individual voter or to the
members of an interest organization – there is always a tendency for
an increase of claims and an overstraining of the political system.
This is said to result from the fact that the side effects of the
demands (such as inflation) are diffuse and therefore will not be
considered by the individual making the demands.

The complexity argument also plays a role in explanations of the
relatively or even absolutely decreasing steering capacity of the
state. Basic to these explanations is the claim that an exponential
growth occurs in the number of strategic criteria that must be
observed by state institutions when processing policy demands.
Also basic is the claim that there is a corresponding increase in the
veto power of those whose co-operation is essential for the

realization of such programmes.[30] Another widely disseminated argument, one that is found in democratic theory, and that seeks to account for deficient governmental steering capacity, is that which asserts that party competition and periodic election campaigns obstruct governmental action and planning (which are necessarily long-term in nature). It is claimed that these discontinuities constantly hamper both the conceptualization and implementation of governmental programmes.[31] It is evident that both of these arguments provide a direct grounding of and functional justification for attempts to extend the system of 'liberal corporatism' (and in this specific sense hasten the 'socialization' of public policy-making). The partial delegation of political-administrative decisions to 'mixed', semi-governmental authorities appears, at first glance, to be advantageous, in that the partner in the strategic planning and execution of policy can to a certain extent be bound and sworn to co-operation. The proposal to delegate policy also has the additional advantage of relatively insulating such decision procedures against the rhythm and disruptive influence of election periods and election campaigns.

What is conspicuous in this certainly incomplete list of explanations of the ungovernability phenomenon is the fact that it says little about the concrete objects of conflict that constitute the substance of the demands and expectations. It also says little about the character of those matters that both require regulation, but which also confound the steering capacity of the state. Of course, the proposed remedies for the problem of ungovernability identify, at least indirectly, which categories of demands and expectations must be reduced and neutralized, namely the individual and collective reproduction needs of labour power. And they also identify the specific obstacle on which the steering capacity of the state founders, namely, the fact that the social power as well as the blackmail capacity of capital (its ability to abstain from investing) can repel state intervention. At any rate, no great interpretive effort is required to decipher the stated ungovernability crisis as a manifestation – one no longer amenable to political mediation – of the class conflict between wage-labour and capital or, more precisely, between the political reproduction demands of labour power and the private reproduction strategies of capital. In this way, to be sure, no more is accomplished than an exercise in translation. One conceptual language is decoded with the aid of another. The satisfaction that might be derived from this is lessened, I believe, by the recognition that while this translation results in the loss of a few details that are explained quite convincingly by the theories advanced, no answer is given in response to the second question, that concerning the conditions for the success or failure of the five reorganization strategies I have distinguished.

The claims and the strengths of the Marxist response to the ungovernability and state crisis theories cannot be based merely on disclosing the fact that the contradictions and discrepancies of political-governmental organizations are rooted in socio-economic conditions, or that they are capable of being described in class categories. Rather, the Marxist response must be based on a demonstration of the fact that the opposition in capitalist societies between living and dead labour, between labour power and capital, is such a basic and chronic structural defect of these social systems that the therapeutic repertoire employed by the ungovernability theorists must be regarded as being so hopelessly inadequate that it in fact aggravates the crisis.

What, then, do the ungovernability theories have to offer with regard to the causal and, hence, effective character of the proposed therapy, as opposed to its symptom-suppressing or even symptom-intensifying properties? To be sure, not much here deserves the name of social-scientific argument. Instead, a resolute pragmatism or a simple utopianism predominates. Friedman's doctrine of the restoration of market mechanisms and the defusing of political crises through depoliticization owes its apparent logic, as Macpherson and many others have shown, solely to the fact that it ignores the differences between labour markets and all other markets.[32] Those who would like to reactivate pre-political cultural disciplinary practices already demonstrate their helplessness by their rabid tone[33] and by their complete lack of agreement as to which cultural and ideological traditions should furnish the norms that could restrain the much-lamented inflation of social demands. The dilemma of the conservatives consists precisely in the fact that they can neither rescue nor create anew those traditions and rules of collective life in whose name they do battle against reform politics and other manifestations of so-called political rationalism. They are thus left with no option – as Hanna Pitkin convincingly argues in her critique of Oakeshott – other than that of invoking elements of a tradition that has become fictional or of suppressing, both in theory and in practice, forms of political conflict.[34]

The New Objectivity of those like Biedenkopf and Schelsky, who place their trust in technocratic structures or in the Federal Constitutional Court also becomes entangled in the difficulty of having to justify political domination through non-political considerations. This is particularly evident in strategies that seek to increase administrative rationality and governmental performance capacity by simplifying the manner in which the state apparatus relates to its social environment. These strategies are recognized by their own proponents to be inadequate, for reasons having less to do with a failure in their methods of calculation than with insufficiencies in the consensual base upon which they depend – a point that is not, however, explained.

Finally, a self-reproach has been advanced against neo-corporatist proposals that seek to eliminate the problem of ungovernability through a far-reaching 'socialization' of state policy, or through alliances between large organizational groups and the state. According to this self-reproach, the state's overly extensive deployment of the scaffold for organized interests could bring about that scaffold's collapse. Organized interests would thus be devalued in their function as guarantors of stability in direct proportion to their institutional appropriation.[35]

It is clear that the conservative theoreticians of crisis – and, for that matter, their social democratic opponents – cannot, with any theoretically grounded certainty, grasp the causes of the crisis that they observe. Nor can their proffered remedies be shown to be causal therapies. The eclectic quality of their explanations of the political crisis of ungovernability is matched by the arbitrary and incoherent character of their proposed therapies. On the one hand, there is a diffuse lament regarding the societal conditions produced in the political and economic process of modernization; on the other hand there is an appeal to politicians and actors in the public sphere, urging them to leave behind their conventional scruples and to set out on the path back to stability and 'order'. In the conservative world view, the crisis of governability is a disturbance in the face of which the false path of political modernization must be abandoned and 'non-political' principles of order (such as family, property, achievement and science) must again be given their due. The polemic against political modernization – against equality, participation and socialism – therefore appears to require no consistent justification, no political programme, and no theory of political transition. Its proponents are content to forge a negative political coalition of those who (actually or purportedly) are threatened by reform. They do so through nebulous appeals to authoritative powers – which serious theoretical consideration would show to be either without substance or altogether subversive of their own appeals.

Capitalist development and 'ungovernability'

By contrast, Leftist theories of crisis actually do take seriously the difficult task of proving their claims. For them, crises are not only disturbances; they are also constellations that can be made historically productive. At the same time, crises are not contingent events that, like accidents, could just as well *not* occur; they are seen to be manifestations of tensions and structural defects inherent in the organizing principles of a particular social formation. Finally, Leftist theories infer that crises are problematic sequences of events, whose outcomes cannot be dealt with by certain models of the overcoming of crisis. The two most important questions raised by these theories can be stated as follows: what is the decisive structural defect of social systems labouring under symptoms of ungovernability? And, further, what arguments can be marshalled to provide a prognosis of failure for the strategies of reorganization that are unfolding before our eyes?

I shall examine these questions by way of conclusion, but not in order to attempt, even in outline, an answer to them. I merely wish to indicate, through a few observations, how difficult it is today to provide a concrete answer from the perspective of Marxist and other critical theories of society. (It was of course in the context of these critical theories that the framing elements of crisis theories originated – elements now being employed for purposes other than those originally intended.) Such an answer is of course necessary if the neo-conservative prophets and their pragmatic concepts are to be opposed theoretically (and not just politically).

Crisis theories can be constructed either in an objectivist or subjectivist manner; in other words, they can apply either to the being or to the consciousness of a social formation. If we understand crises as more than sudden eruptions and threatening exceptional circumstances within a social system, and if, in addition, we include in their definition the notion that in a crisis the economic and political principles of social organization are called into question (for otherwise we would have to speak either of recessions or accidents), then exclusively objectivist or exclusively subjectivist attempts to argue for the insurmountability of crisis tendencies in capitalist industrial societies must be judged as unsuccessful. Even if there were scientifically promising theories concerning the accumulation process, the rate of profit, and technological change, it would from today's perspective remain an entirely open problem where, if indeed anywhere, an economic crisis of this type would give rise to a consciousness capable of calling into question the foundations of the political and economic organization of capitalist society. For we know that economic crises promote not only the motivation to engage in fundamental opposition, but also the readiness to conform and adapt. It is likewise an open problem whether a far-reaching augmentation of demands, an increase in claims and a drastic withdrawal of moral support would indeed seriously impede the functioning of the accumulation process. Objectivist and subjectivist crisis theories that claim a measure of certainty are undermined today by one historical example or another, for they do not adequately take into account the elasticity of the different subsystems of welfare state capitalism. Hence any crisis theory based on the limited conceptual model of constantly increasing problems of valorization or of the growth of consciousness that is critical of the system, or of the interplay between the two, no longer seems very defensible. This is especially the case if one takes into account not only particular periods and actual economies but also the structure of the capitalist system as a whole.

By contrast, the term ungovernability is meant to refer to a special case of a general pathology of the system. All social systems are reproduced through the normatively regulated, meaningful action of their members, as well as through the mechanisms of objective functional connections. This distinction between social integration and system integration, between rules that are followed and subjectless, nature-like regularities that assert themselves, is basic to the entire sociological tradition. Pairs of concepts such as use-value and exchange-value, ego and id, action and structure, state and society, reasons and causes are expressions and applications of this fundamental distinction. By employing them we can also define more carefully the nature of the pathology indicated by the concept of ungovernability. Social systems may be said to be ungovernable if the rules their members follow violate their own underlying functional laws, or if these members do not act in such a way that these laws can function at the same time.

Given this schematization, one may note two diametrically

opposed sets of conditions under which a discrepancy between social and system integration, between acting and functioning definitely *cannot* arise. Social systems are reliably immune to pathologies of the ungovernability type if they either control and determine their functional conditions themselves through actions guided by meanings and norms or, conversely, if they erect a completely impenetrable barrier between socially significant motives and systemic functions, thus assuring that the functional laws are reliably protected against disturbances originating in the domain of action. Neither alternative finds real or complete counterparts in the societies with which we are acquainted; they are hypothetical or 'ideal' solutions, which in opposing ways aim to abolish any potential interference between system and social integration, between the sphere of rule and the sphere of regulations.

The peculiarity of capitalist industrial societies consists in the paradoxical fact that they pursue *both* 'ideal solutions', attempting to solve the problem of their reproduction in contradictory ways. The ownership of the means of production, market competition and the private use of capital are institutional means that serve to separate the problem of system integration from the process of will-formation, collective action and societal control. For an essential feature of markets is that they *neutralize* meaning as a criterion of production and distribution. In the process of capitalist industrialization, material production is uncoupled, step by step, from wilfully mediated (political and traditional) steering mechanisms and delivered over to the laws of exchange relations. 'Interests' take the place of both 'passions' and virtues.[36] The political and normative neutralization of the sphere of production and markets is connected with the phenomenon of secularization. The validity of norms is refined and relativized by the causality of market laws. But this equation underlying the process of modernization can prove itself only if the norm-free self-regulation of the market process is adequate for guaranteeing systemic integration or balance. This is not the case, however, for two reasons. First, markets can only function if they are *politically* institutionalized, that is, embedded within a framework of rules established by the state (such as the monetary system or contractual law). To use the classic metaphor, the clock must still be set, wound and occasionally repaired by a skilled – and at the same time consciously self-restraining – ruler. Second, because the market mechanism functions only by virtue of the action of those who are included in it as 'living' labour power, their normative claims and willingness to perform are the resources upon which the accumulation process stands or falls. The institution of the labour 'market' and 'free wage-labour' is a fiction, since what is of interest, positively and negatively, in the commodity called labour power is indeed what distinguishes it from all other commodities, namely, that it is in fact living labour power that, one, does not arise for the purpose of saleability, two, cannot be separated from its owner, and three, can be set in motion only by its owner. This inextirpable subjectivity of labour power implies that in wage-labour the categories of action and functioning, of social and system integration are inextricably intertwined. Thus, while the emergence of a differentiated and normatively neutralized or 'private' market sphere tends to solve the problem of societal reproduction precisely by segregating the functional level from the level of action (i.e., anonymous regularities from rules that are followed consciously), the organizing principle of wage-labour, which emerges as the other side of the privatization of capital, presses towards the opposite solution. Action orientations and functional conditions fuse into one another, because labour power is governed simultaneously by will and by the market, and because the process of accumulation does not function without political regulation that requires legitimation.

Capitalist societies are distinguished from all others not by the problem of their reproduction, that is, the reconciliation of social and system integration, but by the fact that they attempt to deal with the basic problem of all societies in a way that simultaneously entertains two solutions that logically preclude one another: the differentiation or privatization of production *and* its politicization or 'socialization' (in the Marxian sense). These two strategies thwart and paralyse each other. As a result the capitalist system is confronted constantly with the dilemma of having to abstract from the normative rules of action and the meaningful relations between subjects without being able to disregard them. The political neutralization of the spheres of labour, production and distribution is simultaneously confirmed and repudiated. Developed capitalist industrial societies do not have at their disposal a mechanism with which to reconcile the norms and values of their members with the systemic functional requirements underlying them. In this sense, these societies are always ungovernable, and it is largely due to the favourable circumstances associated with a long wave period of economic prosperity prior to the mid 1970s that they were able to live with this phenomenon of ungovernability. Only if one ignores these structural conditions of ungovernability can one be affected by the mood of alarm being spread by the neo-conservative crisis literature. Only on the basis of this ignorance could one imagine that the problem of ungovernability could be tackled successfully by trimming to size the rules and norms proper to action, so that they might again harmonize with the functional imperatives and 'objective laws' underlying the system. In fact it is the potency of these imperatives themselves that must be curbed and rendered capable of subordination to political-normative rules. (This contrary conclusion is of course identical to the one drawn by the Left from the same analytic scheme.) Only then would it be possible to mediate social norms and claims with imperatives that had been freed from their rigidity.

In the Federal Republic, the neo-conservative crisis literature performs the function, among other things, of preventing discussion of political solutions to the governability crisis; instead, it pretends to initiate this discussion. Its proposals for adapting consciousness to some poorly-defined moral traditions and for adjusting claims to lowered expectations constitute a pseudo-solution to the problem of ungovernability. In this respect the Anglo-Saxon (not to mention the Italian) political science literature is far superior, at least in regard to its impartiality. In the past few years, I have encountered within this literature many references to the following statement by Gramsci. This statement assigns a good part of the German ungovernability literature its historical place: 'The crisis consists precisely in the fact that the old is dying and the new cannot be born; in this interregnum a great variety of morbid symptoms appear'.[37]

Notes and references

1 Since 1974 the concept of ungovernability has become a standard topic in international political science and political journalism. In the meantime a number of prominent social scientists have participated in its scholarly utilization. See the following collections: W. Hennis *et al.*, *Regierbarkeit: Studien zu ihrer Problematisierung*, vol. 1 (Stuttgart 1977); M. Crozier *et al.* (eds.), *The Crisis of Democracy* (New York 1975); M. Th. Greven, B. Guggenberger and J. Strasser (eds.), *Krise des Staates? Zur Funktionsbestimmung im Spätkapitalismus* (Darmstadt/Neuwied 1975); G. K. Kaltenbrunner (ed.), *Der überforderte*

schwache Staat: Sind wir noch regierbar? (Munich 1975); A. King
(ed.), *Why Is Britain Becoming Harder To Govern?* (London 1976); D.
Frei (ed.), *Überforderte Demokratie* (Zurich 1978).

2   C. Koch and W. -D. Narr, 'Krise – oder das falsche Prinzip Hoffnung',
Leviathan, 4 (1976), pp. 291–327.

3   S. Huntington, 'The United States', in Crozier *et al.*, *The Crisis of
Democracy*, p. 73.

4   Quoted from p. 39 of B. Guggenberger, 'Herrschaftslegitimierung
und Staatskrise – Zu einigen Problemen der Regierbarkeit des
modernen Staates', in Greven *et al.*, *Krise des Staates?*, pp.
9–59.

5   ibid., p. 41.

6   A. Wolfe, *The Limits of Legitimacy, Political Contradictions of Contemporary Capitalism* (New York 1977).

7   H. M. Enzensberger, 'Zwei Randbemerkungen zum Weltuntergang',
Kursbuch, 52 (1978), pp. 1–8.

8   The growing functional weakness of political parties as a medium for
political articulation and integration in capitalist democracies is a
finding that can throw light on parallel phenomena. In any case, the
'suspicion that in the developed societies of the OECD world traditional party democracy is no longer a viable means of effecting necessary changes' unites, in a striking way, observers from the Right, the
Centre, and the Left. The quotation is from R. Dahrendorf, 'Krise der
Demokratie? Eine kritische Betrachtung', in Frei (ed.), *Überforderte
Demokratie*. The view from the Right is typified by S. Brittan, 'The
economic contradictions of democracy', in King (ed.), *Why Is Britain
Becoming Harder To Govern?*; and by W. Hennis, *Organisierter
Sozialismus: Zum 'strategischen' Staats-und Politikverständnis der
Sozialdemokratie* (Stuttgart 1977), and 'Parteienstruktur und
Regierbarkeit', in Hennis *et al.*, *Regierbarkeit*, pp. 150–95. For the
view from the Centre, see S. Berger, 'Politics and antipolitics in
Western Europe in the seventies', *Daedalus* (Winter 1979), pp. 27–50;
and, from the Left, W. -D. Narr (ed.), *Auf dem Weg Zum Einpar-
teienstaat* (Opladen 1977).

9   A. King, 'Overload: problems of governing in the 1970's', *Political
Studies*, 23 (1975), pp. 283–96, especially p. 285.

10   Huntington, 'The United States'.

11   A. Hirschman, *Exit, Voice and Loyalty* (Cambridge, Mass. 1970).

12   See H. von Arnim, *Gemeinwohl und Gruppeninteressen: Die Durch-
setzung allgemeiner Interessen in der pluralistischen Demokratie*
(Frankfurt 1977).

13   ibid.; see also, Hennis *Organisierter Sozialismus*, and 'Parteienstruktur und Regierbarkeit'.

14   F. W. Scharpf *et al.*, *Politikverflechtung: Theorie und Empirie des kooperativen Föderalismus in der Bundesrepublik* (Kronberg 1975).

15   See R. Mayntz and F. W. Scharpf, *Policy Making in the German Federal Bureaucracy* (Amsterdam 1975).

16   F. W. Scharpf, *Die Rolle des Staates im westlichen Wirtschaftssystem: Zwischen Krise und Neuorientierung* (Berlin 1978), p. 16.

17   J. Douglas, 'The overloaded crown', *British Journal of Political Science*, **6** (1976), pp. 483–505, especially pp. 494ff.

18   See C. Offe, 'Die Institutionalisierung des Verbandseinflusses – eine ordnungspolitische Zwickmühle', in U. von Alemann and R. Heinze, (eds.), *Verbände und Staat: Vom Pluralismus zum Korporatismus* (Opladen 1979), pp. 86–7.

19   Douglas, 'The overloaded crown', pp. 499–500.

20   German Communist Party, *Entwurf, Programm der DKP* (1977), p. 20; see also E. Lieberam, *Krise der Regierbarkeit – Ein neues Thema bürgerlicher Staatsideologie* (Berlin/GDR 1977).

21   Wolfe, *The Limits of Legitimacy*, p. 329.

22   R. Inglehart, *The Silent Revolution: Changing Values and Political Styles among Western Publics* (Princeton 1977). See also K. Hildebrandt and R. J. Dalton, 'Die Neue Politik: Politischer Wandel oder Schönwetterpolitik', *Politische Vierteljahresschrift*, **18** (1977), pp. 230–56.

23   J. Habermas, *Legitimation Crisis*, translated by Thomas McCarthy (Boston 1975).

24   D. Bell, *The Cultural Contradictions of Capitalism* (New York 1976).

25   N. Glazer, 'Die Grenzen der Sozialpolitik', in W. -D. Narr and C. Offe (eds.), *Wohlfahrtstaat und Massenloyalität* (Cologne 1978), pp. 335–51.

26   Quoted from p. 196 of L. Klages, 'Wohlfahrtstaat als Stabilitätsrisiko?', in H. Baier (ed.), *Freiheit und Sachzwang: Beiträge zu Ehren Helmut Schelskys* (Opladen 1978), pp. 192–207.

27   ibid.; see also M. Janowitz, *Social Control of the Welfare State* (Chicago 1978).

28   U. von Alemann and R. Heinze (eds.), *Verbände und Staat: Vom Pluralismus zum Korporatismus*.

29   H. Schelsky, *Die Arbeit tun die anderen. Klassenkampf und Priesterherrschaft der Intellektuellen* (Opladen 1975).

30   King, 'Overload: problems of governing in the 1970's', pp. 290ff.

31   Brittan, 'The economic contradictions of democracy'.

32 C. B. Macpherson, *The Life and Times of Liberal Democracy* (Oxford 1977). For a critique see J. Goldthorpe, 'The current inflation: towards a sociological account', in J. Goldthorpe and J. F. Hirsch (eds.), *The Political Economy of Inflation* (London 1978), pp. 186–214.

33 Hennis, *Organisierter Sozialismus*.

34 H. F. Pitkin, 'The roots of conservatism: Michael Oakeshott and the denial of politics', in L. A. Coser and I. Howe (eds.), *The New Conservatives – A Critique from the Left* (New York 1977), pp. 243–88.

35 Douglas, 'The overloaded crown', p. 507; similarly, see F. W. Scharpf, *Die Funktionsfähigkeit der Gewerkschaften als Problem einer Verbändegesetzgebung* (Berlin 1978).

36 Hirschman, *The Passions and the Interests*.

37 A. Gramsci, *Selections from the Prison Notebooks* (New York 1971), p. 276.

3 Social policy and the theory of the state*

Controversies concerning a social scientific theory of the state

In the liberal social sciences, the study of the state and social policy is guided by *formal* concepts. Liberal definitions of the sociological nature of the parliamentary-democratic constitutional state generally refer to the forms, procedures, rules and instruments of state activity, and not to state functions, their consequences and the contending interests within the state. For example, the Weberian definition of the state as the 'monopoly of physical violence' refers to the ultimate formal authority of sovereign acts, but reveals nothing of the direction of the relation of violence, i.e., by whom and against whom it is deployed. The concept of politics, understood as the solitary, decisive deeds of 'leaders' unconstrained by reason, becomes irrational, and renders such questions meaningless. The methodological concept of democracy prepared by Weber, and later applied by Schumpeter, has made his work the high court of liberal democratic and pluralist theory: as Weber says, democracy is a 'state-technical' and particularly effective mechanism of generating order, but theory can predict none of its outcomes.

This form of argument – which first posits content as contingent (i.e., as dependent on the will of great individuals, on empirical processes of coalition and bargaining or, finally, upon the variable, scientific-technical 'force of circumstances') and subsequently disregards it theoretically – also prevails in related disciplines like

* This essay, co-authored with Gero Lenhardt, was first presented as a paper to the opening plenary session of the Eighteenth Convention of the Deutsche Gesellschaft für Soziologie, Bielefeld, September 1976. It is here translated (and slightly abridged) from the version later published as 'Staatstheorie und Sozialpolitik – politische-soziologische Erklärungsansätze für Funktionen und Innovationsprozesse der Sozialpolitik', in C. V. Ferber and F. X. Kaufman (eds.), *Kölner Zeitschrift für Soziologie und Sozialpsychologie*, special issue, **19** (1977), pp. 98–127.

constitutional law and administration theory. For example, after the formation of the Federal Republic of Germany E. Forsthoff and W. Weber expended considerable intellectual energy contesting that the normative characterization (as given in the constitution) of the essence of the West German state as a 'welfare state' (*'Sozialstaat'*) was compatible with the formal principles of constitutional statehood. In other words, they sought to reduce the welfare state principle from the constitutional to the legislative level. Similarly, in the science of administration, strategies not determined by content or practicable, normative alternatives – the 'incrementalist' (Lindblom), 'opportunistic' (Luhmann) treatment of problems – are characterized as the empirically predominant form of administrative rationality.

In contrast, what we understand by the theory of the state may be described as the totality of attempts to expose this formalistic blind spot by means of social-scientific research. The reduction of the state and democracy to categories of *procedure* – a persistent and increasing tendency since the First World War – has permeated the flesh and blood of the liberal social sciences so thoroughly that not only do the marked systematic *gaps* in knowledge (of the content and *results* of procedures) go unnoticed as such, but scientific attempts by the respective professions to fill them are as a rule abandoned to official ignorance. This anti-formal social-scientific approach is typically interested in the 'dictatorial element' that 'every bourgeois democracy inevitably bears within it' (Kirchheimer). More generally, this approach is concerned with the concrete sources and material consequences of the deployment of state violence, in so far as these sources and consequences are not merely actual and therefore contingent, but intrinsic functional features of the organization of the bourgeois state apparatus. The point of departure of this kind of substantive investigation is not the establishment of particular modes of procedurally regulating state activity (for example, the constitutional state or democracy) but, rather, hypothetical notions about the functional connection between state activity and the structural problems of a (capitalist) social formation.

The intellectual need for substantive, functional analyses of the state, or of particular areas of state activity, is certainly not peculiar to Marxist social science. Von Ferber provides a recent and (in the German literature on social policy) influential example of the attempt to overcome formalistic definitions of social policy. He mounts an impressive indictment of the West German depiction of social policy as a system of state-allocated legal claims to transfers of money. He claims that this kind of depiction of social policy – one that is defined exclusively by the disciplines of economics and law – results in a 'narrow-mindedness' in the practice and theory of social policy as it relates to individuals or small communities.[1] Although this criticism of attempts to bind political phenomena to formal procedures (for example, 'democracy' to competition among elites for the votes of the population, or 'social policy' to legal claims to income transfers)[2] may be justified and convincing, it is not to fill the existing lacunae with the normative options of the observing social scientist, so that 'social policy' is instead conceptually related to justice, equality, security, freedom from want, and so on. Quite apart from the fact that prescriptions of the content of social policy can raise only narrowly restricted social and temporal claims to validity, little is achieved in such attempts at normative definition. We still do not know what the state, or social policy, *is* in a functional sense. We merely obtain a reply to the undoubtedly less interesting question: by what normative criteria do certain people who happen to be social scientists judge it? When it is claimed that a 'many-sided humane security or improvement of socio-cultural status' is the goal of social policy, or when it is recommended that particular parameters of individuals' life-conditions (for example, income) should 'not be allowed to operate restrictively'[3] the semantic-operative value of such assertions is questionable. Indeed, they serve to outline the preliminary formulation of a sociological investigation of social policy that may be termed the Ought–Is comparison: an image of the deficiencies and omissions[4] of existing practices is drawn, but the political relevance of this evidence of deficits remains doubtful.

These normative investigations are also considered to be the specific concern of sociological research into social policy. The problem, of course, is that the ought-value inputs are more or less directly drawn from the social conscience of the researcher. The research demonstrates that the practice of social policy fails to meet the politically progressive criteria of criticism that the research itself has adopted. Thereby, normative research projects are open to the objection, first, that they are incapable of sustaining the validity and necessity of their normative presuppositions, and, second, that they habitually overestimate their capacity to induce at least some unease among those political and administrative actors to whom proof of the discrepancies between 'ought' and 'is' is presented (and who, as a rule, have the power to finance – or refuse to finance – such research). In any event, any theoretical conception of social policy that seeks to 'stimulate . . . long-term, relevant, and continuous research into welfare-state interests'[5] must find a way to escape this twofold – methodological and political – dilemma.

Despite their opposition to formalistic (particularly economic and juridical) accounts of social policy, the normative[6] approaches actually confirm, rather than overcome, the unreconciled duality of spheres into which social reality is sundered by liberal social science. In both cases, procedural rules are counterposed to needs, 'facts' to 'values', formal to material rationality. It seems to us that both the formalistic and normative approaches to the study of social policy avoid the question that is of central importance within recent social-scientific discussions of the theory of the state, especially those stimulated by authors of a Marxist persuasion. How does state policy (social policy in this case) arise from the specific problems of an economic and class structure based on the private utilization of capital and free wage-labour, and what *functions* does this policy perform with regard to this structure?

Speaking generally, this question can be reformulated as follows: how does a given historical society reproduce itself while maintaining or altering its identity? What structures and mechanisms engender its continuity and identity or bring about breaches in that continuity? It is easy to show that the insight that this continuity is problematic, or at least is not guaranteed by any meta-social factors (for instance, human nature) is at the heart of any effort, whether by Comte or Marx, to formulate a *theory* of society. It is with this insight that sociology first becomes possible. Sociology masters this original, undiminished, central and ever-present problem to the extent that it is able to identify the *structural problems* that make the cohesion and historical continuity of society problematic rather than self-evident, and identifies the means of social 'integration' through which a given social system overcomes, or fails to overcome, its specific structural problems. In the theoretical tradition of historical materialism, the reference to the state regulation of bourgeois society has always played a role in hypothetically answering this latter question. Clearly, this hypothesis must be measured against evidence concerning both the specifically repressive, regulative, ideological and other functions of the state apparatus and its unique organizational components and policies. In what follows, we shall adopt this approach with respect to the domain of social policy.

On the social function of social policy institutions and the problem of functional frames of reference

Any analysis of social policy that seeks to answer such questions is well advised to begin with the hypothetical construction of a functional frame of reference, which must then prove its worth as the key to the explanation of empirical political processes.[7] We suggest that one such hypothetical point of reference for the functional explanation of social policy is: social policy is the state's manner of effecting the lasting transformation of non-wage-labourers into wage-labourers. This hypothesis is based on the following consideration. The process of capitalist industrialization is accompanied – and by no means only at its historical origins, when the phenomenon is especially evident – by the disorganization and mobilization of labour power. The spread of relations of competition to national and then world markets, the continual introduction of labour-saving technical changes, the undermining of agrarian labour and forms of life, the impact of cyclical crises: these and other factors effectively destroy, to a greater or lesser extent, the hitherto prevailing conditions of the utilization of labour power. The individuals affected by such events find that their own labour capacities – whose conditions of utilization they control neither collectively nor individually – can no longer serve as the basis of their subsistence. But this, of course, does not mean that they automatically hit upon the solution to their problems by alienating their labour power to a third party in exchange for money. Individuals do not automatically enter the supply side of the labour market. To assume such an automatism would be to tailor the historical norm to something that seems sociologically self-evident, thus losing sight of the mechanisms that must exist if the 'normal case' is to actually occur.

A distinction between 'passive' and 'active' proletarianization may be helpful in presenting this problem more precisely. It should be uncontroversial that massive and continuous 'passive' proletarianization, the destruction of the previously dominant forms of labour and subsistence, has been an important socio-structural aspect of the industrialization process. Sociologically speaking, however, there is no reason why those individuals who find themselves dispossessed of their means of labour or subsistence should spontaneously proceed to 'active' proletarianization by offering their labour power for sale on the labour market. To assume this would be to regard the consequences of 'passive' proletarianization – hunger and physical deprivation – as factors of sociological explanation.

Quite apart from methodological considerations, this assumption must be ruled out for the simple reason that, in theory, a range of functionally equivalent 'escape routes' from passive proletarianization have existed historically, and continue to exist. Migration in order to re-establish a now-destroyed independent existence elsewhere; the securing of subsistence through more or less organized forms of plunder; the flight to alternative economic and life-forms, often sustained by religious inspiration; the reduction of the level of subsistence to the point that begging and private charity suffice for survival; the extension of the phase prior to entry into the labour market, so that there is a stretching of the phase of adolescence, either within the family system or, more often, through the institutions of the formal educational system; offensive efforts to root out the causes of passive proletarianization (for example, machine-smashing, political demands for protective tariffs), or the development of political movements (revolutionary socialist mass movements) whose goal is the liquidation of the commodity form of labour power itself: these possibilities provide an incomplete and unsystematic list of real alternatives, both past and present, to 'active' proletarianization through wage-labour. Given this range of alternatives, an explanation is required as to why only a minority (however large quantitatively) has opted for them. Clearly, the large-scale transformation of proletarianized labour power into wage-labour, i.e., the rise of a labour *market*, is not a 'natural' outcome. Even if the destruction of traditional forms of subsistence is presupposed as a fact, the process of industrialization is inconceivable without also presupposing massive 'active' proletarianization.

Given that the structural problem of proletarianization, of the incorporation of labour power into a labour market, is not resolved 'by itself' in any serious social-scientific sense, what component social structures in fact functionally contribute to its effective resolution? We propose the thesis that the wholesale and complete transformation of *dispossessed* labour power into active wage-labour was not and is not possible without *state policies*. While not all of these policies are conventionally considered part of 'social

policy' in the narrow sense, they do perform the function of incorporating labour power into the labour market.

Our central problem – that 'active' proletarianization does not
follow naturally from 'passive' proletarianization – may be subdivided into three component problems.

1   If a fundamental social reorganization of the kind that did
occur in the course of capitalist industrialization is to be possible,
then dispossessed potential workers must in the *first* place be prepared to offer their capacity for labour as a commodity on the
market. They must consider the risks and burdens associated with
this form of existence as *relatively* acceptable; they must muster the
cultural motivation to become wage-labourers.

2   Socio-structural pre-conditions are necessary for wage-
labourers to function as wage-labourers. Because of their special
living conditions, not all members of society could function as
wage-labourers unless certain basic reproduction functions
(especially in the domain of socialization, health, education, care
for the aged) are fulfilled. A range of special institutional facilities is
therefore required, under whose aegis labour power is, so to speak,
exempt from the compulsion to sell itself, or in any event is
expended in ways other than through exchange for money-income
(the housewife is a case in point). The functional indispensability of
such non-market subsystems as family, school and health-care facilities may be considered less problematic than the answer to the
question of why these forms of organization must fall within the
province of *state* policy. Two points may be offered to support the
thesis that forms of existence outside the labour market must be
organized and sanctioned by the state if the transformation of
labour power into wage-labour is to be possible. To begin with,
those subsystems that dealt with living conditions in the pre-
industrial and early industrial phase (particularly the family, but
also private and church charity, as well as other primary-group
forms of social welfare) lose their ability to cope in the course of
industrial development and have to be replaced by formal political
regulations. Second – this point is quite compatible with the first,
and probably no less important – only the 'statization' of these
flanking subsystems makes possible ruling-class control over the
living conditions of that segment of the population who are per-
mitted access to that special form of life and subsistence that stands
outside the labour market, and who are, therefore, temporarily or

permanently exempt from the compulsion to sell their labour power on the labour market. The nub of this second argument is that the 'material' pre-conditions of reproduction and, equally, of ruling-class control over wage-labourers, make it necessary to *politically* regulate who is and who is not a wage-labourer. Without this argument, it would be hard to explain why nearly everywhere the introduction of a common educational system (i.e., the replacement of family forms of training and socialization) was accompanied by the introduction of a general and definite period of *compulsory* education (which amounts to the obligatory organization of certain periods of life outside the labour market). The reliable and permanent incorporation of 'additional' labour power into the wage-labour market can be guaranteed only by strictly regulating the conditions under which non-participation in the labour market is possible (and where purely repressive measures like the punishment of begging and theft do not suffice). The choice between a life of wage-labour and forms of subsistence outside the labour market must accordingly not be left to the discretion of labour power. When, and for how long, individuals remain outside the labour market, the decision whether someone is too old, sick, young, disabled, or has a valid claim to be part of the education system or to social provision must be left neither to individual needs nor to the momentary chances of subsistence outside the market. These choices must be positively regulated through politically defined criteria, for otherwise there would be incalculable tendencies for wage-labourers to evade their function by slipping into the flanking subsystems. This is why a pre-condition of the constitution of a class of wage-labourers is the political institutionalization – and not merely the *de facto* maintenance – of various categories of non-wage-labourers.

3 Finally – this is the *third* component problem – there must be, in the long run, an approximate quantitative balance between those who are 'passively' proletarianized (whether through enforced flight from agricultural forms of reproduction, dismissal as a result of recession or technological change, etc.) and those who are able to find employment as wage-labourers given the volume of demand on the labour market.

The first of the component problems mentioned above is dealt with by all those state policies emanating from the 'ideological' and 'repressive' sections of the state apparatus (to use the terminology of the French structuralists). It is not only that the entry of workers into the wage-labour function – the transformation of labour power into a commodity – is problematic and by no means inevitable at the beginning of the process of industrialization. In addition, during the course of the development of industrial capitalism this problem constantly engenders another: that of containing workers within the wage-labour function. According to the Marxist anthropology of labour and theory of alienation, the special character of wage-labour implies that the willingness of workers to actually sell their labour power cannot be regarded as self-evident. With private ownership of the means of production, a particular form of division of labour is institutionalized together with a particular mode of distribution of goods. Workers have been largely deprived of the possibility of structuring the labour process, especially with regard to their own interests. The capitalist organization of labour typically makes labour power as completely directable and controllable from the outside as possible. From the standpoint of the organization of labour, then, the fact of 'dispossession' means that individuals are deprived of the material resources and symbols upon which a satisfying self-image depends. Hence, to the extent that private economic rationality prevails, labour cannot overcome its character as a means by immediately satisfying its need. This fact seriously prejudices work motivation, not only at the beginning of the industrialization process (when the efficacy of pre-capitalist value orientations still had to be reckoned with), but also today. This deep-seated problem of the 'social integration' of wage-labour must be dealt with by mechanisms of social control that are not reliably engendered by the labour market itself. Examples of this include the criminalization and prosecution of modes of subsistence that are potential alternatives to the wage-labour relation (from the pro-hibition of begging to repressive acts like the Bismarckian Socialist Law) and the state-organized procurement of norms and values, the adherence to which results in the transition to the wage-labour relation. Only the long-term application of these two mechanisms of state policy produce a situation in which the working class 'by education, tradition, and habit looks upon the requirements of that mode of production as self-evident natural laws'. This transfor-mation of dispossessed labour power into wage-labour is itself a constitutive socio-*political* process whose accomplishment cannot be explained *solely* by the 'silent compulsion of economic relations'.[8]

Moreover, even if the organizational form of wage-labour is politically established as the dominant mode of subsistence, this does not at all mean that it will be automatically sustained over time. The structural problem of proletarianization is continuously generated by the specific industrial-capitalist forms of utilization of wage-labour.[9] These forms of utilization imply that the psychological and physical tolerance limits of workers are not usually taken into account in maintaining labour capacity. This is not solely a consequence of the restrictions institutionalized through technical design or the form of personal authority. Even if the work actually carried out is minimally regulated and open to some initiative, workers are compelled to face decisions whose consequences can be quite injurious to their health. Risky encounters with technical equipment which violates safety regulations, a ruinous work-pace, and excessively long working hours are some of the modes of conduct that are enforced by the operation of the productivity-wage system. The powerlessness of workers in this regard is reinforced by the fact that management itself takes only limited account of physical safety and health. If the labour power of an employee is somehow impaired, employers typically react by dismissing the affected worker and hiring fresh, able-bodied labour power. Employers therefore have little reason to enact preventive labour safety measures or to contribute to the rehabilitation of labour power. The 'marketability' of labour power is also adversely affected by the continual obsolescence of occupational skills. The independent functional relationship between technical and organizational innovations and competition among those offering their labour power for sale generates a permanent imbalance between the job structure and individual abilities, an imbalance which cannot be eliminated by the market itself. To the extent that occupational skills can no longer be acquired or constantly adapted through experience, and in as much as general cultural skills are not sufficient to obtain a job, the prospects of being able to participate in the labour market deteriorate constantly. As a rule, it cannot be expected that management will provide training facilities, even if these are designed to produce skilled labour power. Since the contract under which labour power is ceded to the employer can be revoked by the worker at any time, management has no guarantee at all of any return on its investment in training programmes.

The endogenous mechanisms of capitalist production weaken the capacity to perform work – a capacity determined by the health and skill level of individual workers. These mechanisms reduce the exchangeability of labour on the labour market to such an extent that 'catchment areas' outside the labour market must be established in which labour power can be accommodated either permanently (old-age pensions, payments for disabled workers) or temporarily (institutions of health care and further education). But this process entails a second condition: such 'catchment areas' must not be freely selectable; access to them must be coupled with administratively controlled admission requirements, since otherwise a slackening of the 'compulsion to sell' able-bodied labour power would be likely.[10]

In this respect, social policy is a state strategy for incorporating labour power into the wage-labour relation, a relation that was able to attain its contemporary scope and 'normality' *only by virtue of the effectiveness of this strategy*. Understood in this way, social policy is not some sort of state 'reaction' to the 'problem' of the working class; rather, it ineluctably contributes to the *constitution* of the working class. The most decisive function of social policy is its regulation of the process of proletarianization. In other words, the process of proletarianization cannot be thought of as a massive, continuous and relatively smooth process without also thinking of the constitutive functions of state social policy.[11]

In addition to the preparation and stabilization of proletarianization through repression and socialization policies and the compulsory collectivization and processing of its risks, the third component of state social policy is the *quantitative control* of the proletarianization process. The process of capitalist industrialization occurs through leaps and abrupt transformations that are marked by sharp disproportions. Because of the pattern of the process – and even if both the readiness and aptitude for entering the labour market were maintained – it seems unlikely that exactly (or even only approximately) the same amount of labour power will fall victim to 'passive' proletarianization at any given point in time as can be 'accommodated' within the wage-labour relation under the prevailing spatial and occupational-structural conditions.

In so far as the dispossession of labour power, or the ejection of already employed wage-labourers exceeds the absorption capacities of the labour market, an (at least temporary) 'excess supply' of labour that at best functions as a 'reserve army' must be reckoned with as a permanent possibility. Such disproportions are probable in part because the 'commodity' labour power differs from other commodities in that the quantity, place and time of its appearance are not dependent on strategic choices based upon the criterion of 'saleability'. In other words, labour power is indeed treated *as a commodity* but, unlike other commodities, its coming into being is not *based on* strategic expectations of saleability.[12] This structural problem of a long-term discrepancy between demand and supply, and in particular the potential excess of supply, necessitates quantitative regulation in order to establish an equilibrium between 'passive' and 'active' proletarianization. It is precisely because the 'anarchic' fluctuations of the supply and demand sides of the labour market are socially generated but not socially controlled, that 'social "catchment areas" outside the process of production are required to ensure the reproduction of labour power even when no actual employment within the production process results'.[13] This problem of the institutional 'storage' of that portion of the social volume of labour power which (because of conjunctural and structural changes) cannot be absorbed by the demand generated by the labour market becomes acute as traditional forms of caring for such labour power become ineffective. This thesis may be substantiated more closely through the results of a social history-oriented study of the sociology of the family,[14] and through studies of the loss of function of private welfare and charity institutions.

Our conclusions so far may be summed up in the following way. The dispossession of labour power generates three structural problems: the incorporation of labour power into the supply side of the labour market; the institutionalization of those risks and areas of life that are not 'subsumed' under the wage-labour relation; and the quantitative regulation of the relationship between supply and demand on the labour market. These structural problems are by no means resolved automatically by the 'silent compulsion of economic relations', whose participants are somehow left no choice but to submit to the ineluctable imperatives of capitalist industrialization. If 'economic relations' compel anything, it is the invention of social institutions and relations of domination that in turn are not at all based on *mute* compulsion. The transformation of dispossessed labour power into 'active' wage-labour does not occur through the market alone, but must be sanctioned by a political structure of rule, through state power. The owner of labour power first becomes a wage-labourer as a citizen of a state. Thus, we understand the term social policy to include the totality of those politically organized relations and strategies that contribute to the resolution of these three structural problems by continuously effecting the trans-formation of owners of labour power into wage-labourers.[15] A more thorough analysis would probably confirm our impression that, while these three basic problems – the *willingness, ability* and *objective 'sales prospects'* of labour power – can be precisely delineated at the analytic level, 'multi-functional' devices nevertheless prevail at the level of the corresponding social policy measures. These devices are constructed so that, simultaneously and in shifting combinations, they seek to control motives, adjust labour capacities and quantitatively regulate the labour supply. From a strategic-conceptual point of view, the predominance of such social policy devices, which may be characterized as 'broad band therapy' for these structural problems, makes it appear somewhat unwise to exclude from the concept of social policy the rather repressive measures of social control (or the problem-solving strategies of education, housing and health policies), especially since the connections between these individual measures are clearly recognized today within the state administration itself. The scope of state activities designated as part of social policy therefore should not be deduced from their departmental allocation. These activities should instead be determined on the basis of their functional orientation to that objective structural problem to whose treatment the various state institutions, departments and intervention strategies contribute: the problem of the constitution and continuous reproduction of the wage-labour relationship.

Approaches to the explanation of processes of political innovation in the field of social policy

The goal of state-theoretical investigation into the historical and contemporary forms and changes of social policy is to explain this policy on the basis of its substantive functions. The functional linking of state social policy to the structural problems of the social-ization of labour proposed in the previous section offered only preliminary indications of this goal. Questions concerning the driving forces or crucial influences determining the historical development of the instruments and institutions of social policy remain open. Indeed, the institutions of social policy are not fixed, but are subject to constant development and innovation. We have, so far, only outlined and illustrated a theoretical frame of reference for state-theoretical research on social policy, one that seeks to examine and understand the 'existence' of social policy institutions in relation to the structural problem of the 'integration of labour power into social production in the form of wage-labour'. But even if these institutions have completely fulfilled the three functions discussed above, they do not do so once and for all. It is also necessary to explain the regularity of the changes in their existence, the 'laws of motion', so to speak, of the development of social policy. In discussing this 'dynamic' aspect we shall base ourselves *inter alia* on the theoretical perspectives and conclusions of a case study of the development and implementation of a special field of legislation in the domain of the labour market and social policy – a domain whose pattern of development requires political and socio-logical clarification.[16]

In reply to this question concerning the driving forces of policy development, two forms of argument have been offered in the political science literature. Each of these has its specific difficulties. They may be distinguished as follows.

Explanation of the genesis of state social policy in terms of interests and needs

We said earlier that wage-labour could be successfully established as the dominant organizational form only if the specific risks faced by the owner of the 'commodity' labour power were made accept-able, and only if any 'escape' from the wage-labour relation – whether in the form of regression to pre-capitalist or progression to socialist forms of organization – was simultaneously prevented. This suggests the hypothesis that the further development of the institutions and operations of social policy are impelled by the actual risks of the process of capitalist industrialization, and also by the organizational strength of the working class, which raises and enforces appropriate *demands* on the state. Developments in social policy may thus be analysed as the result of objective risk-burdens and the political implementation of demands.

The obvious problem in this explanatory approach is that it presupposes that the system of political institutions is constituted so that it actually concedes the demands of working-class organiz-ations in exactly the measure and combination corresponding to the prevailing conditions of objective risks and the political strength of these organizations (workers' parties and trade unions). But the achievement of this type of correspondence is itself an open question. Those who seek to explain social policy developments with reference to interests or needs, or to demands for various changes must therefore provide additional explanations of how it is that the system of political institutions is, first, sufficiently responsive and reactive to become aware of such demands so that they are accorded the status of political 'issues'; but, second, not *so* responsive and reactive that these 'inputs' might be significantly registered and dealt with in ways that are not *necessarily* linked with either the level of objective risks facing wage-labour or with the political strength of organized workers. This consideration leads at least to the conclusion that policy development cannot be fully explained by needs, interests and demands alone, and that the process of the conversion of 'demands' into 'policies' is always refracted and mediated through the internal structures of the political system, which is what determines whether or not 'needs' are acknowledged as themes worthy of treatment. [17]

Explanation of developments in social policy by 'objective' imperatives of the process of valorization of capital

The explanatory approaches that may be grouped under this type of argument maintain that the causal variables of developments in social policy are not 'demands' of the working class, but functional exigencies of the capitalist valorization process. A crucial characteristic of this process is its 'extravagance' in devouring labour power, the consequence of which is the wholesale destruction of labour capacities and, therewith, the foundations of future accumulation. [18]

State social policy is thus explained by capital's long-term self-interest in the maintenance of the 'material' substance, the level of skill and availability of labour power, and in its protection against short-sighted and excessive exploitation. Apart from the fact that this explanatory approach must exclude any measures of social policy that cannot be unconditionally related to the maintenance of the material substance of labour power (or must bracket them under the perplexing concept of 'non-system-specific social policy', as do Funke *et al.*), [19] methodological objections, or at least queries, can also be raised. First, this approach must clarify the extent to which it can be assumed that state agencies command the requisite foresight and analytical capacity for diagnosing the functional exigencies of capital more accurately than the bearers of the valorization process themselves. And second, even if the state administration were staffed by veritable super-sociologists, this approach is forced to clarify under what circumstances state agencies are in a position to freely respond to the perceived exigencies with suitable measures and innovations in social policy.

A more complex and less problematic model of explanation may be obtained by combining the two approaches. There are two different ways to do this, the first of which – an extrapolation, it seems to us, of Marx's analysis of the determination of the normal working day – predominates in a good part of Marxist analysis on the subject.[20] This first argument may, without too much simplification, be condensed into the following thesis: when the (existing) organizations of the working class propose and politically enforce demands for security through social policy from the state, they only ever bring about conditions that are necessary – in the long run, at any rate – for the interests of capital and a cautious modernization of the relations of exploitation.[21] The organizations of the working class thus merely force capital to 'concede' what then turns out to be in the latter's own well-understood interests. At least, this is said to be true in the sense that capital, in exchange for the costs it must pay for concessions in social policy – costs that are possibly burdensome in the short term but tolerable in the medium term – is compensated in the long run with the advantages of a physically intact and properly skilled workforce, as well as a secured social peace that an increasingly ideologically immunized working class will willingly observe. Such hyper-functionalist constructions imply that the state apparatus, or rather the parties and trade unions that effectively function as its components, have at their disposal fine-tuning and balance mechanisms of colossal complexity and unerring accuracy. If the suggested hypothesis is to be plausible, these mechanisms must be able to ensure that all those, or only those, demands that lead to social policy measures and innovations *at the same time* have the effect of satisfying the long-term functional exigencies of accumulation.

In contrast to such markedly 'harmonistic' interpretations of the genesis and function of social policies of the state, we seek to defend the thesis that the explanation of social policy must indeed take into account as causal factors both 'demands' and 'systemic requirements', that is, problems of 'social integration' and 'system integration' (Lockwood), the political processing of both class conflict and the crises of the accumulation process. As the reaction to *both* these sets of problems, social policy development can never deal with these problems consistently. The solution to one set of problems in no way coincides with the solution to the other; they are mutually contradictory. Accordingly, we maintain that the pattern of development of the strategies and innovations of state social policy is determined through treatment of the 'meta-problem' that may be summed up by this question: how can strategies of social policy be developed and existing institutions modernized so that there can be a satisfaction of *both* the political demands 'licensed' in the context of the prevailing political rights of the working class *and* the foreseeable exigencies and labour and budgetary prerequisites of the accumulation process? The crucial functional problem in the development of social policy and, thus, the key to its social-scientific explanation is that of the *compatibility* of the strategies through which the ruling political apparatus must react to 'demands' and 'systemic requirements' in the framework of existing political institutions *and* to the relationship of social forces channelled through them.

This thesis proposes that particular social policy measures and innovations should be conceived as 'answers' to neither specific demands nor perceived modernization imperatives generated by the problems of the valorization of capital. As is manifest in the themes and conditions of the formation of social policy innovations, social policy instead consists of answers to what can be called the *internal* problem of the state apparatus, namely, how it can react *consistently* to the two poles of the 'needs' of labour and capital – in other words, how to make them mutually compatible. The problem to which state policy development in the social policy domain reacts is that of the precarious compatibility of its own institutions and performances.[22] Our functional reference-point for the explanation of innovations in social policy is therefore the problem of the *internal rationalization* of the system of performance of social policy; in this view, the corresponding *pressure* for rationalization results from the fact that the conflicting 'demands' and requirements faced by the political-administrative system continually call into question the compatibility and practicability of the existing institutions of social policy.

Administrative rationalization and the implementation of innovations

This view of the 'compatibility problem', we contend, depicts the causal condition and driving force of innovation in social policy, and is quite accessible to empirical sociological analysis. Accordingly, it would be possible to test the thesis that those actors (in the ministries, parliaments and political parties) who are responsible for social policy institutions and innovations within the state apparatus actually do find themselves constantly faced with the dilemma that many legally and politically sanctioned demands and guarantees remain unreconciled to exigencies and capacities of the budgetary, financial and labour-market policy of the capitalist economy. They are brought into conflict with this policy by uncontrollable environmental factors. The initiatives to innovate in matters of social policy are chronologically and substantively tailored to the specific parameters of this dilemma. If this thesis were confirmed, we would be entitled to assert that such state policy innovations do not 'serve' the needs or exigencies of any particular social group or class, but instead react to the internal structural problems of the welfare state apparatus.

This thesis would be incomplete and misleading, however, unless it was added that the state's efforts at political innovation, though 'goal abstract' and related solely to its own internal problems (namely, the integrity of its legal, physical and institutional organizational resources), have effects that are not at all *limited* to these internal spheres of state organization. On the contrary, every measure of internal rationalization – whether technical, medical, administrative-organizational or fiscal – always entails more or less far-reaching 'external effects' upon the level of wealth and power resources of social groups. This is quite obvious in cases in which social policy innovations – new laws, decrees and institutional procedures – explicitly and manifestly modify the balance of burdens and benefits among particular categories of people. A (comparatively trivial) sociological example would be the raising of taxes or the cutting of services in the course of efforts to balance the budget. The connections are less transparent (and therefore require sociological explanation) if the external effects of social policy innovations are not regulated explicitly but are enacted wholesale as a more or less indeterminate and latent function of the process of administrative rationalization. An instance of this would be the organizational changes in the management of municipal youth, or social services. However such measures of administrative reform are enacted in a given case, it is certain that there is no such thing as an administrative reform that is *nothing but* an administrative reform; it always entails changes in the quality of the available social services, their accessibility to clients, the composition of the clientele, and so on.

Finally, of the greatest interest to sociological investigations of social policy developments and rationalization strategies are political innovations of a third type. In this case, the real social effects ('impact') of a law or institutional service are not determined by the wording of laws and statutes ('policy output'), but instead are generated primarily as a consequence of social disputes and conflicts, for which state social policy merely establishes the location and timing of the contest, its subject matter and the 'rules of the game'. In these cases of extra-political or 'external' implementation of social policy measures state social policy in no way establishes concrete 'conditions' (for example, the level of services, specific insurance against difficult living conditions). Instead, it defines the substance of conflict and, by differentially empowering or dis-empowering the relevant social groups, biases the extent of the specific 'utility' of the institutions of social policy for these groups. An illustration of this relationship is the function of youth labour protection laws, which do not entail effective protection and security for young employees at all, but merely define the framework within which the relevant power positions of suppliers and buyers on the labour market are brought into play. Thus, the legal regulation of particular quality standards relevant to the jobs of young people can, as often happens, become a serious handicap to their job prospects, whose possible violation of the legal requirements, may, in turn, be tolerated as necessary. As this example indicates, between the legal and social realities of state social policy lie power processes that direct the transformation of 'output' into 'impact'. It is not only suppliers and buyers on the labour market who are involved in these power processes; depending on the particular social policy issue being legally regulated, these processes also include administrative personnel, members of the (medical, educational, legal, etc.) professions, organized interests and the mass media. What is important to us here is only that aspect that concerns research strategy: the developments and innovations of state social policy can be conceived not as the *cause* of concrete social conditions or changes, but only as the initiator of conflictual interactions, the outcome of which is open and ambivalent precisely because it is determined by the structural relationship of power and the constellation of interests. From this observation we draw the conclusion that the task of any specifically sociological investigation of social policy cannot be the prescriptive development of 'policy designs' and 'policy outputs', but is pre-eminently that of offering an explanatory description of the conditions of socially implementing policy regulations. It is only this knowledge that supplies the foundation for the expression of political recommendations in non-normative and non-voluntaristic ways.

The considerations and hypotheses developed so far yield a schema of sociological analysis of social policy development that comprises three steps. First, it must be shown that, when the modalities of the generation, financing and distribution of social policy activities are altered, the actors in the state apparatus actually find themselves in the dilemma of reconciling 'licensed' demands or recognized needs, on the one hand, with the perceived 'exigencies' or tolerance of the capitalist economy for 'unproductive' social policy expenditures, on the other hand. The pervasive relevance of this basic problem, only hinted at here, may be tested by establishing whether the timing of the appearance, issues and effects of social policy innovations are linked to such concrete 'compatibility problems'. If this is the case, then the second step is to identify the solution strategies that – aside from the specific themes and tactics of political self-representation that tend to accompany such innovations – are applied within the administration itself to the consistency problem – a problem that is usually not designated as such. Finally, in the third step, there must be an uncovering of the 'external effects' of such solution strategies, their more or less latent benefits and burdens, the consequent increases and decreases of power, together with the pattern of conflict that strategically guides the process of socially implementing social policy innovation.

These processes of social implementation may be categorized according to whether (at one extreme) they result in the essentially undistorted attainment of the goals declared in the official 'policy outputs' of administrators and legislators, or whether (at the other extreme) they encounter more or less organized acts of obstruction by social power groups, which in turn pose fresh consistency problems within the state apparatus and which may possibly require actual repeal of the innovations. It would be of great theoretical and practical interest to be able to locate concrete social policy innovations at particular points along this scale of 'implementation consequences', as well as to identify the relations of social power and conflicts responsible for the given result. But in view of the limited theoretical and empirical foundations of current sociological policy research, it seems inevitable, for the time being at least, that such investigations will be retrospective rather than prospective; abandoning any intention of producing advice and 'improvement', their goals will be empirical-analytic rather than normative-analytic. Their aim will be that of empirically reconstructing the social 'history of effects' of past innovations in social policy.

We may thus expect sociological investigations of this type to elucidate questions like: what immediate benefits, burdens and business prospects were generated by a new programme in social policy? What categories of 'persons affected' were placed in relations of competition and/or co-operation by this programme? To what extent were those affected really able to claim advantages, or to counter or obstruct regulations disadvantageous to them? From whom and to whom can the group-specific burdens be shifted, and which social power groups are able to block the administrative implementation of the programme? The answer to such questions is not only not deducible from the texts of the relevant laws and decrees: it also cannot be known with certainty by state policy-makers themselves. The material effects of social policy innovations will be forged only in the course of their social implementation, and the ambivalence of new measures and agencies will be resolved into unambiguous 'impacts' only when the socio-structurally conditioned relations of power and conflicts have bestowed this unambiguity upon them.

The thesis that these social policy innovations with which the state apparatus responds to its own inherent consistency problem are ambivalent in principle, and the accompanying thesis that official 'outputs' are converted into factual 'impacts' outside the state, may be clarified by a few examples. Here our analysis is based on a few models of rationalization that represent, as it were, the strategic common denominators of more specific innovations in social policy. Although a more exact analysis cannot be provided here, these schemata highlight the ambivalence within the respective rationalization strategies, and therefore the need for these strategies to be completed 'outside' the state. At the very least, we may expect these schemata to challenge the widespread supposition that state social policy by itself produces such conditions as the 'quality of life', 'social security', and so on. In contrast to that supposition our thesis is that the function of 'shaping society' of state social policy is limited to the definition of the themes, times and methods of conflict and, thus, to the establishment of the political-institutional *framework* – and not the *outcome* – of processes of social power.

Strategies of rationalization

A range of rationalization schemata may be detected in the object domain of social policy development. To some extent, these schemata are explicitly recognized and recommended in official social policy reports as strategic calculations that overlap with other fields.

Prevention

A first example concerns the idea of enhancing the effectiveness of social policy by relying increasingly on preventive (instead of retrospective, 'curative') problem-solving strategies. The practice of social policy innovation is guided by this idea in initiatives in various areas: in health policy (reduction of pathogenic living and working conditions, preventive medical examinations); educa-tion/policy (pre-school education, emphasis on 'flexibility' and 'key skills' in occupational training); and in the field of labour relations (the 'humanization' of work, health and safety regula-tions, laws covering the employment of youth labour, etc.). In all such cases, the state organs have an interest in a cost-advantageous settlement of institutionalized claims and functions at the earliest point in the development of the problem. But the question of whether this settlement really serves the state interest is not (positively) answered at all; it is merely raised by the enact-ment of the corresponding measures and laws. As is generally known, the extent to which the volume of finance earmarked for medical protection can be really effective depends on the relative latitude of physicians and hospitals to set prices; whether or not intended programmes of humanization and other measures of labour protection are implemented depends on the strength of company or trade union representation (or on the degree of their immunity to the threat of rationalization-based and conjunctural threats of unemployment). In these and numerous other cases, state policy simply does not command the requisite social 'media of control' necessary for guaranteeing a preventive outcome. This is why the 'success' of social policy is determined by the conflictual 'strategies of utilization' of the various social classes and groups involved.

Final programmes

A similar correlation is displayed within a second rationalization schema, namely, in the efforts to render social policy more effective by replacing conditional with final programmes.* This is a matter of relativizing legal structures that link given rights and claims to abstractly defined conditions and of introducing situation-dependent decision criteria, which are obtained according to the 'discretionary' viewpoints of political opportunity. In this connection we may mention the extensive use of decree provisions in laws relating to social policy, as well as the latitude for judgement afforded by such concepts (which are frequently found in German labour market legislation) as 'suitability for labour-market policy' or 'desirability'; legal texts concerning the regulation of training and working conditions in factories similarly operate as a rule with clauses about 'necessity' and 'desirability'. In this type of innovation, the reference to internal state consistency problems is also evident: a relaxation of rigid legal forms facilitates the dismissal of claims whose satisfaction is not considered 'appropriate' in the light of concrete circumstances, while the binding power of precepts can be softened if the fiscal consequences of their implementation (like unemployment and the lowering of the tax yield) seem too serious. Of course, what has been judged appropriate, desirable, necessary, etc., and accordingly recognized as grounds for a decision by the administration and the courts typically depends both directly and indirectly upon the balance of power between social interests and their respective ability to threaten and sanction. Whether a retraining proposal is considered appropriate from the standpoint of labour-market policy, and thus whether it will be adapted must, for instance, be determined by the state employment office in the light

---

* *Editor's note*: This distinction between 'conditional' and 'final' modes of legal intervention draws upon a typology developed by recent German sociologists of law (for example, Niklas Luhmann). A 'conditional' intervention comprises a programme of legal decisions that is automatically implemented if certain *antecedents* (as specified within the law) are present. A 'final' programme, by contrast, is contingent upon the perceived effectiveness of the intervention in achieving specified *outcomes*.

of the conceivable strategies of potential buyers of the re-trained labour power and in accordance with these buyers' decisions on such matters as site location and labour recruitment procedures. The definition of a 'suitable' job by the employment office is similarly governed by the degree to which employers can engage in individual or collective conflict.

Institutionalized assistance

A third rationalization schema concerns the frequently-noted circumstance that the share of services and payments in kind rises continually in relation to the totality of state social policy tasks. In addition to transferring (and partially replacing) purchasing power, social policy operates through institutionalized relations of schooling, care, attention, healing, socialization, re-socialization, consultation, instruction, etc., in other words, through non-monetary means of regulation.[23] This form of social policy is also definitely linked to the internal state management problem of balancing institutionalized claims and the financial and institutional means with which they can be satisfied. In so far as claimants are not only endowed with money, but are also (or instead) drawn into relations of 'treatment', the 'inappropriate' expenditure of transfer income – always an option as long as only monetary assistance is provided – can be brought under control. Moreover, categories of goods and services that would otherwise be inaccessible, or available only at considerably higher costs, can be provided for. (Transfer payments to students, for example, would have to be raised substantially if their reproduction needs were covered by normal goods and services markets, and not by special, subsidized public facilities such as dormitories.) No doubt, this economizing effect of institutional assistance applies primarily to clients who accept a more or less far-reaching renunciation of freedom of choice, which is indeed enjoyed by market 'buyers', but not by 'clients of service institutions'. This form of need satisfaction – and herein lies the specific ambivalence of this rationalization schema – affords those who establish, control and apportion the institutional supply of services considerable power to define the norms governing the needs of the clients. On the other hand, however, clients undergo a de-individualization as their status is shifted from that of individual 'buyers' to members of a collectivity of 'users', whose potential power may very well become a counterweight to the monopoly of definition held by the management of the institution. To that extent, when social policy agencies switch from income-substitutional policies to institutional forms of assistance (or vice versa) it is not at all certain from the outset whether the material consequence of such innovations will be the bureaucratic disabling of the clientele through the professional imposition of 'appropriate' needs, or rather, the mobilization and rising independence of the clientele (aided by the collective character of institutional assistance), who thereby win the opportunity of entering actively into the process of definition and satisfaction of their own needs. As numerous studies of the political dilemma of the social work profession confirm, this question is decided only in the course of the 'social implementation' of state social policy innovations.[24]

Reprivatization

A fourth rationalization schema, prominent in current developments in social policy, is evident in attempts to save on fiscal expenditures (and on the costs of political conflict!) by shifting public tasks to either parafiscal financing systems or to private or quasi-public ('self-administering') forms of organization of the decision-making process. The assignment of public tasks to institutions financed by contributions; the plans, now under discussion in some quarters, to finance particular functions of social policy through special taxes and charges (on vocational training, the labour market, foreigners); the trends towards private contributions to the costs of health care in the framework of health insurance – these are all examples of this strategy of rationalizing state social policy. Here too, the strategic focus is on eliminating a dilemma within the state: financial and decision-making burdens are to be shifted from the central state level to the sphere of the immediate participants, to those 'on the scene'. Again, it is evident that the relative economic strength of these 'participants' determines how the respective burdens and benefits will eventually be distributed.

The scientization of politics?

Our enumeration and differentiation of the models of rationalization that currently play a role in the development of social policy – we make no claim to even approximate completeness – must be discontinued at this point in order to indicate another type of rationalization strategy. We are referring to a trend that has also been observed and discussed in many other political domains: the 'scientization' of politics, i.e., the authoritative participation of scientific experts in the development and evaluation of political programmes. This question of the 'scientization' of state social policy affords an opportunity to recall the problems discussed in the first section of this essay. The scientization of the development of social policy programmes is above all motivated by a range of manifest and latent functions that can readily be related to the problem of the 'compatibility' of institutional claims and the available means for their satisfaction, and therefore to the internal consistency problem of the state. Science is expected to provide recommendations to enhance both the 'efficient' and 'effective' realization of social policy programmes. Scientization thus functions to unburden the system of political decision-making both socially (the demands and interpretations of reality of anyone who cannot establish their 'scientific legitimacy' can be placed to one side) and temporally (while information is gathered and alternative programmes weighed, a temporal buffer zone can be interposed between the identification of problems and the enactment of problem solutions; more importantly, those affected can prepare themselves for possible trench-warfare and impending changes in their position and power prospects).

Strategies that seek to rationalize and de-activate problems of internal state organization are, nevertheless, characteristically ambivalent in their explicit effects. They are open to interpretation by contending social interests, while their real effects on social policy emerge only in the course of conflict-ridden attempts to apply them. They are, therefore, not determined in advance by the respective rationalization strategies. This is as true of the scientization of the development of social policy programmes as it is of the rationalization schemata discussed above. The more state social policy seeks to rationalize itself by making demands upon the services of the scientific establishment, the greater are the chances – especially if additional filters and mechanisms of discrimination are not brought into play, or if the scientific establishment's members do not defend themselves – that oppositional political-theoretical concepts will flourish and become important in both the formulation and social implementation and application of state programmes. In our view, the decisive conflicts in both political theory and political life which are provoked and intensified by the increasing scientization of social policy (and perhaps education policy as well) may be summed up in these questions: will academic social policy model itself on the theoretical concepts of law and economics and cling, in the manner of an *étatiste-oriented* 'policy science', to a counterfactual self-understanding of its role as producer of 'efficient', 'effective', 'practical', 'correct', or even 'socially just' policies?[25] Or will it grasp the danger of this technocratic misconception and instead act on the basis of the insight that the institutional and legal structures of 'policy outputs' in no way define the social and political 'impact' of social policy? Will the study of social policy thereby come to understand that it is the legally and politically sanctioned relations of social power, the ability to impose exactions and threats, combined with the conflicts of interest dependent on them, which determine the degree to which 'social justice' can be brought about by state social policy? And, finally, is it therefore not the case that *sociological* research into social policy has no other legitimate option than that of exposing these concrete mechanisms and conditions of the social implementation of state social policy?

Notes and references

1   C. von Ferber, *Sozialpolitik in der Wohlstandgesellschaft* (Hamburg 1976), pp. 76ff; cf. also F. Tennstedt, 'Zur Ökonomisierung und Verrechtlichung in der Sozialpolitik', in A. Murswieck (ed.), *Staatliche Politik im Sozialsektor* (Munich 1976), pp. 139ff.

2   Referring to B. Külp and W. Schreiber (eds.), *Soziale Sicherheit* (Cologne and Berlin 1971), p. 12, Murswieck states that the predominant theoretical position within the science of social policy is that of 'a value-free, positive science, whose goal is to explain that which is designated in the realm of politics as social policy measures' (A. Murswieck, 'Perspektiven einer Theorie des Wohlfahrtsstaates in der BRD', *Ms.* (Autumn 1976), p. 7). Of course, such a treatment of social policy relinquishes the determination of its conceptual foundations to the particular divisions of administrative planning. In a similar sense, cf. the pertinent criticism in J. Kruger, 'Soziale Ungleichheit und Sozialpolitik', *Archiv für Wissenschaft und Praxis der sozialen Arbeit* (1975), p. 251.

3 Tennstedt, 'Zur Ökonomisierung und Verrechtlichung in der Sozial-politik', pp. 139, 149.

4 Cf. F. Böhle and D. Sauer, 'Intensivierung der Arbeit und staatliche Sozialpolitik', *Leviathan*, **3** (1975), p. 52: 'Critical analyses of the effectiveness of state social policy are limited to establishing discrepancies between explicitly stated goals and what is actually realized.'

5 Tennstedt, 'Zur Ökonomisierung und Verrechtlichung in der Sozial-politik', p. 155.

6 There should be no need to insist that our critical argument against the normative approach is only *methodological*, and makes no mention whatsoever of the question of the political-moral correctness of posited ought-norms. The treatment of this question would require political argumentation.

7 In this regard, one should note Goldthorpe's reservations and objections concerning any overestimation of the analytical capacity of a functionalist explanation of social policy: 'It is hard to see how one could ever demonstrate that particular social processes are essential for the actual physical survival of a society in the same way as one can demonstrate the necessity of particular biological processes for the survival of an organism'. There is the danger of an 'explanation of a metaphysical and entirely uninformative kind to which an unthinking and uncritical functionalist approach is likely to give rise'. (J. Goldthorpe, 'The development of social policy in England, 1800–1914', *Transactions of the Fifth World Congress of Sociology*, **4** (1962), pp. 53ff.) However, a functional analysis guided by historical materialism can take this reservation into account with comparative ease since, unlike functionalism, it proceeds from the idea that the functional imperatives that a social system 'must' follow are not simply *given* 'objectively' (for sociologists), but are registered and established in class struggles; in other words, it is *social actors* that make these imperatives problems. It therefore takes care of the question of why the given functional imperatives of a social system '*tend to be regarded as imperative*' (ibid., p. 54, emphasis in original). Goldthorpe's second methodological proviso, that functional analyses tend to unfold at a relatively high level of generalization and thereby fail to explain the choice between functionally *equivalent* solutions, would have to be reckoned with to the extent that the given alignments and processes of conflict and consensus arising from concrete actors and situations were not minimized and ignored as 'surface phenomena', but were seen – both theoretically and politically – as quite unavoidable components of processes through which societies resolve

their structural problems and face the choice between equivalent systems of resolution. (See Claus Offe, *Berufsbildungsreform, Eine Fallstudie über Reformpolitik* [Frankfurt 1975], pp. 45ff.)

8   K. Marx, *Capital, I* (Harmondsworth 1976), p. 899.

9   cf. Böhle and Sauer, 'Intensivierung der Arbeit und staatliche Sozialpolitik'.

10   cf. N. Glaser, 'Die Grenzen der Sozialpolitik', in W.- D. Narr and Claus Offe (eds.), *Wohlfahrtsstaat und Massenloyalität* (Cologne and Berlin 1975).

11   Against the generally accepted idea that social policy is a 'reactive' response to the 'social question' (i.e., class struggle -ed.), R. Funke *et al.*, 'Theoretische Problemskizze für eine Untersuchung der Entwicklungstendenzen im Bereich staatlicher Sozialpolitik', manuscript (Max-Planck-Institut, Starnberg 1976), p. 7 correctly emphasize that 'social policy measures created the pre-conditions for the capital-wage-labour relation in that they ward off those dangers to the continuation of this relation generated by the accumulation process itself'. This formulation is misleading in that this relation need not necessarily be stabilized through social policy measures; it is nevertheless true that the wage-labour form of existence *cannot be preserved without social policy*.

12   K. Polanyi, *The Great Transformation* (New York 1944).

13   Böhle and Sauer, 'Intensivierung der Arbeit und staatliche Sozialpolitik', p. 64.

14   See, for example, G. Heinsohn and R. Knieper, *Theorie des Familienrechts* (Frankfurt 1975).

15   This conceptual framework avoids both the formalism criticized earlier and the complementary defect that seems evident in the normative and 'critical' positions. Instead, the foundation of this conceptual framework is shaped by *definite structural problems*, the reality of which then becomes evident whenever, for any reason, there is a failure of the mechanisms whose function is to deal with these problems – and therewith make them imperceptible *as* structural problems.

16   Offe, *Berufsbildungsreform, Eine Fallstudie über Reformpolitik*.

17   cf. E. Standfest, 'Die Kostenentwicklung in der sozialen Sicherung', *WSI-Mitteilungen*, 29 no. 7 (1976), p. 396. In view of such innovations as parliamentary systems and social democratic parties, it is difficult to ignore the problem of 'optimal' (for capitalist social structures) responsiveness by regarding it as solved once and for all. In other words, the possibility of an infringement of functional harmony, and therefore of the presumed 'optimalness', must always be reckoned with, either in

the direction of a curtailment of the political rights of the organizations of the working class or of an enlargement of these rights to the point where they are no longer compatible with the organizational form of wage-labour. The political system's supports for either *free* wage-labour or (as the case may be) for free *wage-labour* would thereupon crumble.

18 cf. Böhle and Sauer, 'Intensivierung der Arbeit und staatliche Sozial-politik'.

19 Funke *et al.*, 'Theoretische Problemskizze' p. 11 and *passim*.

20 See, for example, W. Müller and C. Neusüss, 'The illusion of state socialism and the contradiction between wage labour and capital', *Telos*, **25** (Fall 1975), pp. 13–90.

21 Thus, for example, E. Talos, 'Zu den Anfängen in der Sozialpolitik', *Österreichische Zeitschrift für Politikwissenschaft*, **2** (1976), p. 151: 'The necessity of state action (in the legislative domain concerning the protection of labour and security) is doubly based:
  – on the development of the workers' movement . . . which constitutes a threat to social and political relations alike;
  – on the danger to the physical existence of workers generated by an unrestricted valorization of labour power. The interest in the maintenance of the valorization of capital compels measures that serve to preserve the existence of workers through guaranteeing their reproduction possibilities'. 'The securing of labour power's reproduction possibilities objectively serves the self-interests of capital' both because of the consequent maintenance of the physical subsistence of labour capacities and also because of the consequent 'appeasement and integration of social contradictions' (ibid., p. 157). Similarly, Funke *et al.*, 'Theoretische Problemskizze', pp. 23–4: through 'innovation thrusts in state social policy . . . the social integration of workers, which had been temporarily endangered, is guaranteed anew (!). . . . This is the price of social innovations.' In such constructions, of course, it remains mysterious how the process of policy formation, which is characterized on the level of *action* by 'conflicts between social classes' and by a 'plethora of political controversies' (Talos, 'Zu den Anfängen in der Sozialpolitik', p. 146), is to lead to results whose *objective function* is to establish, as perfectly as possible, a class harmony. It must at least be explained why this insight has not been communicated to the political organizations of the ruling class, which instead continue to suspect and combat every rise in pensions as creeping socialism, etc. In our view, this is a hyperfunctionalist (or even vulgar Hegelian) blind alley that resembles the maxim, 'Whatever was

was necessary' (cf. Goldthorpe 'The development of social policy in England', p. 56).

22 In this respect, we would *in general* defend an explanatory model of processes of social policy innovation which R. Funke 'Zur sozial-politischen Entwicklung in der Bundesrepublik', manuscript (Max-Planck-Institut, Starnberg 1976), p. 14, emphasizes as only a *particular* feature of the social policy documented in the 1976 *Sozialbericht* (Bonn: Ministry of Labour and Social Affairs): 'At the centre of interest . . . stand not new tasks but the preservation of the status quo within the output and financing systems of social policy.'

23 cf. *Sozialbericht*, p. 101; Murswieck, 'Perspektiven einer Theorie des Wohlfahrtsstaates in der BRD', p. 17; B. Badura and P. Gross, 'Sozialpolitik und soziale Dienste: Entwurf einer Theorie der persönlich Dienstleistung', manuscript (Universität Konstanz 1976); Tennstedt, 'Zur Ökonomisierung und Verrechtlichung in der Sozial-politik', p. 150.

24 cf. E. Standfest, 'Demokratischer Sozial-oder autoritärer Wohlfahrts-staat?', in 'Gewerkschaftsstaat oder Unternehmerstaat', special issue of *WSI-Mitteilungen* (August 1976), p. 14.

25 In view of the widespread euphoria about the prescriptive capability of the social sciences in achieving an 'improved' or 'socially just' state social policy, the retrospective summary drawn by an American social policy researcher concerning the political relevance of social policy research may arouse some disillusionment: 'A principal thesis of this book is that the results of social science research studies generally have been irrelevant or relevant only in macro-negative terms (and, hence, of limited worth) to the key decision issues in federal social policy making for the disadvantaged. . . . That is, the studies indicate how groups . . . are disadvantaged as to education, health, jobs, income, etc. (macro-negative information), *but* not specifically how to over-come these problems' (W. Williams, *Social Policy Research and Analysis, The Experience in the Federal Social Agencies* (New York 1971), p. 58). See also the uncertain report on the German experience by R. Bartholomäi, 'Ressortforschung: Aspekte der Vergabe und Forschungsbegleitung', in Wissenschaftszentrum Berlin (ed.), *Theoretische und praktische Probleme der anwendungsbezogenen Sozialwissenschaften* (Berlin 1975).

4 Theses on the theory of the state*

The following theses briefly outline some of the theoretically relevant findings which the authors have made in two empirical studies of reformist state policies in West Germany. These studies were concerned with the reform of vocational training and with a new programmatic approach to research and development policies.[1] We believe that such case studies of state policies in specific policy areas are necessary for generating both theoretical insights and political perspectives, which cannot be developed through deductive reasoning or immediate experience. For the sake of convenience, the argument is divided into eight theses. These points are intended to provoke discussion and debate and are, of course, tentative in nature.

Marxist theories of the state

In contemporary Marxist theories of the state, there is a cleavage between two approaches. One approach suggests that there is a particular *instrumental* relationship between the ruling class (capital as a whole) on the one side and the state apparatus on the other side. The state is conceived as an instrument for promoting the common interests of the ruling class. We believe that this view is gravely misleading – including the version that is offered in the doctrine of 'state monopoly capitalism', with its stereotyped claim about a 'merger of the monopolies and the state apparatus'. The alternative view is that the state does not favour specific interests, and is not allied with specific classes. Rather, what the state protects and

* Written with the assistance of Volker Ronge, this essay was first delivered as a discussion paper to the 'Conference on the State in the Light of Marxism', Lelio Basso Fondazione, Firenze, Italy, March 1975. It was published in Claudio Pozzoli (ed.), *Rahmenbedingungen und Schranken staatlichen Handelns* (Frankfurt 1976), pp. 54–70. An earlier translation appeared in *New German Critique*, **6** (Fall 1975), pp. 139–47.

sanctions is a set of institutions and social *relationships* necessary for the domination of the capitalist class. In this second view, the state is neither a 'servant' nor an 'instrument' of any one class. While it does not defend the specific interests of a single class, the state nevertheless seeks to implement and guarantee the *collective* interests of all members of a *class society dominated by capital*.

The capitalist state

Considered at the most abstract-general level, the concept of the capitalist state describes an institutional form of political power which is guided by the following four functional conditions:

1   *Private production*   Political power is prohibited from organizing material production according to its own 'political' criteria; property, whether in labour power or capital, is *private*. Hence, it is not political power, but private decisions that determine the concrete use of the means of production.
2   *Taxation constraints*   Political power depends indirectly – through the mechanisms of the taxation system – on the volume of private accumulation. Those who occupy positions of power in a capitalist state are in fact powerless *unless* the volume of the accumulation process allows them to derive (through taxation) the material resources necessary to promote *any* political ends.
3   *Accumulation*   Since state power depends on a process of accumulation which is beyond its power to organize, every occupant of state power is basically interested in promoting those political conditions most conducive to private accumulation. This interest does not result from an alliance of a particular government with particular classes or social strata also interested in accumulation; nor does it necessarily result from the privileged access of the members of the capitalist class to centres of state decision-making, a privilege which in turn makes it possible for that class to 'put pressure' on the incumbents of state power to pursue their class interest. Rather the *institutional self-interest* of the state in accumulation is conditioned by the fact that the state is denied the power to control the flow of those resources which are nevertheless indispensable for the exercise of state power. Although the agents of accumulation are not primarily interested in 'using' the power of the state, state actors must be interested – for the sake of their own power – in guaranteeing and safeguarding a 'healthy' accumulation process.

4   *Democratic legitimation*   In parliamentary-democratic political regimes, any political group or party can win control over institutional state power only to the extent that it wins sufficient electoral support in general elections. This mechanism plays a key role in disguising the fact that the material resources of state power, and the ways in which these are used, primarily depend upon the revenues derived from the accumulation process, and not upon the voting preferences of the general electorate. In other words, there is a dual determination of the political power of the capitalist state: the institutional *form* of this state is determined through the rules of democratic and representative government, while the material *content* of state power is conditioned by the continuous requirements of the accumulation process.

Commodification

Is there any method by which these divergent structural conditions of the capitalist state can be reconciled through the policies of a particular government? In our view, there is *one* such method. If conditions can be created so that *every* citizen becomes a participant in commodity relationships, all four constitutive elements of the capitalist state are taken into account. As long as every owner of a unit of value can successfully exchange his/her value as a commodity, there is no need for the state to intervene in private economic decision-making; there is no lack of the material resources required by the state; there is no problem in maintaining a steady process of accumulation (which is only the net result of equivalent exchanges between the owners of capital and the owners of labour power); and, finally, there is no legitimation or consensus problem for political elites who manage to maintain this universe of commodities. Only to the extent that economic units of value *fail* to operate in the commodity form does the structure of the capitalist state become problematic. The commodity form is the general point of equilibrium of both the capitalist state and accumulation, which continues as long as every value appears in the form of a commodity. The link between the political and the economic substructures of capitalist society is the commodity form; the stability of both substructures depends upon the universalization of this form.

The paralysis of the commodity form

The key problem of capitalist societies is the fact that the dynamics of capitalist development seem to exhibit a constant tendency to *paralyse* the commodity form of value. Values cease to exist in the commodity form as soon as they cease exchanging for money or other values. To be sure, in an economic system regulated by private exchanges, it is never certain that one particular item offered for sale on the market will actually find a buyer. But in this simple case the failure of a value offered for exchange is supposed to be *self-correcting*: the owner of the exchange-seeking value will either be forced to lower the price or to offer an alternative good, the use-value of which increases its chances of being bought. At least in the theoretical world of Jean Baptiste Say, a fully commodified economy is self-stabilizing and perpetuating: the failure of a good as a commodity automatically results in other goods less likely to fail. Similarly, in the course of an economic depression, elements of labour and parts of capital which are temporarily expelled from the commodity form are supposed to create, through the very fact of their idleness, the pre-conditions for a new boom (on the condition that there is downward flexibility of prices). The functioning of this 'healthy' self-corrective mechanism, however, does not seem to be the regular case, particularly in late capitalist societies.

Marxist economic theory has developed various, though controversial, theorems which could explain the failure of such equilibrating mechanisms. For example, Baran and Sweezy argue that the monopolization of the economy leads to the downward inflexibility of prices on the one side and, on the other, to a constant flow of 'surplus profit' which cannot find investment outlets. Another explanation is based on the increasingly social character of capitalist production. This explanation points to the increasing division of labour within and among capitalist enterprises, the increased specialization of every single unit of capital and labour, and hence the diminished flexibility and adaptability of capital and labour to alternative uses. Third, it has been argued that the periodic destruction of large parts of value through unfettered economic crises is by itself a healthy economic mechanism which will improve the chances for the remaining values to 'perform' as commodities. In this view, the social conflict associated with this 'draining off' of superfluous values tends to become explosive to the extent that these automatic crisis mechanisms are blocked by state intervention and Keynesian policies.

Whatever the correct and complete explanation may be, there is plenty of everyday evidence to the effect that both labour power and capital are expelled from the commodity form, and that there is little basis for the liberal belief that they will be reintegrated automatically into exchange relationships.

The maximization of exchange opportunities

The most abstract and inclusive common denominator of state policy in late capitalist societies is the securing of exchange relations between individual economic actors. Again, this does not mean that the capitalist state guards the interests of a particular class; rather, it sanctions the general interest of all classes on the basis of capitalist exchange relationships. For instance, it would be a mistake to argue that state policies of education and training are designed to provide the necessary labour power for certain industries, since no one, least of all the state bureaucracy, has any reliable information concerning the type, timing and volume of skills required by capitalists. Such policies are instead designed to provide a *maximum of exchange opportunities* for both labour and capital, so that individuals of both classes can enter into capitalist relations of production. Similarly, research and development policies designed and funded by the state are by no means directed towards concrete beneficiaries, such as industries which can use the resulting technologies. Rather, these policies are designed to open up new markets and to shield the domestic economy against the intrusion of foreign competitors; in short, to create and universalize the commodity form of value, in whose absence values become non-existent in a capitalist society.

Administrative recommodification

The exclusive concern of all state policies with the problem of guarding the commodity form of value is a relatively new phenomenon. In some capitalist states, like the USA, it is still subject to substantial political and ideological controversies. What are the alternative strategies open to the state in order to deal with the structural problem of values failing to perform as commodities? The 'classical' strategy seems to be *inaction*, i.e., hoping for the operation of the self-corrective mechanism of the market, as a consequence of which those units of value that have been expelled from the commodity form are supposed to return to the market. The assumption is that the more unpleasant unemployment (of labour or capital) is, the sooner the owners of those values will return to the market-place. The flaw in this logic lies, however, in supposing that owners of values do *not* have an option other than that of returning to the commodity form. Contrary to the assumptions of bourgeois ideology, they do in fact have other options, of which emigration, delinquency and political revolt are only a few historical examples.

The second alternative open to state policy is that of the subsidized protection of values. In this case, those owners of labour power and capital who can no longer participate in exchange relationships are allowed to survive under conditions artificially created by the state. Their economic existence is protected although they have dropped out of the commodity form, or they are 'artificially' prevented from dropping out because they are granted income (for example, transfer payments) derived from sources other than the sale of value. The problem with this 'welfare state' strategy of producing 'decommodified' values is that it becomes too costly in fiscal terms, thus sharpening the fiscal crisis of the state. Subsidizing the owners of values that have been rendered obsolete as commodities is particularly costly for the state because it entails a category of expenditures which are by no means self-financing. These expenditures do not increase, but rather reduce the basis of future state revenues.

On the basis of these theoretical considerations, we wish to argue that since the mid 1960s the increasingly dominant and exclusive strategy of the capitalist state is to solve the problem of the obsolescence of the commodity form by politically creating conditions under which legal and economic subjects can function as commodities. More specifically, this strategy develops in three directions: first, the saleability of labour power is enhanced through measures and programmes directed towards education, training, regional mobility and improving the general adaptability of labour power. Second, the saleability of capital and manufactured goods is enhanced through the transnational integration of capital and product markets, research and development policies, regional development policies, etc. Third, those sectors of the economy (identifiable according to particular industries, regions and labour market segments) which are unable to survive within the commodity form on their own strength are allowed, according to plan, to fall victim to market pressures. At the same time, these sectors are urged to modernize, i.e., to transform themselves into 'marketable' goods. We suggest that the term 'administrative recommodification' might be an appropriate label for this most recent strategy of the capitalist state; it is basically different from both the *laissez-faire* and 'welfare state-protection' types of strategy sketched out above.

Instruments of state policy

Policies which pursue the general goal of reorganizing, maintaining and generalizing market exchange relationships rely upon a specific sequence of political instruments. These instruments of political regulation can be categorized in the following way. First, there are *regulations and financial incentives* which are designed to control 'destructive' competition and to make competitors subject to rules which enable the economic survival of their respective market partners. Usually these regulations consist of measures and laws which try to protect the 'weaker' party in an exchange relationship, or which support this party through various incentives. Second, there is the broad category of *public infrastructure investment* which is designed to assist certain categories of commodity owners (again: both labour and capital) to engage in exchange relationships. Typical examples are various kinds of schools, transportation facilities, energy plants, and measures for urban and regional development. Third, and most recently, we find attempts to introduce schemes of *joint decision-making* and *joint financing*. These are designed to force market partners to agree in an organized way upon conditions of mutually acceptable exchange *outside* the exchange process itself, so that the outcome is predictable for both sides. Such state-sanctioned schemes of mutual accommodation among associations and collective actors (recently described as neo-corporatism) are to be found not only in the area of wage bargaining, but equally in areas like housing, education and environmental protection.

Structural contradictions of late capitalism

These attempts to stabilize and universalize the commodity form and exchange process by political and administrative means lead to a number of specific structural contradictions of state capitalist societies, which in turn can become the focus of social conflict and political struggle. Such contradictions can be found on the economic, political and ideological levels of society. On the *economic* level, the very state policies which are designed to maintain and expand exchange relationships often have the effect of threatening the continuity of those relationships. This is because all three instruments of state policy-making mentioned above (regulations, infrastructure investment and mutual accommodation) deprive the owners of capital of value to varying degrees, either in the form of capital that is 'taxed away', or in the form of labour power, or in the form of their freedom to utilize both of these in the way they deem most profitable. To the extent that state policies of 'administrative recommodification' are 'effective', they are bound to put a burden upon the owners of capital. This, in turn, has the paradoxical effect of *threatening* the effectiveness of state policies. Since, in a capitalist society, all exchange relationships depend upon the willingness of owners of money capital to invest, i.e., to exchange money capital for constant capital and variable capital; since this willingness depends upon the expected profitability of investment; and since all state policies of recommodfication do have the empirical side effect of depriving capital of either capital or labour power or the freedom to use both in profitable ways, the remedy turns out to be worse than the illness. That is to say, reformist policies of the capitalist state by no means unequivocally 'serve' the collective interests of the capitalist class: very often they are met by the most vigorous resistance and political opposition of this class. Social conflicts and political struggles, especially those with socialist potential, by no means emerge automatically from this systematic contradiction between state policy and the 'interests' of capital. These struggles are usually waged by political forces which are willing and able to consciously defend and utilize the reformist policies of the capitalist state *against* the power and obstructive resistance of the capitalist class itself.

A second structural contradiction is related to the organizational *power structures* created by reformist state strategies. It has often been observed by both liberal and Marxist social scientists that, under late capitalist conditions, those sectors of the economy which are not immediately controlled by market mechanisms tend to absorb an ever greater proportion of the overall quantity of labour power and social product. The most obvious example is public administration and all the agencies that are created and controlled by it (such as schools, transportation facilities, post offices, hospitals, public service agencies, welfare bureaucracies, the military, etc.). What is the explanation for the growing importance of these organizations? Expressed simply, it is because the state's attempts to maintain and *universalize* the commodity form require organizations whose mode of operation is no longer subject to the commodity form.

This can be demonstrated in the case of teachers. Although it is true that their labour power is exchanged for wages, it is not true that the immediate *purpose* of their labour is to produce commodities for profit on the market (which is the case in capitalist enterprises). The purpose of the labour is, rather, to produce the use-values (knowledge, skills, etc.) which put workers in a position to actually sell their labour power on the market. Schools do not sell their 'products', although they help to maintain and improve the saleability of those commodities (labour power) which are the recipients of their 'products'. The 'products' of the work of teachers are distributed to the recipients through channels different from those of exchange. The same is true in such domains as public housing authorities, hospitals, transportation systems, prisons and other branches of the state apparatus. Although nominal *fees* (as opposed to *prices*) play a mediating role in the allocation of their products and services, the prevailing allocating mechanism is not *sale* but such things as legal claims, compulsory rules, acknowledged need or simply rights to free use. It is therefore not surprising that one of the most controversial and unresolved issues in the fields of liberal public economics and political science concerns the mechanism of production and distribution of 'public goods' that could be substituted for the market exchange mechanism that is inapplicable in the realm of public production – an expanding realm of production designed to maintain and to universalize the commodity form of property.

This strategy of maintaining the commodity form presupposes the growth of state-organized forms of production that are exempt from the commodity form. This, again, is a contradiction only in a *structural* sense – a possible source of conflicts and destabilizing developments which in turn remain contingent upon conscious political action and organization directed at the 'weakest links' in the world of exchange relations. Although it is still a puzzle to many

Marxists who consider themselves 'orthodox', it is evident that the major social conflicts and political struggles that took place in America and Western Europe during the 1960s did *not* take place within the exchange relationships between labour and capital. Instead, they occurred as conflicts over the control of the organizations of social production that *serve* the commodity form without themselves being *part* of the commodity nexus. Conflicts in schools, universities, prisons, military organizations, housing authorities and hospitals are cases in point. We suggest that an explanation of this conflict can and must be based on the consideration that such administrative organizations represent the most advanced forms of erosion of the commodity form within capitalist exchange relationships themselves.

A third contradiction can be located on the *ideological* level, or in the normative and moral 'infrastructure' of capitalist society. The functioning of the commodity form presupposes two related norms with which individual actors must comply. First, they must be willing to utilize the opportunities open to them, and they must constantly strive to improve their relative position in the exchange process (*possessiveness*). Second, they must be willing to accept whatever material outcome emerges from their particular exchange relationship – particularly if this outcome is unfavourable to them. Such outcomes must, in other words, be attributed to either natural events or to the virtues and failures of the individual (*individualism*).

For a capitalist commodity economy to function, the normative syndrome of possessive individualism must be the basis of both the behaviour of actors, and their interpretations of the actual and future behaviour of others. Our point is that the contradiction of welfare state capitalism on the ideological level results in the *subversion* of this syndrome of possessive individualism. To the extent that exchange relationships are no longer 'naturally' given, but are created and maintained through visible political and administrative state strategies, the actual exchange value of any unit of labour or capital on the market can be seen as determined as much through *political* measures as through the *individual* management of one's property and resources. These individual resources thus come to be seen as something resulting from, and contingent upon, political measures. Considerations such as whether or not individuals can sell their labour power, and how much they receive for it, increasingly become – at the level of normative orientation and actors' self-understanding – a matter of adequate or inadequate state policies in such areas as education, vocational training and regional economic development. For owners of capital, similarly, market success depends less upon such factors as the willingness to take risks, inventiveness and the ability to anticipate changes in demand, and more upon state policies in such areas as taxation, tariffs, research and development, and infrastructure investment. The structural weakening of the normative and moral fibres of a capitalist commodity society – which is caused by the very attempts to stabilize and universalize the commodity form through state policy measures – again does not imply any automatic tendency towards crises or the 'breakdown' of capitalism. It can, however, become the focus of social conflict and political struggle which is oriented towards overcoming the commodity form as the organizing principle of social reproduction.

Notes and references

1   Editor's note: The authors refer here to Volker Ronge's *Forschungspolitik als Strukturpolitik* (Frankfurt 1977), and to Offe's interpretation of the failures of the SPD federal government's vocational training reform policies between 1969 and 1974, in *Berufsbildungsreform, Eine Fallstudie über Reformpolitik* (Frankfurt 1975); cf. their earlier analysis of the limits of state attempts to rationalize the West German construction industry, in 'Fiskalische Krise, Bauindustrie und die Grenzen staatlicher Rationalisierung', *Leviathan*, 2 (1973), pp. 189–220.

5 Legitimacy versus efficiency*

The attempt to describe structural problems of advanced capitalist societies through conceptual dichotomies is, at best, a starting point for discussion and analysis. Professor W. Baldamus, the British sociologist, has pointed out that such dichotomies play a vastly different role in liberal social theory on the one hand and the Marxist theoretical tradition on the other. Whereas in the former tradition they are employed either for the descriptive classification of social phenomena (for example, low versus high educational status) or as theoretical constructs that conceptualize polar opposites of a historical continuum (for example, mechanical versus organic solidarity), such dichotomies are used in Marxist thought in order to point to an *asymmetrical* or hierarchical social relationship: for example, capital versus labour, exchange value versus use value, ruling class versus proletariat. What the analyst is interested in within the latter tradition is not merely descriptive or conceptual *distinctions*, but historical *contradictions* that exist within relationships of domination in general and particularly in the capital-labour relationship.

The concept of 'contradiction'

It is not obvious at first glance in which of these two strategic perspectives of social theory the dichotomy of 'legitimacy versus efficiency' actually belongs. One can argue, on a descriptive level, that to maintain both legitimacy and efficiency is a major task of modern democratic regimes, and that various branches and

* This is a slightly shortened and edited version of 'Introduction to Part III', in Leon Lindberg et al. (eds.), *Stress and Contradiction in Modern Capitalism* (Lexington, Mass. 1975), pp. 245–59. It was first presented to the international conference on 'Patterns of Change in Advanced Industrial Society: Priorities for Social Science Research in the 1970s and 1980s', held in November 1973 at Monterosso-al-Mare, Italy.

institutions of the political system do specialize in providing either one of these functional prerequisites. One can argue that providing legitimation and providing efficiency are separate though simultaneously performed functions of the political process; this is what Edelman has analysed as the 'symbolic' and the 'instrumental' aspects of state agencies. On a more theoretical level, one can argue that the need to perform those two functions simultaneously tends to cause certain strains and tensions in such political systems that, therefore, must be resolved through strategies which are able to reconcile the two requirements. For instance, the German political scientist Fritz Scharpf has argued that the real and most important obstacles to the efficient performance of governments is in the institutionalized and fragmented pressure of specific demands to which governments have to comply in order to maintain their basis of legitimation and popular support.[1] Other authors argue that a solution to this dilemma becomes increasingly difficult to find, exactly because those values (like instrumental rationality and intellectual discipline) that are necessary for the efficient conduct of government are subverted and paralysed by 'irrational' cultural trends.[2]

Whether or not this contributes to the sharpening of a dilemma or actually constitutes a 'contradiction', as Bell maintains, is probably largely a matter of what we mean by the term 'contradiction'. If we mean the incidence of opposing demands and conflicting pressures that have to be absorbed by a particular institutional setting (be it a political system, a family, or a business enterprise), then the concept approximates the term 'dilemma'. Dilemmas, however, are fairly common and virtually universal in social relationships, and it adds little to our understanding of social reality if we call them 'contradictions'.

An alternative use of the concept 'contradiction' might be sketched out in the following way. Any human society operates through an institutionalized set of rules. A part of these rules determines the process by which the society reproduces itself materially, and thereby transcends the lifetime of its individual members. More specifically, these institutionalized rules of material reproduction regulate three things; namely, the effective control over human labour power, over the material means and resources of production, and over the product itself. Numerous mechanisms of control, or modes of production, which regulate these three elements of material reproduction, can be distinguished historically. Each has its own specific economic, political, and cultural requirements on which it depends in order to secure its continuity as a societal mode of production. Now, a contradiction is not simply a situation in which these indispensable requirements of a certain mode of production are absent or inadequately fulfilled. If that were the case, catastrophes (like floods or epidemics and also 'social catastrophes' like wars) would indicate contradictions. This would hardly be an adequate use of the term. What we mean by contradictions is rather narrower and more precise. A contradiction is the tendency inherent within a specific mode of production to destroy those very pre-conditions on which its survival depends. Contradictions become manifest in situations where, in other words, a collision occurs between the constituent pre-conditions and the results of a specific mode of production, or where the necessary becomes impossible and the impossible becomes necessary.

Without a single exception, all Marxist theorems that try to elucidate the nature of capitalism are based upon this concept of contradiction. A few theorems that have been explored by Marx and Marxist authors can be mentioned here (without implying that all of them are valid or remain valid under the conditions of advanced capitalism). The 'law' of the falling rate of profit maintains that what is necessary for the accumulation process of capital (namely, the introduction of labour-saving technical change) turns out to make further accumulation impossible (due to the decreased share of variable capital out of which surplus value and hence profit can solely be extracted). Similarly, the theorem of underconsumption maintains that what is necessary to maximize profits (namely, the reduction of the wages of labour) renders impossible further capitalist accumulation because of the resulting decline in 'effective demand' and the consequent 'realization' problem. In the same way the organizational strength and political struggle of the working class is analysed in various Marxian theories as a direct consequence of the very mode of capitalist production that systematically creates the conditions under which the working class can engage in anti-capitalist struggles.

Numerous other theorems, based on the same concept of contradiction, could be mentioned. For the purpose of illustration, however, it may be sufficient to point out that in all of them the term contradiction is not used as an attribute of a particular actor in a particular situation, or as a condition that prevails in a specific institutional sector of society. The term contradiction is rather used as an analytical concept related to the dominant mode of production by which a society reproduces itself. Contradictions are not contingent, but rooted in the mode of production, which is *itself* seen to be contradictory, that is, self-paralysing and self-destructive.

Here the obvious questions emerge: how can something exist at all in historical reality that is inherently contradictory by nature? How can it become and remain operative as a mode of production? Does its very existence (and duration over time) invalidate the concept of contradiction as applied to a mode of production? Such paradoxical conclusions can only be avoided if we assume that:

1   the structural contradictions of the capitalist mode of production are not *uniform* throughout the history of a capitalist development, but become larger and more pervasive as accumulation proceeds;
2   the concept of 'contradiction' does not imply any automatic 'breakdown' or 'crisis' of the capitalist mode of production.

In other words, the self-destructive tendencies of the capitalist mode of production evolve in a historical process, and their destructive and revolutionary potential can well be controlled and kept latent through various adaptive mechanisms of the system, at least temporarily. The expectation that the ability to reconcile emerging contradictions through such adaptive measures is limited, and that contradictions will finally result in a *crisis* of the capitalist mode of production, is not based on any utopian hopes, but on the consideration that there is no actor or agency within the capitalist mode of production that is sufficiently unaffected by those contradictions that are to be reconciled to be able to act in such a way as to counteract them.

Whatever the particular contributions of the Marxist theory of society are, it should have become clear by now that this theory proceeds according to a fundamental theoretical model in which the concepts of the 'mode of production', 'contradiction' and 'crisis' are closely and inseparably interconnected.

But what does all of this have to do with the problem that is alluded to by the dichotomy of legitimacy versus efficiency? I argued a moment ago that the theoretical link between contradiction and crisis is to be found in the fact that such corrective or adaptive mechanisms in society as could perform the function of repressing or reconciling contradictions are themselves involved in the contradictions inherent in the capitalist mode of production.

Both liberal and Marxist theorists see the state as the major institutional system in advanced capitalist society that could assume the function of overcoming contradictions. The central analytical controversy, however, concerns the question of whether the state is actually able to perform this function effectively or whether there are systematic contradictions *on the level of state activity itself* that prevent the state from dealing successfully with the contradictions of the capitalist mode of production. It is this controversy that provides a theoretically relevant background for the discussion of 'legitimacy versus efficiency'. The exploration of these two concepts, or aspects of state activity, may contribute to the resolution of the controversy between liberals and Marxists about the nature of the state.

Legitimacy and efficiency

Before discussing this question, I should like to consider some alternative meanings of the two terms legitimacy and efficiency. Since the famous typology of Max Weber, legitimacy is conceived as the essential and indispensable basis of political authority. According to Weber there are different historical modes of legitimating political authority, and one of these modes, the legal-rational one, tends to become the dominant one in the modern world. The great advantage of this mode of legitimation[3] relative to the historically older ones consists of the fact that authority becomes legitimate independently of who is the incumbent in political office or what the intentions of the incumbents are. The only thing that decides the legitimacy of political authority is whether or not it has been achieved in accordance with general formal principles, for example, election rules. These legal principles endow political power, whatever use is made of it, with legitimacy. Compared with those older forms of legitimation, the legitimating mechanism is shifted from the *substance* of authority of the *person* or the ruler to the *mode* by which office holders are recruited.

Those selection principles[4] that regulate the access to political authority and that carry the burden of legitimating it operate in two directions. They constitute binding directions for both the rulers and the ruled. In modern democratic regimes these formal principles oblige the (prospective) office holders to pass the test of general elections, to obey the rules of the constitution while in office, and to resign from power as soon as a competing party elite achieves an electoral victory. Conversely, such constitutional rules of democratic government also bind the behaviour of the citizens who are subject to state authority. This is most obvious in the obligation to comply with the laws made by government, and it is also clear in the fact that the citizens are prohibited from promoting their individual and collective interests through political means other than those provided by the constitution. In other words, the legitimating power of formal constitutional rules reaches as far, and only as far, as the governing elites comply with these rules *and* as far as the ruled are willing to refrain from modes of political behaviour that are not covered by the set of options provided for them by the constitution.

If this is true, a question now emerges: what are the conditions under which these legitimating rules find universal *acceptance*, and under what conditions do they fail to find such acceptance (either on the part of the rulers or of the ruled)? It is exactly because these rules are formal that they cannot win acceptance because of the advantages they imply. Their acceptance must depend not upon what *they* are, but what the *consequences* or likely *results* of their application are. We do not drive on the right-hand side of the road because there is any inherent preference for doing so, but because we assume that general compliance to this formal rule will result in greater safety of transportation, etc. In the same way the preference for democratic government is not based on the rules themselves but on the expectation that this form of government will contribute to common and individual welfare and other desirable ends. The ability of governments actually to produce such ends – or at least to create the appearance that it is able to achieve such ends – may consequently be considered as one major determinant of what we have called acceptance of the legitimating rules that, as formal rules, have themselves to be legitimated. The problem of legitimacy thus turns out to be caught in the dialectic of form and content.

The concept of efficiency is equally in need of some clarification. In the academic disciplines of business administration and organization theory a distinction is made between *efficiency* and *effectiveness*. Marginal gains in efficiency occur if the same amount of output can be produced at lower costs. Effectiveness, on the other hand, measures the ability of an organization to achieve its stated goals. The typical dilemma of the management of a private firm is to find a combination of the two – often inversely related – performance criteria that maximize profits. Both efficiency and effectiveness are sub-goals relative to the overriding goal of *profitability* of private firms who buy and sell their inputs and outputs on *markets*. Where – as in the case of governmental organizations or the state in general – both the criteria of profitability and market relationships are absent, it becomes difficult to attribute a clear-cut meaning to such terms as efficiency and effectiveness. If, for instance, the postal services and mail distribution are closed on Saturdays in order to save costs and to reduce the chronic deficit of most government-run post offices, this measure looks like an economizing, hence efficiency-increasing, act. Upon closer inspection, however, we see that this is not necessarily the case: it implies greater inconvenience for the users of postal services as well as a reduction of the number (or wages) of postal employees, and only a government that was in a position to consider these side effects as irrelevant (both politically and economically) could congratulate itself on having achieved a gain in efficiency. In the absence of this highly unlikely condition of the irrelevance of side effects, the state agency would have to take into account the trade-off that exists between the saving of expenditure and the increase in user inconvenience. But since only one of these variables, namely expenditure, can be calculated in monetary terms, whereas the other one (user inconvenience) does not reflect a market process, the comparison between the two is not amenable to calculation. Hence, it is hardly demonstrable that in fact an efficiency gain has been achieved through any particular government measure.

A similar difficulty occurs in the case of the *effectiveness* of government activity. Within the jurisdiction of a particular agency and within the framework of given goals, the effectiveness (or ability to achieve stated goals) of a given agency can easily be determined. However, since the governmental system of organizations does not receive its goals from the market (like a business firm), it has to organize a process by which goals are defined, their priority in time and funds is determined, and the responsibility for the achievement of this goal is assigned to a particular agency. Again, in the absence of market relationships and the profit criterion, the term effectiveness becomes ambiguous. For instance, a particular agency may be highly effective in implementing goals that are determined through a highly ineffective political process of decision-making. School administrators may be very effective in implementing a programme of school reform that turns out not to serve the purposes it was designed to serve in the first place, and a similar judgement may be reached in respect to NASA and the decision to send a man to the moon.

We conclude that the rationality operating in the capitalist state (or normatively postulated for its operation) cannot be the type of rationality that prevails in private organizations. The goal that inspires the capitalist state and its detailed operation is not a substantive one and cannot be justified as a substantive one. That is to say, the capitalist state is not oriented towards doing anything efficiently or effectively (because there is no way to determine whether efficiency or effectiveness has actually been advanced through any measure or programme); rather, it is oriented towards putting private actors in a position to increase their efficiency and effectiveness according to the criteria of private exchange and accumulation. Due to the constitutional arrangements that we find in liberal democracies, the state is not even allowed to pursue any substantive ends other than those that constitute the pre-conditions for universal commodity relationships.

This important point can easily be demonstrated. Schooling and training do not have the purpose of providing knowledge and abilities to young people; they do have the purpose of putting individuals in the position to use their labour power as commodities on the labour market, and for this purpose knowledge and abilities are thought to be instrumental variables. How efficiently and effectively educational policies do operate can only be determined by looking at the increases in efficiency and effectiveness that appear in the private sector, that is, in the market interaction of the owners of labour power and the owners of money capital who are willing to pay wages for the use of this labour power. There is no 'internal' criterion of a 'good' policy, independent of commodity interaction. Not only will a policy that manifestly fails to put private units in the commodity form (or to help them to survive in that form) be considered a failure by policy-makers, but also the budgetary basis of such policies will decline. Important trends in the discipline of policy analysis and its practical recommendations point in the direction of modernizing policy design in a specific way; namely, reducing those benevolent welfare-state measures that consist of handing out goods and services to certain categories of people in 'need', and replacing them by measures that are expected to put them in a position to take care of their needs themselves through the sale of their labour power.

The capitalist state is efficient and effective not by its own criteria, but to the extent that it succeeds in the universalization of the commodity form. The ideal state of affairs is a situation in which every citizen can take care of all of his or her needs through participation in market processes, and the inherent test of rationality of policy-making in the capitalist state is the extent to which it approximates this situation. There is no need to equate the capitalist state, either empirically or theoretically, with a political alliance of the personnel of the state apparatus on the one side and the class of the owners of capital (or certain segments of this class) on the other side. For the abstract principle of making a subject of permanent market exchange relationships out of every citizen does more to keep state policies in tune with the class interests of the agents of accumulation than any supposed 'conspiracy' between 'overlapping directorates' of state and industry could possibly achieve. As the most general strategic rule, which is the key to most observable policies and changes in the method of policy-making, the imperative to universalize the commodity form means doing nothing but two things. First, putting every owner of labour power in a position that makes him or her able to find employment on the labour market, the demand side of which is directly or indirectly determined by the profitability criteria of the owners of capital; as soon as labour is made employable under these criteria, the surplus-value extracted from the labour power under conditions of equivalent exchange is guaranteed. Second, putting individual units of capital or capital as a whole in a position in which it actually appears to be profitable to buy labour power. In this sense full employment of all units of value under the exploitative conditions of the capitalist mode of production is in fact the supreme purpose of the capitalist state and the substance of its observable activity.

From this discussion of the concepts of legitimacy, efficiency and effectiveness I wish to suggest one conclusion. There is only one point of general equilibrium in the relationship between legitimacy and efficiency, and that harmonic balance is achieved if:

1   the acceptance of the legitimating rules of democratic and constitutional regimes is reinforced by the material outcomes of governmental measures and policies;
2   if these measures and policies are 'efficient' in the only way a capitalist state can be efficient, namely, in successfully providing, restoring and maintaining commodity relationships for all citizens and for the totality of their needs.

This definition of the state of general balance serves, however, only as a starting point for the attempt to explore causes of possible deviations from this 'harmony' that then could explain the supposed contradictory relationship between the requirements of legitimacy and efficiency.

Hypotheses about contradictions between efficiency and legitimacy

There are three broad categories of empirical phenomena that could disturb such an idealized balance of the legitimacy and efficiency of the capitalist state. They can be very briefly distinguished and illustrated as follows.

First, the problem of securing the commodity form of both labour and capital becomes both more urgent and more difficult to solve in the course of capitalist development. The monopolistic structure of industry that we find in the dominant sectors of most advanced capitalist economies best illustrates this situation. Monopolies tend to make larger profits relative to industries in competitive situations, and hence they need larger investment opportunities in order to maintain their operation at a given level of employment of both capital and labour.[5] In the absence of easy-to-occupy new markets, it becomes more costly for the state to open new investment opportunities for monopoly profits (for example, socializing parts of their private costs or by relieving them of the burden of paying for their social costs), and hence to maintain their rate of growth. But even if state economic policies succeed in keeping the monopolistic sector in operation, they do so at the risk of the declining employment of labour due to the constant introduction of labour-saving technological change taking place in the monopolistic sector. Moreover, the further the process of monopolization has already proceeded at a given point in time, the more difficult it becomes for corporations to find investment opportunities on markets that are already 'closed' by monopolistic practices. These structural problems lead to a situation that is characterized by the existence of a large and permanent 'surplus population', consisting of both owners of labour power unable to find employment and owners of capital unable to find profitable investment opportunities.

The political alternatives that are likely to come up in this situation are either a violation of the legitimating rules (for which support can no longer be provided through state policies) by the occupants of the state apparatus, or a violation of those rules by the ruled. In both cases the dual constraining power in which, as we have seen, the constitutional arrangements of liberal democracy consist, is weakened. If the constitution is broken by the rulers, the commodity form is restored by such measures as increased regressiveness of taxation, the repeal of the right to strike, to engage in union activity or to form militant organizations; and, finally, forced labour for those parts of the labour force that do not find employment on the ordinary labour market. If the constitution is broken by the ruled, the commodity form is tentatively abolished in mass struggles using means of political power that are declared illegal by the constitution and constitutional authorities, and in which the workers insist that their work, their income, and their life should no longer be controlled by capitalist 'market forces', but by rights based upon popular power. One contradiction within the operation of the capitalist state is that by supporting capitalist commodity production it cannot but support those forces of accumulation that result in the opposite of full employment, namely, the irreversible 'dropping out' of growing parts of both labour and capital.[6]

A second contradictory relationship between legitimacy and efficiency is this: in order to prevent the erosion of the commodity form (as well as ruptures in the accumulation process that is based on the equivalent exchange between labour and capital, that is, on the commodity form), numerous and still increasing measures have been initiated by capitalist states and their governments to increase the ability of value units to engage in exchange relationships and to perform as commodities. The already mentioned policies of schooling and training are designed to increase the saleability of labour power. Recent innovations in industrial relations regulations[7] and labour market policies[8] in Western countries pursue the goal of:

1   instituting flexible and at the same time responsible frameworks of wage determination and arbitration that are expected to safeguard both sides in their existence as commodities;
2   facilitating the integration and, if necessary, repeated reintegration of labour power into an economy that is characterized by unforeseeable and abrupt economic and technical changes.

A similar rationale seems to be pursued in the area of research and development policies (which are expected to provide the chance to participate in competitive accumulation processes to individual capital units and whole industries) as well as in the area of regional development, where policies are also designed to keep capital and labour competitive; that is, connected with exchange opportunities.

Such state-organized provisions for exchangeability do imply two alternative contradictions. Such 'far-sighted' programmes may fail to win the support of those parts of the capitalist class (and occasionally the working class) who are the beneficiaries of the status quo of the actual or imminent disappearance of certain values from the market. For it is by no means self-evident that there is a universal and consistent interest in the general 'commodification' of value. For instance, if one firm has the prospect of achieving a monopoly position and out-competing its former competitors, it will hardly be in favour of state measures that help the prospective victim survive. Similarly, if one industry derives its profits mainly from the employment of cheap and unskilled youth labour, it will be opposed to state training programmes that would increase the range of alternative market options open to its workers and hence threaten its profits. The political creation of market options for certain categories of labour or capital or both (as in the case of regional development) will always be at the expense of some others, and where competitive relationships among categories of labour prevail (for example, professionals versus semi-professionals, male versus female workers), there is no exception to this rule. The fact that such programmes of political and administrative commodification tend to be costly in their share of the budget and have to be financed out of tax money often makes it easy for the specific opponents of such programmes to win allies among the mass of taxpayers and to launch vigorous political resistance and obstruction to such programmes. The underlying contradiction of such familiar political issues and conflicts is that the attempt of the state apparatus to maintain and universalize the commodity form is not only not in the common and long-term interest of capital as a whole, but also clearly against the particular and short-term interest of many owners of both labour and capital who are negatively affected by such programmes. To the extent the capitalist state fails to impose its policies upon the resisting factions of capital and labour, we are at the same point as before, namely, in a situation where there is a manifest surplus population of both labour power and capitalists unable to participate in exchange relationships.

But even if state policies succeed in restoring and maintaining commodity relationships (at the expense and against the resistance of those in whose particularistic interest the absence of options of exchange of others lies), the problem is by no means settled. The contradiction that becomes apparent under these conditions is the following one: the restoration of commodity relationships through the state and its administrative agencies takes place under social arrangements that are themselves external to commodity relationships.[9] The problem with which experts in public economies and infrastructure investment have dealt in various ways can be summarized by the questions: how can state authorities serve the market by means that in fact suspend market relationships? How can commodities be created in a 'decommodified' way?

Obviously, the relationship between a worker and an employer or between a department store and its customer, on the one side, and the relationship between a teacher and a student, or a highway authority and the users of highways, on the other side, differ in one crucial aspect: in the first case, the transaction is determined through effective demand, supply, and individual profitability criteria, whereas in the second case the transaction is structured by such parameters as politically perceived and determined needs, budgetary decision-making, and administrative expertise. Occasionally there are desperate attempts, especially among conservative political forces in all advanced capitalist countries, to turn back the wheel of supposedly unproductive state expenditures for public goods and public services, to 'reprivatize' them, or at least to create a public goods market so that the rules of production and allocation of public goods may eventually become analogous to those rules governing the exchange of commodities.

The powerful political thrust to get rid of this administrative mode of control over labour and material resources is often, but not exclusively, motivated by the need to relieve the economy of the burden of taxation, and to overcome the fiscal crisis of the state.[10] A second argument is of similar importance. It is the fear that the administrative form of control over material resources could become politicized to such an extent that it would no longer be subservient to, but subversive of the commodity form. This fear is well grounded in many facts. We see that wherever the state expands services and infrastructure, they become the focus of conflicts that, on the most general and abstract level, can be described as conflicts between the function of commodification such services are designed to serve and the decommodified form in which they try to do this.

Such conflicts cannot occur under pure commodity relationships,

because the great virtue of the commodity form of social organization is that it settles conflict automatically. If two individuals need
the same good, no conflict can arise because it is given to the one
who is able to pay a higher price; and if two suppliers compete for
the money of one purchaser, no conflict can arise between them,
because the purchaser decides according to individual quality or
price considerations. It is exactly this peace-making function of the
market mechanism that is removed from the administrative form of
providing goods and services. There is no accepted formula by
which it could be decided what is to be learned at school, how many
miles of highway should be built in what region, and so on. Sometimes the resulting political conflicts are merely about what specific
category of capital or labour should be served by such investments
and services to maintain their commodity existence, but often the
very commodity form itself is at issue in such conflicts. This is the
case when the question is brought up – and sometimes fought out in
militant struggles – concerning whether schools, universities,
hospitals, welfare systems, prisons, housing authorities, conserva-
tion projects, etc., should aim to provide or restore marketable
labour power and material resources, or whether they should serve
some alternative needs and social purposes.

The contradiction within state-organized production of goods
and services is one of form and content. By virtue of their origin and
functional content, such organizations are designed to create
options of exchange for both labour and capital. By virtue of their
formal administrative mode of operation, they are exempt from
commodity relationships: use values are produced and distributed
without being controlled and dominated by exchange values. This
tends to open up such state agencies to demands that sometimes (as
was the case in the student revolt) are directed against the
commodity form itself as well as against a state apparatus that is
seen to be subservient to this form. By expanding social services and
infrastructure investment, the state not only exacerbates the
symptoms of the fiscal crisis, it also makes itself the focus of conflict
over the mode in which societal resources should be utilized.[11] The
state does not so much, as liberal reformers believe, become a force
of social change and social progress, but rather it increasingly
becomes the arena of struggle; it provides the rudimentary model of
organization of social life that is liberated from the commodity form
without being able to live up to the promise implicit in that model.
State agencies project an image of themselves that suggests that use

values like education, knowledge, health, welfare and other ingredients of a 'decent' life actually are the final purpose of its measures and policies. The experience that this image is misleading, and that the state produces all these services not in order to satisfy the corresponding needs, but only to the extent that is required to keep in motion the universe of commodities with its implicit exploitative relationships of production – this experience must cause specific conflicts and attitudes of frustration over 'false promises'.

The increasingly visible conflict between the promise and experience, form and content of state policies can lead – and this is the major hypothesis related to the legitimacy/efficiency dichotomy – to a growing difficulty for state policies to win acceptance for the legitimating rules on which political power is based. The most active state policies that try to maintain and to restore exchange opportunities for every citizen through a huge variety of economic and social strategies of intervention are – according to their form and the image they project of themselves – a model of social relations that is liberated from the commodity form. In actual fact, however, these policies are forced to operate as supportive mechanisms of the commodity form, and within the fiscal and institutional limits of the universe of commodity relationships. A dual and inconsistent standard of 'goodness' of policy-making results from this structure. Policies will be measured both by the exchangeability they produce for labour and capital *and* by their promise to satisfy needs of people through alternative, non-market means of social production. The very concepts of health (the ability to work versus physical well-being), education (the marketability of labour power versus personality development) and all other social services are characterized by this dual reference to the commodity form *and* to need. This duality makes it increasingly difficult for the political system to gain support and acceptance for those legitimating rules of democratic government on which political power is based.

A third contradiction must be briefly mentioned. It has been argued[12] that the terms of acceptance of the legitimating rules of political power undergo a structural change that itself is propelled by the consequences of some state services. For instance, expanded education is said to exert effects upon the moral consciousness of people, and these effects tend to make them unwilling to accept the apparent universalism inherent in the rules of liberal democracy and representative government. Consequently, the terms of acceptance become more demanding and the willingness of people to engage in 'non-constitutional' forms of struggle is increased. This makes the difficulties of the political regime even greater. To be sure, there is no functional need for explicit legitimation as long as 'everything goes well' and role acceptance is forced upon citizens either by their own utilitarian/instrumental motives and/or, at least, by the absence of feasible alternative roles and social mechanisms. To put it in slightly different terms, as long as every citizen takes part in market relationships that allow him or her to do so continuously, there is no apparent reason to challenge the legitimating rules of political power or even to think about them in cognitive terms. As everyday experience teaches, and as I have argued in the preceding sections, this happy condition of normality can hardly be assumed to be the normal case. Either the 'commodity existence of every citizen' is visibly and clearly threatened, or the organizational arrangements by which state policies try to maintain and to restore exchange relationships do themselves open up political alternatives by which those half-conscious attitudes of 'institutional fit' become subverted. While it is true, as Mann cogently demonstrates, that 'capitalism is distrusted by intellectuals',[13] he fails to give any indication as to why, after all, intellectuals are not the only ones to distrust capitalism and the legitimating rules of the capitalist state.

Notes and references

1   F. Scharpf, *Planung als politischer Prozeß* (Frankfurt 1973).

2   cf. D. Bell, 'The Cultural Contradictions of Capitalism', *The Public Interest*, **21** (Fall 1970).

3   For recent discussions of the concept of legitimacy cf. P. Graf Kielmannsegg, 'Legitimität als analytische Kategorie', *Politische Vierteljahresschrift*, **12** no. 3 (1971); P. Green and S. Levinson (eds.), *Power and Community* (New York 1970), pp. 276–327; and J. Habermas, *Legitimation Crisis* (Boston 1975).

4   The concept of selection principles is used and elaborated in C. Offe, 'Structural Problems of the Capitalist State', *German Political Studies* (London 1974), vol. 1, pp. 31–57.

5   This is the key argument in P. Baran and P. M. Sweezy, *Monopoly Capital* (New York 1964).

6   For a very detailed and original analysis of the emerging 'surplus

population' see various works of J. O'Connor, above all his *Fiscal Crisis of the State* (New York 1974).

7   cf. J. Goldthorpe, 'Industrial Relations in Great Britain, A Critique of Reformism', paper prepared for a conference on 'Sources of Discontent and Institutional Innovation in Advanced Industrial Societies', Columbia University, March 1974.

8   C. Offe, *Berufsbildungsreform, Eine Fallstudie über Reformpolitik* (Frankfurt 1975).

9   For an elaboration of this point, see C. Offe, 'The abolition of market control and the problem of legitimacy', *Working Papers on the Kapitalistate*, no. 1 (1973) and *idem.*, *Strukturprobleme des Kapitalistischen Staates* (Frankfurt 1973).

10 cf. O'Connor, *Fiscal Crisis*.

11 cf. *ibid.*, Chapter 9.

12 See Habermas, *Legitimation Crisis*.

13 Michael Mann, 'The ideology of intellectuals and other people in the development of capitalism', in Leon Lindberg *et al.* (eds.), *Stress and Contradiction in Modern Capitalism* (Lexington, Mass. 1975), pp. 275–307.

6   Some contradictions of the modern welfare state*

The welfare state has served as the major peace formula of advanced capitalist democracies for the period following the Second World War. This peace formula basically consists, first, in the explicit obligation of the state apparatus to provide assistance and support (either in money or in kind) to those citizens who suffer from specific needs and risks which are characteristic of the market society; such assistance is provided as a matter of legal claims granted to the citizens. Second, the welfare state is based on the recognition of the formal role of labour unions both in collective bargaining and the formation of public policy. Both of these structural components of the welfare state are considered to limit and mitigate class conflict, to balance the asymmetrical power relation of labour and capital, and thus to overcome the condition of disruptive struggle and contradictions that was the most prominent feature of pre-welfare state, or liberal, capitalism. In sum, the welfare state has been celebrated throughout the post-war period as the political solution to societal contradictions.

Until quite recently, this seemed to be the converging view of political elites both in countries in which the welfare state is fully developed (for example, Great Britain, Sweden), and in those where it is still an incompletely realized model. Political conflict in these latter societies, such as the USA, was not centred on the basic desirability and functional indispensability, but on the pace and modalities of the implementation of the welfare state model.

This was true, with very minor exceptions, until the mid 1970s. From that point on we see that in many capitalist societies this established peace formula itself becomes the object of doubts,

* This essay was first presented as a paper to the Facoltà de Scienze Politiche, Università di Perugia, Italy, February 1980. It is here reprinted, with minor alterations, from the version published in *Praxis International*, 1 no. 3 (October 1981), pp. 219–29.

fundamental critique, and political conflict. It appears that the most widely accepted device of political problem-solving has itself become problematic, and that, at any rate, the unquestioning confidence in the welfare state and its future expansion has rapidly vanished. It is to these doubts and criticisms that I will direct our attention. The point to start with is the observation that the almost universally accepted model of creating a measure of social peace and harmony in European post-war societies has itself become the source of new contradictions and political divisions in the 1970s.

Historically, the welfare state has been the combined outcome of a variety of factors which change in composition from country to country. Social democratic reformism, Christian socialism, enlightened conservative political and economic elites, and large industrial unions were the most important forces which fought for and conceded more and more comprehensive compulsory insurance schemes, labour protection legislation, minimum wages, the expansion of health and education facilities and state-subsidized housing, as well as the recognition of unions as legitimate economic and political representatives of labour. These continuous developments in Western societies were often dramatically accelerated in a context of intense social conflict and crisis, particularly under war and post-war conditions. The accomplishments which were won under conditions of war and in post-war periods were regularly maintained, and added to them were the innovations that could be introduced in periods of prosperity and growth. In the light of the Keynesian doctrine of economic policy, the welfare state came to be seen not so much as a burden imposed upon the economy, but as a built-in economic and political stabilizer which could help to regenerate the forces of economic growth and prevent the economy from spiralling downward into deep recessions. Thus, a variety of quite heterogeneous ends (ranging from reactionary pre-emptive strikes against the working-class movement in the case of Bismarck to socialist reformism in the case of the Weimar social democrats; from the social-political consolidation of war and defence economies to the stabilization of the business cycle, etc.) converged on the adoption of identical institutional means which today make up the welfare state. It is exactly its multi-functional character, its ability to serve many conflicting ends and strategies simultaneously, which made the political arrangement of the welfare state so attractive to a broad alliance of heterogeneous forces. But it is equally true that the very diversity of the forces that inaugurated and supported the welfare state could not be accommodated forever within the institutional framework which today appears to come increasingly under attack. The machinery of class compromise has itself become the object of class conflict.

The attack from the Right

The sharp economic recession of the mid 1970s has given rise to an intellectually and politically powerful renaissance of neo-*laissez-faire* and monetarist economic doctrines. These doctrines amount to a fundamental critique of the welfare state that is seen to be the illness of what it pretends to be the cure: rather than effectively harmonizing the conflicts of a market society, it exacerbates them and prevents the forces of social peace and progress (namely, the forces of the market-place) from functioning properly and beneficially. This is said to be so for two major reasons. First, the welfare state apparatus imposes a burden of taxation and regulation upon capital which amounts to a *disincentive to investment*. Second, at the same time, the welfare state grants claims, entitlements and collective power positions to workers and unions which amount to *a disincentive to work*, or at least to work as hard and productively as they would be forced to under the reign of unfettered market forces. Taken together, these two effects lead into a dynamic of declining growth and increased expectations, of economic 'demand overload' (known as inflation) as well as political demand overload ('ungovernability'), which can be satisfied less and less by the available output.

As obvious as the reactionary political uses are that this analysis is usually meant to support or suggest, it may well be that the truth of the analysis itself is greater than the desirability of its practical conclusions. Although the democratic Left has often measured the former by the latter, the two deserve at least a separate evaluation. In my view the above analysis is not so much false in what it says but in what it remains silent about.

For instance, to take up the first point of the conservative analysis: is it not true that, under conditions of declining growth rates and vehement competition on domestic and international markets, individual capitalists, at least those firms which do not enjoy the privileges of the monopolistic sector, have many good reasons to consider the prospects for investment and profits bleak, and to blame the welfare state, which imposes social security taxes and a great variety of regulations on them, for reducing profitability even further? Is it not true that the power position of unions, which, in turn, is based on rights they have won through industrial relations, collective bargaining, and other laws, is great enough to make an increasing number of industrial producers unprofitable or to force them to seek investment opportunities abroad? And is it not also true that capitalist firms will make investment (and hence employment) decisions according to criteria of expected profitability, and that they consequently will fail to invest as soon as long-term profitability is considered unattractive by them, thus causing an aggregate relative decline in the production output of the economy?

To be sure, no one would deny that there are causes of declining growth rates and capitalists' failure to invest which have nothing to do with the impact of the welfare state upon business, but which are rather to be looked for in inherent crisis tendencies of the capitalist economy such as overaccumulation, the business cycle, or uncontrolled technical change. But even if so, it still might make sense to alleviate the hardship imposed upon capital – and therefore, by definition, upon the rest of society, within the confines of a capitalist society – by dropping some of the burdens and constraints of the welfare state. This, of course, is exactly what most proponents of this argument are suggesting as a practical consequence. But after all, so the fairly compelling logic of the argument continues, who benefits from the operation of a welfare state that undermines and eventually destroys the production system upon which it has to rely in order to make its own promises become true? Does not a kind of 'welfare' become merely nominal and worthless anyway that punishes capital by a high burden of costs and hence everyone else by inflation, unemployment, or both? In my view, the valuable insight to be gained from the type of analysis I have just described is this: the welfare state, rather than being a separate and autonomous source of well-being which provides incomes and services as a citizen right, is itself highly dependent upon the prosperity and continued profitability of the economy. While being designed to be a cure to some ills of capitalist accumulation, the nature of the illness is such that it may force the patient to refrain from using the cure.

A conceivable objection to the above argument would be that capitalists and conservative political elites 'exaggerate' the harm imposed upon them by welfare state arrangements. To be sure, in the political game they have good tactical reasons to make the welfare state burden appear more intolerable than it 'really' is. The question boils down then to what we mean by – and how we measure – 'reality' in this context. In answering this question, we will have to keep in mind that the power position of private investors includes the power to *define* reality. That is to say, whatever they *consider* an intolerable burden in fact *is* an intolerable burden which will *in fact* lead to a declining propensity to invest, at least as long as they can expect to effectively reduce welfare-state-related costs by applying such economic sanctions. The debate about whether or not the welfare state is 'really' squeezing profits is thus purely academic because investors are in a position to *create the reality – and the effects – of 'profit squeeze'*.

The second major argument of the conservative analysis postulates that the effect of the welfare state is a disincentive to work. 'Labour does not work!' was one of the slogans in the campaign that brought Margaret Thatcher into the office of the British Prime Minister. But, again, the analytical content of the argument must be carefully separated from the political uses to which it is put. And, again, this analytical argument can, often contrary to the intentions of its proponents, be read in a way that does make a lot of empirical sense. For instance, there is little doubt that elaborate labour protection legislation puts workers in a position to resist practices of exploitation that would be applied, as a rule, in the absence of such regulations. Powerful and recognized unions can in fact obtain wage increases in excess of productivity increases. And extensive social security provisions make it easier – at least for some workers, for some of the time – to avoid undesirable jobs. Large-scale unemployment insurance covering most of the working population makes unemployment less undesirable for many workers and thus partially obstructs the reserve army mechanism. Thus, the welfare state has made the exploitation of labour more complicated and less predictable. On the other side, as the welfare state imposes regulations and rights upon the labour–capital exchange that goes on in production, while leaving the authority structure and the property relations of production itself untouched, it is hardly surprising to see that the workers are not, as a rule, so intrinsically motivated to work that they would work as productively as they possibly could. In other words, the welfare state maintains the control of capital over production, and thus the basic source of industrial and class conflict between labour and capital; by no means does it establish anything resembling 'workers control'. At the same time, it strengthens workers' potential for resistance against capital's control – the net effect being that an unchanged conflict is fought out with means that have changed in favour of labour. Exploitative production relations coexist with expanded possibilities to resist, escape and mitigate exploitation. While the *reason* for struggle remained unchanged, the *means* of struggle increased for the workers. It is not surprising to see that this condition undermines the 'work ethic', or at least requires more costly and less reliable strategies to enforce such an ethic.[1]

My point, so far, is that the two key arguments of the liberal–conservative analysis are valid to a large extent, contrary to what critics from the Left have often argued. The basic fault I see in this analysis has less to do with what it explicitly states than with what it leaves out of its consideration. Every political theory worth its name has to answer two questions. First, what is the desirable form of the organization of society and state and how can we demonstrate that it is at all 'workable', i.e., consistent with our basic normative and factual assumptions about social life? This is the problem of defining a consistent *model* or goal of transformation. Second, how do we get there? This is the problem of identifying the dynamic forces and *strategies* that could bring about the transformation.

The conservative analysis of the welfare state fails on both counts. To start with the latter problem, it is extremely hard today in Western Europe to conceive of a promising political strategy that would aim at even partially eliminating the established institutional components of the welfare state, to say nothing about its wholesale abolition. That is to say, the welfare state has, in a certain sense, become an irreversible structure, the abolition of which would require nothing less than the abolition of political democracy and the unions, as well as fundamental changes in the party system. A political force that could bring about such dramatic changes is nowhere visible as a significant factor, Right-wing middle-class populist movements that occasionally spring up in some countries notwithstanding. Moreover, it is a well-known fact from political opinion research that the fiercest advocates of *laissez-faire* capitalism and economic individualism show marked differences between their *general* ideological outlook and their willingness to have *special* transfers, subsidies, and social security schemes abandoned from which they *personally* derive benefits. Thus, in the absence of a powerful ideological and organizational undercurrent in Western politics (such as a neo-fascist or authoritarian one), the vision of overcoming the welfare state and resurrecting a 'healthy' market economy is not much more than the politically impotent day-dream of some ideologues of the old middle class. This class is nowhere strong enough to effect, as the examples of Margaret Thatcher and – hypothetically – Ronald Reagan demonstrate, more than marginal alterations of an institutional scheme that such figures, too, have to accept as given when taking office.

Even more significant, however, is the second failure of the conservative analysis; its failure to demonstrate that 'advanced-capitalism-*minus*-the-welfare-state' would actually be a workable model. The reasons why it is not, and consequently why the neo-*laissez-faire* ideology would be a very dangerous cure even *if* it could be administered, are fairly obvious. In the absence of large-scale state-subsidized housing, public education and health services, as well as extensive compulsory social security schemes, the working of an industrial economy would be simply inconceivable. Given the conditions and requirements of urbanization, large-scale concentration of labour power in industrial production plants, rapid technical, economic and regional change, the reduced ability of the family to cope with the difficulties of life in industrial society, the secularization of the moral order, the quantitative reduction and growing dependence of the propertied middle classes – all of which are well-known characteristics of capitalist social structures – the sudden disappearance of the welfare state would leave the system in a state of exploding conflict and anarchy. The embarrassing secret of the welfare state is that, while its impact upon capitalist accumulation may well become destructive (as the conservative analysis so emphatically demonstrates), its abolition would be plainly disruptive (a fact that is systematically ignored by the conservative critics). The contradiction is that while capitalism cannot coexist *with*, neither can it exist *without*, the welfare state. This is exactly the condition to which we refer when using the concept 'contradiction'. The flaw in the conservative analysis is in the one-sided emphasis it puts on the first side of this contradiction, and its silence about the second one. This basic contradiction of the capitalist welfare state could, of course, be thought to be a mere 'dilemma' which then would be 'solved' or 'managed' by a circumspect balancing of the two components. This, however, would presuppose two things, both of which are at least highly uncertain: first, that there *is* something like an 'optimum point' at which the order-maintaining functions of the welfare state are preserved while its disruptive effects are avoided; and, second, if so, that political procedures and administrative practices will be sufficiently 'rational' to accomplish this precarious balance. Before I consider the prospects for this solution, let me first summarize some elements of the contending socialist critique of the welfare state.

The critique from the socialist Left

Although it would be nonsensical to deny the fact that the struggle for labour protection legislation, expanded social services, social security and the recognition of unions led by the working-class movement for over a century now has brought substantial improvements of the living conditions of most wage earners, the socialist critique of the welfare state is, nevertheless, a fundamental one. It can be summarized in three points which we will consider in turn. The welfare state is said to be:

1   ineffective and inefficient;
2   repressive;
3   conditioning a false ('ideological') understanding of social and political reality within the working class.

In sum, it is a device to stabilize, rather than a step in the transformation of, capitalist society.

In spite of the undeniable gains in the living conditions of wage earners, the institutional structure of the welfare state has done little or nothing to alter the income distribution between the two principal classes of labour and capital. The huge machinery of redistribution does not work in the vertical, but in the horizontal direction, namely, *within* the class of wage earners. A further aspect of its ineffectiveness is that the welfare state does not *eliminate the causes* of individual contingencies and needs (such as work-related diseases, the disorganization of cities by the capitalist real estate market, the obsolescence of skills, unemployment, etc.), but *compensates for* (parts of) the *consequences* of such events (by the provision of health services and health insurance, housing subsidies, training and re-training facilities, unemployment benefits and the like). Generally speaking, the kind of social intervention most typical of the welfare state is always 'too late', and hence its *ex post facto* measures are more costly and less effective than a more 'causal' type of intervention would allow them to be. This is a generally recognized dilemma of social policy-making, the standard answer to which is the recommendation to adopt more 'preventive' strategies. Equally generally, however, it is also recognized that effective prevention would almost everywhere mean interfering with the prerogatives of investors and management, i.e., the sphere of the market and private property which the welfare state has only very limited legal and *de facto* powers to regulate.

A further argument pointing at the ineffectiveness of the welfare state emphasizes the constant threat to which social policies and social services are exposed due to the fiscal crisis of the state, which, in turn, is a reflection of both cyclical and structural discontinuities of the process of accumulation. All West European countries experienced a sharp economic recession in the mid 1970s, and we know of many examples of cutting social policy expenditures in response to the fiscal consequences of this recession. But even if and when the absolute and relative rise of social policy expenditures as a percentage of GNP continues uninterrupted, it is by no means certain, as Ian Gough and others before him have argued, that increases in the expenditures are paralleled by increases in real 'welfare'. The dual fallacy, known in the technical literature as the 'spending-serving-cliché', is this: first, a marginal increase in expenditures must not necessarily correspond to a marginal incre-ment in the 'outputs' of the welfare state apparatus; it may well be used up in feeding the bureaucratic machinery itself. But, second, even if the output (say of health services) *is* increased, a still larger increase in the level of risks and needs (or a qualitative change of these) may occur on the part of the clients or recipients of such services, so as to make the net effect negative.

The bureaucratic and professional form through which the welfare state dispenses its services is increasingly seen to be a source of its own inefficiency. Bureaucracies absorb more resources and provide less services than other democratic and decentralized structures of social policy could. The reason why the bureaucratic form of administering social services is maintained in spite of its inefficiency and ineffectiveness, which becomes increasingly obvious to more and more observers, must, therefore, be connected with the social control function exercised by centralized welfare bureaucracies. This analysis leads to the critique of the *repres-siveness* of the welfare state, its social control aspect. Such repressiveness is, in the view of the critics, indicated by the fact that, in order to qualify for the benefits and services of the welfare state, the client must not only prove his or her 'need', but must also be a *deserving* client – a client, that is, who complies with the dominant economic, political, and cultural standards and norms of the society. The heavier the needs, the stricter these requirements tend to be defined. Only if, for instance, the unemployed are willing to keep themselves available for any alternative employment (often considerably inferior to the job they have lost) that eventually may be made available to them by employment agencies are they entitled to unemployment benefits; and the claim for welfare payments to the poor is everywhere made conditional upon their conformity to standards of behaviour which the better-to-do strata of the population are perfectly free to violate. In these and many other cases, the welfare state can be looked upon as an exchange transaction in which material benefits for the needy are traded for their submissive recognition of the 'moral order' of the society which generates such need. One important pre-condition for obtaining the services of the welfare state is the ability of the individual to comply with the routines and requirements of welfare bureaucracies and service organizations, an ability which, needless to say, often is inversely correlated to need itself.

A third major aspect of the socialist critique of the welfare state is to demonstrate its *political-ideological* control function. The welfare state is seen not only as the source of benefits and services, but, at the same time, as the source of false conceptions about historical reality which have damaging effects for working-class consciousness, organization and struggle. First of all, the welfare state creates the false image of two separated spheres of working-class life. On the one side, the sphere of work, the economy, production and 'primary' income distribution; on the other, the sphere of citizenship, the state, reproduction and 'secondary' distribution. This division of the socio-political world obscures the causal and functional links and ties that exist between the two, and thus prevents the formation of a political understanding which views society as a coherent totality-to-be-changed. That is to say, the structural arrangements of the welfare state tend to make people ignore or forget that the needs and contingencies which the welfare state responds to are themselves constituted, directly or indirectly, in the sphere of work and production, that the welfare state itself is materially and institutionally constrained by the dynamics of the sphere of production, and that a reliable conception of social security does, therefore, presuppose not only the expansion of 'citizen rights', but of 'workers rights' in the process of production. Contrary to such insights, which are part of the analytical starting points of any conceivable socialist strategy of societal transformation, the inherent symbolic indoctrination of the welfare state suggests the ideas of class co-operation, the disjunction of economic and political struggles, and the evidently more and more ill-based confidence in an ever-continuing cycle of economic growth and social security.

The welfare state and political change

What emerges from our sketchy comparative discussion of the 'Right' and the 'Left' analyses of the welfare state are three points on which the liberal–conservative and the socialist critics exhibit somewhat surprising parallels.

First, contrary to the ideological consensus that flourished in some of the most advanced welfare states throughout the 1950s and 1960s, nowhere is the welfare state believed any longer to be the promising and permanently valid answer to the problems of the socio-political order of advanced capitalist economies. Critics in both camps have become more vociferous and fundamental in their negative appraisal of welfare state arrangements.

Second, neither of the two approaches to the welfare state could and would be prepared, in the best interest of its respective clientele, to abandon the welfare state, as it performs essential and indispensable functions both for the accumulation process as well as for the social and economic well-being of the working class.

Third, while there is, on the conservative side, neither a consistent theory nor a realistic strategy about the social order of a non-welfare state (as I have argued before), it is not perfectly evident that the situation is much better on the Left where one could possibly speak of a consistent theory of socialism, but certainly not of an agreed-upon and realistic strategy for its construction. In the absence of the latter, the welfare state remains a theoretically contested, though in reality firmly entrenched, fact of the social order of advanced capitalist societies. In short, it appears that the welfare state, while being contested both from the Right and the Left, will not be easily replaced by a conservative or progressive alternative.

To be sure, there are a number of normative models of the social and economic order which are, however, advocated by intellectuals and other minorities rather than being supported by any broad political current. One is the neo-*laissez-faire* model according to which the welfare state can and should be abolished so that the resurrection of the free and harmonious market society can take place. This solution is typically supported by political forces from the old middle class, such as farmers and shopkeepers, who also often favour tax-resistance movements. The political problem with this solution is that the further and more evenly capitalist modernization has taken place within one country, the smaller the social base of this backward-looking alternative will be. Its polar opposite is a model favoured by elements of the new middle class, combining 'post-material' values with certain ideas inherited from the anarchist and syndicalist tradition of political thought. This model would imply that the functions of the welfare state could be taken over by libertarian, egalitarian and largely self-reliant communities working within a highly decentralized and debureaucratized setting.

Typically, both of these alternative models have no more than a very marginal role to play as long as they fail to form alliances with one of the principal classes, respectively, and the political forces representing them. But such alliances, either between the old middle class and the centres of capital or the new middle class and the established working-class organizations, are immensely difficult to form and sustain. Nevertheless, it would probably not be too speculative an assumption to expect such struggles for new alliances to occupy the stage of social policy and welfare state reform in the years to come. In my view, three potential alternative outcomes of these political efforts can be envisaged.

First, under conditions of heightened economic crisis and international tension, a relative success of the neo-*laissez-faire* coalition, based on an alliance of big capital and the old middle class, is not entirely to be excluded as a possibility. Second, in countries with a strong social democratic (and possibly also in those with a strong Euro-communist) element, it is more likely that new forms of interest intermediation and relatively peaceful accommodation will emerge which are designed to determine the 'right dose' of welfare state expansion, i.e., one that is compatible both with the requirements of accumulation as well as with the key demands of working-class organizations. This model would involve the extensive reliance on 'neo-corporatist' or 'tripartite' modes of decision-making, carried out by representatives of highly centralized employers' organizations and unions under the supervision of specialized agencies of the state. This second conceivable configuration, however, will operate, especially under economic crisis conditions, at the expense not only of the old middle class, but also of those sectors of the working class which are less well organized and represented within such highly exclusive frameworks of inter-group negotiation and decision-making. Not entirely inconceivable is, third, a type of alliance that combines working-class organizations and elements from the new middle class on the basis of a non-bureaucratic, decentralized, and egalitarian model of a self-reliant 'welfare society'. Proponents of this solution are to be found within the new social movements who find some resonance in the theoretical ideas of authors like Illich, Gorz, Touraine, Cooley and others.

Rather than speculating about the likely outcome of this configuration of forces and ideas, which would require a much more detailed analysis than is possible within the confines of this essay, I want to turn in my concluding remarks to the nature of the political process which will eventually decide one or the other of these outcomes. This process can best be conceived of as consisting of three tiers, or three cumulative arenas of conflict. The first and most obvious is the arena of political *decision-making within the state apparatus*. Its actors are political elites competing with each other for electoral victories and scarce resources. They decide on social policy programmes, legislations and budgets. This is the most superficial and most visible level of politics, the one publicized by the media and involved whenever the citizen is called upon to act in his or her political role, for example, as voter.

But this is by no means the only level at which political power is generated, distributed and utilized. For the space of possible decisions of political elites is determined by societal forces that, on a far less visible level, shape and change the politicians' view and perception of reality, i.e., of the alternatives open to decision-making and the consequences to be expected from each of the alternatives. This is the level at which the agenda of politics and the relative priority of issues and solutions is determined, and the durability of alliances and compromises is conditioned. On this level, it is more difficult to identify specific actors; the forces operating here are most often the aggregate outcome of a multitude of anonymous actors and actions which nevertheless shape the politicians' view of reality and space of action. Examples of such conditioning forces are events in the international environment (such as wars or revolutions), macro-economic indicators (terms of trade, growth rates, changes in the level of unemployment and inflation, etc.), and changes in the cultural parameters of social life (ranging from the rates of secondary school attendance to divorce rates). The experience of these indicators shapes the elites' image of reality, their view of what they can and must do, what they have to expect as consequences of their actions, and what they must refrain from doing. The important point here is this: although the power to structure the politicians' reality, agenda and attention cannot be as easily traced back to personal actors as is the case on the first level of political conflict, there is, nevertheless, a *matrix of social power* according to which social classes, collective actors and other social categories have a greater chance of shaping and reshaping political reality, opening or closing the political agenda, than others. Access to and control over the means of production, the means of organization and the means of communication are highly unevenly distributed within the social structure, and each of them can be utilized, to a different degree of effectiveness, to shape and to challenge what politicians perceive as their *environment of decision-making*. The relative weight of these different resources which, partly, may balance each other, but which also can be concentrated in the hands of one and the same class or group, depends also on cyclical and conjunctural variations which may allow a group to exploit its specific social power to a larger or smaller extent at different points in time.

Underlying this second level of politics (the social power matrix), however, is a third level at which changes within the matrix itself occur, i.e., changes in the relative 'weight' collective actors enjoy in shaping the agenda of politics. If, as we have argued before, the second level consists in the process of shaping the space of political action by the exercise of veto power, blackmail, threat, mobilization and social discourse about political issues, or merely the silent force of 'anticipated reaction', this does not mean that the amount and effectiveness of political resources that each social class and social category controls must remain fixed. That is to say, social power is never great enough to reproduce itself eternally. Power positions are, almost by definition, contested and hence subject to change and redistribution. The struggle for the *redistribution of social power* is what takes place on the third, and most fundamental, level of politics. For instance, the market power, or political legitimacy, or the organizational strength that one group or class has enjoyed so far may be restricted (with the effect of making the political agenda less vulnerable *vis-à-vis* this group), or another group may open up new channels of influence, may form new alliances, or win a hegemonic position through the appeal to new values, ideals and visions. Both relative losses of power and relative gains in power can be promoted, facilitated or triggered off (if only through the unequivocal demonstration of failures) on the level of formal politics. The veto power attached to certain groups can be limited and constrained, and the institutional underpinnings of social power can be abolished. It therefore appears that the three levels are interrelated, not in a strictly hierarchical but in a cyclical manner: although the action space of level one ('formal politics') is largely determined by the matrix of social power ('level two'), it may itself facilitate and promote a revision of the distribution of social power ('level three'). And the state of democratic politics would thus have to be looked upon as both determined by, and a potential determinant of, social power.

I trust that I can leave it to the reader to apply this analytical model of the political process to the contemporary controversy about the welfare state that I have reviewed and discussed, and, thereby, to explore the extent of its usefulness. The question with which I wish to conclude is as much of academic as it is of political significance: will the agenda of the welfare state, its space of action and future development, be shaped and limited by the matrix of social power of advanced capitalist social structures? Or will it, conversely, itself open up possibilities of reshaping this matrix, either through its own accomplishments or failures?

Notes and references

1   A corollary argument often used in the conservative analysis is this: not only does the welfare state undermine the *quality* of working behaviour by inducing workers to be more 'demanding' and, at the same time, less willing to spend strong efforts on their work, etc., but also it cuts the *quantity* of available productive labour. This is said to be so because the welfare state ideology puts strong emphasis on public sector services, bureaucratic careers, and especially education and training, all of which drain the labour market of 'productive' labour in a variety of ways.

7 The separation of form and content in liberal democracy*

The liberal-democratic model of politics

To speak about the state, the individual, and the relationships existing between the two involves a difficulty of conceptual distinction. This difficulty lies in the fact that the two concepts appear to refer to phenomena that can be clearly delineated. However, if we look more closely at the relationship between the two, we discover that the matter is more complicated than indicated by a simple logical opposition. Upon reflection, it turns out:

1   that the state, as an institutionalized order of public authority, can be understood only as the historical result of the will and the actions of individuals;
2   that, more importantly, everything that we mean by 'the individual', its subjectivity and dignity, can exist and unfold only to the extent that the state safeguards the rights on which it depends.

Both are creative of each other – this is at least the way in which bourgeois social philosophy, beginning in the seventeenth century, has insisted on construing their mutual relationship. According to social contract theory, the state is based upon *nothing but* the associated individuals who decide to enter into a contract with each other; that is to say, public authority is neither based upon the will of God nor any dynastic privileges of the prince, but on the (hypothetical) will of its subjects. Inversely, the purpose of such authority is to provide the subjects with 'individuality' – with legal rights and physical protection of their life and property. Underlying the distinction of the state and the individual, there is a fundamental relationship of mutual creation.

* An earlier version of this essay was first presented to the conference, 'The Individual and the State', Centre for International Studies, University of Toronto, Canada, February 1979. It was later published in *Studies in Political Economy*, 3 (Spring 1980), pp. 5–16.

The most prominent way in which this mutual relationship is mediated in the modern state is the democratic political process. *Democratic politics is the bridge between the citizen and the state*. I need only mention here the links out of which this bridge is built: the civil liberties and political rights attributed to the individual citizen, the majority principle, political parties, elections, parliament and the state executive. According to liberal-democratic theory, the traffic that moves over this bridge determines – and determines exclusively – the uses to which state power is put.

The functions of this bridge are twofold. Seen from the point of view of the *individual*, who is granted access to the bridge by the constitution or constitutional practices of a state, the bridge provides the opportunity to articulate interests, engage in debates and conflicts over those interests, form coalitions, win majorities, and eventually determine public policies. Seen from the angle of conflicting interests that exist within civil society, the bridge is the arena of what one of the more optimistic analysts of liberal democracy has called 'the democratic class struggle' (Lipset).

If we look upon the same process from the other end of the bridge, i.e., the state as an institutionalized order of public power, the political process appears as the *resolution of conflict*, leading to the universal recognition of a supreme public authority. This is the dual function that the political forms of which the bridge consists perform: they allow for the articulation *and* resolution of conflict, they determine the scope of possible participants and duration of conflict, and they define its ultimate resolution in unity and legitimate government. Thus, political forms are at the same time generators of conflict and peacemakers. Their logic is to organize diversity *and* unity – thereby providing a continuous link between the individual and the state.

Conflict is allowed to be carried out *only to the extent* it takes place in political forms which make sure that it will *not* be permanent and universal. Electoral campaigns are an example: they are as intensive as they often are because they are short-lived and relatively infrequent. Political rights are granted only to the extent that their exercise does not interfere with the political rights of others. Thus, every political form of the liberal-democratic state, or every link of the bridge between the individual citizen and the state, involves a stop-rule which *limits* the conflict to which it gives rise. Something like this, at least, is the model which liberal political theorists have in mind when thinking about the relationship between the state and the individual: individuality and authority, conflict and harmony are made possible by one and the same political forms which mediate between the individual and the state.

At this point, some may feel that something must be wrong with this model if we compare it to the political realities of advanced capitalist democracies. I fully agree with those who do, but that does not provide us with an answer as to what is wrong, and for what reason, with such a notion of the political mediation between the state and the individual.

What I want to explore, then, are some symptoms and reasons for the breakdown of a bridge which today is not considered particularly solid anywhere – be it in the apocalyptic visions of contemporary conservatives, the confessions of theoretical bankruptcy of political liberalism, or the heated controversies of the Left about the possible and desirable forms of socialism.

Problems of 'governability'

One of the most fashionable terms among conservative political theorists and commentators has been 'ungovernability'. Its connotations are 'rising expectations' on the part of competing interest groups and parties, disseminated by the media; a resulting 'overload' of the state bureaucracies which find themselves, under the impact of fiscal constraints, unable to satisfy such expectations; a breakdown of government authority which would be required for a firm resistance to proliferating demands; an increasing level of distrust, suspicion and frustration among the citizens in their attitudes *vis-à-vis* the state, and a creeping paralysis of the foundations of economic stability and growth potential.[1] All of which means, in terms of our bridge metaphor, that the *conflict-generating* potential of the institutions of the democratic polity by far outweighs their *conflict-resolving* capacity. As a consequence, the state becomes increasingly unable to reconcile the demands transmitted through democratic institutions with the requirements of the national and international economy. Symptoms of disintegration, breakdown and chaos are predicted to increase dramatically in the near future.

Such alarmist diagnoses suggest both a cause and a cure. The cause is seen to be wage demands and, in particular, social consumption demands, made by the working class and its organizations; the cure, although mostly less clearly articulated, is some form of strengthening of the forces of discipline, moderation and self-restraint, both by a change in political institutions and practices (for example incomes policy) and by an alteration of cultural norms as they are transmitted through the educational system and mass communications.[2]

One may have some doubts about the correctness of the causal interpretation as well as about the feasibility and effectiveness of the proposed cure. As to the former, 'rising expectations' may often turn out to be a misnomer for increased insecurity and structurally induced need. To illustrate the point, one could compare a chicken living in the natural environment of a farm to a chicken being raised in the technologically advanced environment of a modern chicken factory. It is clear that the latter, deprived of the opportunity to practise its instincts which lead it to control and adapt to its physical environment, becomes dependent upon all kinds of support systems supplying it with the right food, temperature, amount of fresh air, infra-red light, antibiotics, etc. It would be absurd to speak here of any increased needs as constituting 'rising expectations' or increased demands, whereas it is obvious that they result from utter helplessness and dependency. And so do most of the physical and social needs that people under highly urbanized, socially and economically insecure conditions of life address to the welfare state. And it is equally unlikely that the support systems of the welfare state could even partially be switched off in the absence of a major reorganization of social institutions that would restore a measure of autonomous control of people over the process of production and reproduction of their social and physical lives.[3] In the absence of such transformation, the state must accept the obligation to provide those reproductive services – which are reproductive of both capital and labour power. The consequence is that virtually all parameters of life are perceived as being determined by, and therefore can be altered by, the state. There is very little left which could be considered as lying beyond the realm of public policy – a point to which I will return later.

At the other end of the political spectrum, we find an entirely different diagnosis. The view from the Left is that economic strain and instability such as experienced by all Western capitalist countries since the mid 1970s does result in a *narrowing* of the scope of political conflict admitted to democratic politics, and sometimes in the authoritarian transformation of democratic polities, character-ized by large-scale political repression. Such tendencies may at least partly have to do with the increased weight that the veto power of capital, and especially large corporate investors, achieves under conditions of economic instability and low growth rates. The economic imperatives which impose themselves upon governments in such conditions then result in the imposition of stricter con-straints upon those political forces whose uninhibited articulation could do damage to 'business confidence' and the 'investment climate'.[4]

Contradictory as the two diagnoses, the conservative one and the one from the Left, appear, it may well be the case that both of them are true. That is to say, in spite of attempts to reduce the scope of conflict that can be transmitted through democratic institutions, the remaining volume of conflict is of an order of magnitude that causes symptoms of 'ungovernability'. In other words, *both* the institutional functions of *conflict articulation* and of *conflict resolution* are reduced; and the polity becomes *repressive* and *un-manageable* at the same time. *Neither* of the two functions which, according to liberal-democratic theory, are to be performed by the institutional bridge linking the state and the individual can be performed.

If this is what is going on, and I believe it is, we should expect to find two interrelated developments in the political structures of capitalist democracies. First, if democratic institutions such as the party system, elections and parliamentary government are reduced in their ability to provide for the articulation of the political conflict, *alternative channels of conflict are likely to develop and to absorb the political energies of people.* Second, if those institutions also fail in their potential for reducing conflict to manageable proportions and generating a condition of governability, we would expect govern-ments to *rely increasingly upon criteria and standards of perform-ance that are derived from other sources than the democratic political process.* It is my thesis that both the location of major political conflicts and struggles and the institutional location at which state policies are formed shift away from those institutions which demo-cratic theory assigns to these functions. As a consequence, the mediation that democratic theory postulates between the state and the individual breaks down as an operative mechanism, without, however, being formally abolished. At the same time, *alternative political forms* of both the articulation of conflict and the resolution of policy issues appear for which at the present there exists no normative political theory. Behind the façade of parliamentary democracy, both political conflict and the resolution of policy issues increasingly take place within organizational settings which are unknown to democratic theory.

To start with the formation of policy decisions within the state, the mode in which such decisions are produced is familiar to every newspaper reader. The mode equally deviates from parliamentary control of the executive, from party control over the executive, and from the Weberian ideal of a political top executive directing a bureaucratic apparatus according to his own responsible vision. Very often, decisions on key political issues emerge instead out of a highly informal process of negotiation among representatives of strategic groups within the public and the private sectors.[5] Consultation, negotiation, mutual information and inconspicuous techniques of estimating potential resistance and support for a specific policy assume a role in public policy-making which is by no means restricted to a supplementary one. Apart from its highly informal character, two other aspects are characteristic of this mode of public policy-making. One is the strong element of *functional* representation, and the other its lack of democratic legitimation. Such para-parliamentary, as well as para-bureaucratic, forms of decision-making have therefore been described as neo-corporatist methods of interest intermediation. Corresponding to these characteristics, there is every reason for the participants to keep their delicate exchange of proposals, information and threats as remote as possible both from the general public eye and from the segmental constituencies which participants represent. Such a setting is used not only in the international and supranational arena, where it probably has the longest tradition, but increasingly also in domestic policies, particularly in the areas of economic policy. It involves participants coming from federal, state and local governments and major corporate groups whose only 'legitimation' resides in the fact that they control a considerable 'obstruction potential' that they can bring to bear upon the policy in question. The consensus that underlies major state policies is a consensus that does not result from a democratic process as formally provided for by democratic institutions, but a consensus resulting from informal, highly inaccessible negotiations among poorly legitimized representatives of functional groups. It is a *substitute* consensus replacing a democratic mechanism, the potential of which for creating unity has become highly doubtful.

An equally familiar method of providing some degree of legitimacy and acceptability to this para-parliamentary mode of decision-making is the involvement of scientists in such procedures. While this can in part be attributed to the complexity of issues and the decision-maker's dependence upon expertise, it remains an open question whether such considerations are the only ones that make scientists participants in neo-corporatist modes of interest intermediation[6] or whether, in addition, they serve the function of rejecting potential claims of 'non-experts' to be heard; for as soon as an issue is institutionally defined as requiring *scientific* advice and expertise, the scope of legitimate participants is drastically reduced. This mechanism, as it is used for instance within councils of economic advisers, has provoked the vehement objections of unions who felt that the exclusion of their point of view was the real intent and function of surrounding policy-makers with a council of economic policy experts. By replacing democratic procedures of consensus building by such other methods of conflict resolution, government elites *avoid* the 'official' institutions of politics in a constant search for *non-political forms of decision-making*.

As governing elites bypass the democratic chain of institutions and turn to alternative mechanisms for the resolution of conflict, at the other end of the bridge, so do individual citizens. Although the overwhelming majority of citizens does vote in general elections, this behaviour often seems to be more of a ritualistic rather than a purposive nature. Empirical evidence provided by recent surveys both in the United States and Western Europe demonstrates a great increase in distrust and even cynical views that people hold about political parties.[7] Non-conventional methods of expressing one's political will and fighting for one's interests are both considered to be more effective and practised more often than membership in political parties. Citizens action groups (*'Bürgerinitiativen'*) addressing themselves to such issues as urban renewal, educational policies, energy and environmental protection have become a major movement in West Germany and other West European countries during the last decade, involving more individuals as active participants than all political parties taken together.[8] The most intense and innovative articulation of political conflict takes place within the institutions and via institutional channels which, according to democratic political theory, should play at best a marginal role in the 'formation of the political will of the people' – a task that the West German Constitution explicitly assigns to political parties. For instance, to take examples from West German politics, the *churches*, in particular the Protestant church, have been the institutional origin of a number of foreign policy initiatives, including those related to the East European countries and the Third World. The *universities* have been the scene where major domestic policy reforms originated and where a democratic socialist opposition formed that could not find acceptance within the party system. The *unions* – not any of the political parties – have brought up such issues as 'humanization of work' and 'quality of life'. And literature, art and the mass media have articulated standards of a democratic political culture that political parties were unable to establish. To be sure, some of these new issues, demands and concerns have been absorbed within the political party system – although often highly selectively and with much delay. This has been, for instance, the case with new social movements such as the women's movement, the anti-nuclear energy movement, and various regionalist movements which now exist in a majority of West European countries.

The reasons why political parties *do* increasingly fail to attract and absorb the political energies of people are numerous. One reason is the over extension of the strategy of the 'catch-all party' which tries to win votes from wherever they come, denying any class-specific base of its programme and politics. The ensuing contradiction is a highly increased level of factionalism and centrifugal tendencies *within* parties both of the Left and the Right, leading, in the eyes of the voter, to a loss of party-identities, and to the impression that the differences contained *within* any of the parties are greater than those *between* parties. Political sociologists have also shown that the more a party approaches the model of the catch-all party, i.e., the *broader* the range of electoral support it tries to win, the *narrower* the range of social backgrounds from which its leaders, members of parliament and government personnel tend to be recruited.[9] This is due to a powerful tendency towards the professionalization of political careers which are accessible to fewer and fewer segments of the social structure. This highly non-representative composition of the party leadership is in turn likely to diminish the trustworthiness of political parties. Also, many observers agree that an inversion of governing parties has taken place in their relation to the state executive. Whereas they are expected to be instruments of the direction and control of government, giving political direction to the conduct of government, they often appear to work more effectively in the opposite direction, namely as some kind of public relations agencies working for the particular government which they only nominally 'control'. Within many West European social democratic, liberal and conservative parties one begins to hear concerns voiced about how to restore the trust of the electorate such that political parties are in fact appropriate and effective organizations to which people can turn in order to have their particular political interests and demands transmitted to the state apparatus.

If the governability crisis is responded to through the resort of *governing elites* to para-parliamentary, non-public, informal and poorly legitimized forms of resolving policy-issues often described as *neo-corporatist*, the participation crisis is responded to by *citizens* in a parallel retreat from the official channels of conflict articulation. My thesis is that, as a consequence of both processes, politics in *both* of the conventional meanings of the term: politics as the *struggle over substantive issues* and politics as the *institutional form of conflict resolution* degenerates into informal and mutually disconnected modes of struggle and decision. The constitutional bridge that democratic theory takes for granted is in the process of breaking down. If we extrapolate this tendency into the future, we can anticipate an *unmediated* opposition between the individual and the state, or the most extreme form of political alienation. This takes place not in the course or as a consequence of an open challenge to the official institutions of the democratic polity, but as an *inconspicuous loss of function and relevance* of these institutions which are increasingly bypassed rather than destroyed by both sides.

The separation of the state and politics

To be sure, the direction of change that I have sketched out and that we see taking place in the relationship between the individual and the state, or between citizens and governing elites, cannot be explained by reference to political and institutional dynamics alone:

they have their base in changing relationships of *economic power* and *value changes* that occur beyond the level of the political institutions itself. Let us consider a few of them. Many observers would agree that the uncoupling of decisions about the use of state power from the mechanisms of democratic politics has to do with the issues that have to be resolved and for which the competitive party system and parliament are unsuited to produce workable solutions. This is particularly the case in the field of *economic policy-making*, concerning problems of stability, growth, employment, international competitiveness and fiscal crisis. All of these problems are direct manifestations of the dynamics – that is, the anarchic ups and downs – of the accumulation of capital in the private sector. The more severe these problems become, the less governments can afford to allow the type and exact timing of their policy measures to be determined by whatever consensus does – or does not – emerge from the process of democratic politics. Only if economic policy-makers loosen their institutional ties to their parties and parliaments can they hope to remain effective in responding to rapidly changing economic imperatives.

Similarly, only if political parties cultivate a selective blindness towards certain interests, demands and concerns of particular constituencies can they hope to avoid antagonizing those parts of the electorate whom they need for parliamentary majorities. In other words, only class parties or parties representing highly homogeneous groups can afford to be highly responsive to their voters and members. Where a system of class parties does not exist, and where a condition prevails that in the late 1950s was celebrated as the *end of ideology*, it is likely that class interests are at least partly expressed through channels *other* than the party system.

The intensity of class antagonism and/or of economic crisis thus appears to be one determinant of whether the institutional link provided by the institutions of the democratic polity holds or breaks, whether conflict is absorbed and reconciled through the parliamentary and party systems or whether unofficial strikes and militant political movements proliferate at the same pace as unofficial consultations between government and corporate groups within the framework of a creeping corporatism. However, whatever the role of class antagonism and economic crisis is in explaining the breaking of the institutional bridge, it is, in advanced Western capitalist democracies, only part of the explanation.

In addition to class conflict, there appear to be other categories of issues which are – or are likely to become – beyond the capacity of the liberal-democratic polity to absorb and to reconcile. These issues result from *changes in values* and concerns of people whose relation to social classes, as defined in economic terms of wealth and income, are at best indirect. Some political scientists[10] and political sociologists speak of a value change that is going on which points in the direction of an increasing predominance of what are called 'post-materialist' or 'post-acquisitive' values over those that have to do with income, satisfaction of material needs and social security. Such post-materialist values focus instead on participation, equality and the development of the self in its intellectual, aesthetic and physical dimensions. This hypothesis, which is confirmed by a number of surveys conducted in various European countries, relates to a phenomenon that we find predominantly, although not exclusively, within the *urban new middle class*, a stratum that has been growing in the past both in its numbers and political weight. The change from 'materialist' to 'post-materialist' values is seen by some authors to be a result of the experience of long-term prosperity and security which have rendered 'material' concerns about incomes and jobs somewhat less urgent. Most importantly, however, it appears to be the case that *even if* those problems of income, jobs, inflation, social security and growth *do* re-emerge in periods of cyclical or permanent recession of the economy, it is at best highly uncertain whether those groups, once they have adopted 'post-material' values, are prepared to switch back to 'material' ones. There appears to be an *irreversibility* in the sequence of value change. Consequently, in a period of economic strain not only the clash of material interests, but, in addition, a broad spectrum of post-material interests and causes (most conspicuously represented by the women's movement and the ecological movements) will together make up the scenario of political conflict.

For movements growing out of such 'post-materialist' concerns, the channels of party politics are fundamentally inappropriate forms of organization, even if the political parties, and the party system as a whole, were more 'open', i.e., able to absorb conflict, than is actually the case. The reasons for this are easy to understand: whereas it is the logic of political *parties* to maximize votes in order to occupy positions of state power and to conduct the entire business of government, *social movements* based upon 'post-materialist' values contradict this logic in all its aspects; they win their strength by concentrating on *one* issue or set of issues, thereby antagonizing rather than registering the support of a great number of other groups. Their demands are of a nature that cannot primarily be implemented through *state power* but which would require, in addition, a change in the cultural and economic norms and ways of life shared by large parts of the population – for example, males, racial or ethnic majorities, or producers. Finally, these concerns and values – in contrast to political programmes of parties – are unable to provide directives for the *entire range* of issues that the holders of state power find on their agenda. To illustrate, there is no feminist principle which could help to decide the general course of a desirable tax reform, nor is there an ethnic or regionalist guideline in such policy areas as the regulation of foreign trade.

In short, advanced capitalist societies appear to generate mass values and concerns which have high priorities for individuals for the sake of the expression of their individual and collective identity, but which, at the same time, are inaccessible to the established forms of articulation and resolution of political conflict and the definition of the concrete use of state power. This condition adds to a situation that I have earlier described as the breakdown of the institutional mediation between the state and the individual. If politics has to do with the working out of visions about the just order of social life, and the conflict among divergent visions of such order, then it is, given this condition of a blocked mediation, only a slight exaggeration to say that we experience a condition in which politics and the state have become divorced from each other.

The politics of production

To this, one could react by joining those conservative philosophers and social scientists who maintain that, after all, the age of politics is over, and the individual is doomed to fatalistic acceptance of the state's administration of technical and economic imperatives. I want to conclude with some thoughts about why this idea, the proponents of which want to make us accept the post-liberal and post-democratic dissociation of the state and politics, is utopian in the worst sense (and a reactionary utopia at that).

The ultimate separation of state power from the will and the moral and political aspirations of individuals in the way of a benevolent technocracy would presuppose that the effects of state power do not significantly affect the life of the individual. This, at least according to liberal ideology, may have been the case under conditions of a *laissez-faire* economy which consequently was not dependent upon – and in fact ideologically opposed to – any mechanism of democratic mediation between the state and the individual: the respective spheres of markets and policies, private and public affairs were relatively clearly delineated. But the opposite is clearly the case in advanced capitalist systems. While the *institutional* link between the individual and the state has been attenuated for the reasons I have discussed before, the *actual* links between the state and the individual become ever more *direct*. The contradiction is clear: as *politics* move beyond the reach of the citizen, state *policies* move ever closer. If this is true, the fatalistic acceptance of a technocratic state administration is certainly not what we could expect to follow from the breakdown of institutionalized mediations.

Let me explain what I mean by state policies moving closer to the individual citizen. It is quite commonplace among political scientists to speak of a secular trend towards increasing state intervention within capitalist societies. This secular trend becomes manifest in the proliferation of more and more specific regulations of all aspects of the behaviour of citizens. What is less often observed is that such intervention can take either of two forms: it can focus upon the behaviour outputs of citizens, for instance by attaching positive or negative sanctions to certain modes of behaviour which are thereby encouraged or discouraged. And it can, in addition or alternatively, focus upon the input sides of social and economic life. What I want to suggest is that state interventionism has increasingly developed along the second alternative, concentrating more upon the physical substratum or natural material of societal processes. *Nature itself has increasingly become an object of state policy*. Human and physical resources are increasingly managed and manipulated by the state.

Consider, for instance, the prominence of policy areas whose relative importance on the state agenda is, as far as I can see, unparalleled by the issues of fifty or even twenty years ago:

1   state organized and state supported development of science-based technologies;
2   energy, raw materials, even water and air as parameters on the supply side of the economy which have to be provided for by state policies;
3   education, health care, population control as a field of policies aiming at the provision of the right amount, quality and spatial distribution of human resources;
4   land use, regional development and urban renewal as the political determination of territorial or spatial structures of social activity.

In other words, all of the classical 'factors of production' – capital, labour, land – are no longer to be taken as given, but are developed, shaped, distributed and allocated by specific state policies. All of these policies have to do with the direct intervention of the state into non-human and human nature, including the psychic aspects of the latter. The point I am trying to make is the following: these relatively recent and rapidly expanding policy areas have all to do with the interaction between man and nature (inner or outer nature), that is, with a sphere of life that, within any liberal conception of society, was strictly considered a realm of private activities – be it within private production, the family or art.

This configuration of trends is quite paradoxical. Whereas the traditional sphere of politics and the institutional mechanisms that supposedly mediate between the citizen and state authority are in the process of losing their content, as I have argued before, the actual contact between the state and the individual becomes ever closer, and literally physical. Much of the political conflict that goes on has shifted to this poorly institutionalized area where the state gets into physical contact with the individual's body and psyche. Here I refer to struggles in which conflicting ideas about the desirable order not of state and society, but of 'nature' seem to oppose each other. Quite often both the issues and the collective identities of actors of such conflict are defined in 'naturalistic' terms. The following examples come to mind.

On the most superficial level, we experience forms of movements, which, although they are not in any traditional sense 'political', still release astonishing amounts of collective energy mixed with elements of anger and protest. For instance, concerns over the healthiness and safety of goods has been one root of consumerism, often concentrating on issues of nutrition. Conservationist issues receive an unprecedented amount of public attention, and media programmes dealing, for instance, with the plight of endangered species, draw maximum audiences. Also, the mass phenomenon of jogging and other practices to maintain one's physical fitness and health must be sociologically interpreted in these terms. The preservation of historical buildings and urban structures has been an issue, in many countries, that triggered off massive political protests wherever city or other governments attempted to dispose of such structures in the name of 'urban renewal' and 'modernization'.

Further, vigorous social movements have emerged in the last decade or so which have defined themselves in terms of cultural values and collective identities attached to such 'naturalistic' categories as age, sex, race and region. Such movements not only cause difficulties for the organizations of traditional politics and their established political/ideological dividing lines; they are also an embarrassing proof of failure of a whole school of social science which for decades has claimed that, in the course of 'moderniz-ation', so-called 'ascriptive' social roles and conflicts lose their significance and are replaced by criteria of 'achievement'. Finally, a new set of issues has gained prominence in the labour movement, concentrating not on wages and employment, but 'humane' work-ing conditions. Its demands are directed towards the abolition of working conditions characterized by dirt, noise, heat, repetitive-ness and accidents.

If the demands articulated by such movements and trends are 'post-material' in the sense that they do not primarily focus on improvements of the individual's or group's status in the distri-bution of income, they are, at the same time, highly 'materialist' in the sense that they challenge the prevailing mode of production and the effects it has upon the physical and human substance of social life.[11] In this way, politics and political conflict return to a place from which liberal-democratic political institutions were designed to displace it: namely, to the structure and dynamics of social production. While we experience the depoliticization of the state, we also experience a repoliticization of production in the broadest sense that comprises all aspects of the societal appropriation of human and non-human nature.

The separation of form and content in liberal democracy   177

Notes and references

1 For a clear exposition of these points of view, see S. Huntington, 'The United States', in M. Crozier *et al.* (eds.), *The Crisis of Democracy* (New York 1975).

2 I have summarized and analysed the arguments of the new conservative crisis theory in " 'Ungovernability": the renaissance of conservative theories of crisis', in this volume. For a useful collection of American essays on the same topic, see L. Coser and I. Howe (eds.) *The New Conservatives* (New York 1973).

3 For a clear and innovative theoretical model of what such a transformative process could look like under the conditions of advanced capitalist Western democracies, see the recent book by the communist Italian union leader, B. Trentin, *Da sruffati a produttori* (Bari 1977).

4 The mechanism of the interaction between economic power of investors and political power of representative governments is discussed in F. Block, 'The ruling class does not rule: notes on the Marxist theory of the state', *Socialist Revolution*, 7 no. 3 (May–June 1977), pp. 6–28; see also 'Theses on the theory of the state', in this volume.

5 cf. L. Panitch, 'Corporatism in Canada', *Studies in Political Economy*, 1 (Spring 1979), pp. 43–92.

6 cf. the classic essay by P. C. Schmitter, 'Still the century of corporatism?' *Review of Politics* 36 (1974) pp. 85–131.

7 For an overview of the declining role of political parties in Western European politics, see S. Berger, 'Politics and antipolitics in Western Europe in the seventies', *Daedalus* (Winter 1979), pp. 27–50.

8 For the West German context, I rely here on the excellent compilation of data and theoretical views that can be found in B. Guggenberger and U. Kempff (eds.), *Bürgerinitiativen und Repräsentatives System* (Cologne and Opladen 1978).

9 Both citizen participation and recruitment patterns of political party leadership are more 'universalistic' in 'class parties' as opposed to 'catch-all parties'; cf. S. Rokkan and A. Campbell 'Citizen participation in political life: Norway and the United States', *International Social Science Journal*, 12 (1960), pp. 69–99.

10 cf. the widely discussed work of R. Inglehart, *The Silent Revolution: Changing Values and Political Styles among Western Publics* (Princeton 1977).

11 The resurgence and prominence of 'qualitative' (as opposed to quantitative-distributive) issues in the West European working-class movements is a point of agreement among observers with diverse

backgrounds and orientations. For a political and theoretical statement of this 'qualitative' materialism, see Trentin, *Da sruffati a produttori*.

8   Competitive party democracy and the Keynesian welfare state*

Nineteenth-century liberal political theory and classical Marxism were in full agreement on one major point: both Marx and his liberal contemporaries, such as Mill and de Tocqueville, were convinced that capitalism and full democracy (based on equal and universal suffrage) could not mix. Obviously, this analytical convergence was arrived at from diametrically opposed points of view. The classical liberal writers believed that freedom and liberty were the most valuable accomplishments of society. These accomplishments, therefore, deserved to be protected under all circumstances from the egalitarian threats of mass society and democratic mass politics, threats that, in their view, would necessarily lead to tyranny and 'class legislation' by the propertyless, uneducated majority.[1] Marx, for his part, analysed the French democratic constitution of 1848 as a political form that would exacerbate social contradictions by withdrawing political guarantees from the socially dominant and giving political power to the subordinate. Consequently, he argued, democratic conditions could allow the proletarian class to put into question the social foundations of bourgeois society.[2]

Looking at the twentieth-century experience of capitalist societies, there is a lot of evidence *against* this nineteenth-century hypothesis concerning the incompatibility of mass democracy, defined as universal and equal suffrage in a parliamentary or presidential form of government, and bourgeois freedom, defined as production based on private property and 'free' wage labour. The coexistence of the two has come to be known as liberal democracy. To be sure, the emergence of fascist regimes in some of the core

* This is a revised and expanded version of a paper prepared for 'New forms of Governmental Intervention: A Panel in Honor of Andrew Shonfield', XII World Congress of the International Political Science Association, Rio de Janeiro, Brazil, August 1982. Earlier drafts appeared in Stewart Clegg et al. (eds.), *The State, Class and Recession* (London 1983) and in *Policy Studies*, 15 (1983) pp. 225–46.

capitalist countries testifies to the continued existence of tensions and contradictions between the capitalist economy and political democracy, and to the possibility of the outbreak of catastrophic tensions under the impact of economic crises. But, it is also true that most advanced capitalist countries have also been liberal democratic states throughout most of the twentieth century and that 'all major advanced bourgeois states are today democracies'.[3] In view of this evidence and experience, our *problematique* is the reverse of that with which the classical writers of both liberalism and Marxism concerned themselves. While they *prognosticized* the incompatibility, we have to *explain* the coexistence of these two partial principles of social organization. More precisely, we want to know: first, which institutional arrangements and mechanisms can be held responsible for the pattern of coexistence that proved enduring beyond all nineteenth-century expectations, and, second, what, if any, are the limits of such arrangements. These limits, or failures of mediating mechanisms, would be defined analytically as those points at which either capitalist societies turn non-democratic or democratic regimes turn non-capitalist. These are the two questions which I treat in this essay. To put it schematically, the course of the argument starts from the problem of how we *explain* the compatibility[4] of the structural components of 'mass polity' and 'market economy', and then goes on to focus on the level of each of these two structures, on the factors *contributing to* as well as those *undermining* such compatibility. This is done in the sequence of boxes 1–4 within the following schema:

	Factors maintaining stability	Factors paralysing stability
Mode of democratic mass participation (CPD)	1	2
Mode of economic steering (KWS)	3	4

To pose these questions at all is to presuppose, in accordance with both Marx and Mill, that there *is* some real tension between the two respective organizing principles of social power and political power, market society and political democracy, a tension that must be (and possibly cannot indefinitely be) bridged, mediated and stabilized. This is by no means an undisputed assumption. For instance, Lenin and the Leninist tradition deny that there is such tension. They assume, instead, that there is an inherent harmony between the rule of capital and bourgeois democratic forms, with the latter mainly serving to deceive the masses. Consequently, it makes no sense to ask what makes democracy compatible with capitalism and what the limits of such compatibility might be – democracy is simply seen as the most effective and reliable arrangement for capitalist class dominance. 'What is central to Lenin's position is the claim that the very organizational form of the parliamentary democratic state is essentially inimical to the interests of the working class', as one recent commentator has succinctly stated.[5] Plausible and convincing as this view can be when based on the constitutional practice of Russia between 1905 and 1917, its generalization to the present would have, among other and still worse political consequences, the effect of grossly distorting and obscuring the very *problematique* which we want to discuss.[6]

The mirror-image distortion is promulgated by some ideological pluralist-elitist democratic theorists. They claim (more precisely they used to claim in the 1950s and early 1960s) that the tension between the principles governing a capitalist market society and political democratic forms had finally been eliminated in the American political system. According to this doctrine, the class struggle within bourgeois society had been replaced by what Lipset called 'the democratic class struggle', which was seen to make all social arrangements, including the mode of production and the distribution of economic resources contingent upon the outcomes of democratic mass politics. The underlying logic of this analysis can be summarized as follows: 'if people actually wanted things to be different, they simply would elect someone else into office. The fact that they don't is consequently proof that people are satisfied with the socio-political order as it exists.' Hence, we get something like the inverse of the Leninist doctrine: democracy is not tied to capitalism, but capitalism to democracy. Both of these perspectives deny major tensions or incompatibilities between mass democracy and the market economy.

Thus, both the Leninist and the pluralist-elitist conceptions of democracy miss the point that interests us here. The former dogmatically postulates the total *dependence* of democratic forms and procedures on class power, while the latter equally dogmatically

postulates the total *independence* of class and democratically constituted political power. A question that is both more modest and
more likely to lead to insights of both intellectual and practical
significance is, however, this: which institutions and mechanisms
regulate the *extent* to which the two can become incongruent in a
given society, and what are the *limits* of such potential incongruity,
limits, that is, that would constrain the range of potential variance
of class power and democratically constituted political authority?

Marketization of politics and politicization of the private economy

In what follows, I will argue that the continued compatibility of
capitalism and democracy, so inconceivable to both classical liberalism and classical Marxism (including Kautsky and the Second International), has emerged historically due to the appearance and
gradual development of two mediating principles: mass political
parties and party competition, and the Keynesian welfare state
(KWS). In other words, it is a *specific version* of democracy, one
with political equality and mass participation that is compatible with
the capitalist market economy. And, correspondingly, it is a *specific
type* of capitalism that is able to coexist with democracy. What
interests us here are those specificities of the political and economic
structures, the way in which their mutual 'fit' is to be explained by
the functions each of them performs and, furthermore, the strains
and tensions that affect those conditions of 'fit'.

Historically, each of those two structural components of
'democratic capitalism' has in Europe largely taken shape during or
in the aftermath of the two world wars – democracy through party
competition beginning after the First World War and the Keynesian
welfare state coming after the Second World War. Each of these
two principles follows a pattern of 'mixing' the logic of authority and
the logic of the market, of 'voice' and 'exit' in Hirschman's terminology. This is quite obvious in the case of the Keynesian welfare
state, for which the term 'mixed economy' is often used as a
synonym. But it is no less true for the political sphere of capitalist
society which could well be described as a 'mixed polity' and the
dynamics of which are often, and to a certain extent appropriately,
described as the 'oligopolistic competition' of political elites or
political 'entrepreneurs' providing public 'goods'.[7] The logic of
capitalist democracy is one of mutual contamination: authority is
infused into the economy by global demand management, transfers

and regulations so that it loses more and more of its spontaneous and self-regulatory character; and market contingency is introduced into the state, thus compromising any notion of absolute authority or absolute good. Neither the Smithean conception of the market nor the Rousseauian conception of politics have much of a counterpart in social reality. Thus, one of the ways in which compatibility is accomplished appears to be the infusion of some of the logic of one realm into the other, i.e., the notion of 'competition' into politics and the idea of 'authoritative allocation of values' into the economy.

Let us now consider in turn each of the two links, or mediating mechanisms, between state and civil society. Following the *problematique* developed above, we will ask two questions in each case. First, in what way and by virtue of which structural characteristics do political parties and the Keynesian welfare state *contribute to the compatibility of* capitalism and democratic mass politics? Second, which observable trends and changes occur within the institutional framework of both the 'mixed economy' and the 'mixed polity' that *threaten the viability* of the coexistence of capitalism and democracy?

Stabilization through competitive party democracy

The German bourgeoisie's great fear during the first decade of this century was that, once the full and equal franchise was introduced together with parliamentary government, the class power of the working class, due to its numerical strength, would directly translate into a revolutionary transformation of the state. It was the same analysis, of course, that inspired the hopes and the political strategies of the leaders of the Second International. Max Weber had nothing but sarcastic contempt for both these neurotic anxieties and naïve hopes. Together with Rosa Luxemburg and Robert Michels who also conducted the same analysis, though with their own specific accents, Weber was among the first social theorists who understood (and welcomed) the fact that the transformation of class politics into competitive party politics implied not only a change of form, but also a decisive change of content. In 1917, he stated that 'in Germany . . . organisations such as the trade unions, but also the Social Democratic Party, constitute a very important counterbalance against the direct and irrational mob rule typical of purely plebiscitary peoples'.[8] He expected that the bureaucratized political party with its charismatic and demagogic political leader would form a reliable bulwark to contain what he described as 'aimless mass rage' or 'syndicalist putschism'. Rosa Luxemburg's account of the dynamic of political mass organization differs only in its opposed evaluative perspective, not its analytical content. In 1906, she observed the tendency of working-class organizations (i.e., the unions and the party) to follow specialized strategies according to a tacit division of labour and of the organizations' leadership to dominate rather than serve their mass constituencies. The bureaucratic staff of labour's organizations tends, according to Luxemburg, towards 'excessive aloofness', 'the specialization of their methods of struggle and occupation', 'the overrating of the organization, its transformation from a means into an end, and gradually into an end in itself, into a most precious thing', 'the need for calm', 'the loss of sense of the general situation', etc., while at the same time 'the mass of comrades are degraded to a mass incapable of judging'.[9] Biographically, politically and intellectually, Robert Michels absorbed and integrated the ideas of both Luxemburg and Weber in his famous 'iron law of oligarchy' of 1911, in which his observation of the empirical tendencies of organizations was transformed into a proclaimed inexorable historical necessity.[10]

It is probably no exaggeration to contend that the twentieth-century theory of political organization was essentially formed on the basis of the experience and the theoretical interpretation of these three authors, who, interestingly enough, arrived at widely divergent political positions at the end of their lives. Luxemburg died in 1919 as a revolutionary democratic socialist and victim of police murder, Weber in the same year as a 'liberal in despair', and Michels in 1936 as an ardent admirer and ideological defender of Mussolini and Italian fascism. In spite of the extreme diversity of their political views there remains a strong common element in their analysis, one which can be summarized in the following way: as soon as mass political participation is organized through large-scale bureaucratic organization – as presupposed and required by the model of electoral party competition and institutionalized collective bargaining – the very dynamic of this organizational form contains, perverts and obstructs class interest and class politics in ways that are described as leading to opportunism (Luxemburg), oligarchy (Michels) and the inescapable plebiscitarian submission of the masses to the irrational impulses of the charismatic leader and his demagogic use of the bureaucratic party 'machine' (Weber).

According to the shared insight underlying this analysis, as soon as the will of the people is expressed through the instrumentality of a competitive party striving for government office, what is expressed ceases to be the will of the people and is instead transformed into an *artefact of the form itself* and the dynamic put in motion by the imperatives of political competition. This dynamic, in turn, has three major effects. First, the *deradicalization of the ideology of the party*. In order to be successful in elections and in its striving for government office, the party must orient its programme towards the expediencies of the political market.[11] This necessitates, first, maximizing votes by appealing to the greatest possible number of voters and, consequently, minimizing those programmatic elements that could create antagonisms within the electorate; second, the readiness, *vis-à-vis* other parties, to enter coalitions and the restriction of the range of substantive policy proposals to those demands that potential coalition partners might be willing to entertain or negotiate. The combined effect here is to dissolve any coherent political concept or aim into a 'gradualist', temporal structure or sequence, giving priority to what can be implemented at that point in time and with the given resources, while postponing and displacing those demands and projects not yet realistic or feasible.

Second, the fully developed competitive party is forced by the imperatives of competition to equip itself with a highly bureaucratized and centralized organization. The objective of this organization is to maintain a continuous presence on the political market, just as the success of a business firm depends, in part, on the size and continued presence of its marketing and sales organization. The bureaucratic organization of the modern political party performs the tasks of:

1 collecting material and human resources (membership dues, contributions and donations, members, candidates);
2 disseminating propaganda and information concerning the party's position on a great number of diverse political issues;
3 exploring the political market, identifying new issues and monitoring public opinion;
4 managing internal conflict.

All of these activities are normally executed by a professional staff of party officials who develop a corporate interest in the growth and stability of the apparatus that provides them with status and careers.

186   *Contradictions of the Welfare State*

This pattern of internal bureaucratization, to be found in parties of the Right and the Left alike, has two important consequences. One consequence is that the social composition (as measured by class background, formal education, sex, occupation, age, etc.) of the party leadership, its officials, members of parliament and government diverges more and more from both the social composition of the population in general and the party's electoral base in particular. That is to say, the professionalization of party politics leads to the political dominance of professional and managerial party personnel who, by their training and professional experience, typically come from such backgrounds as business administration, public administration, education, the media or interest organizations.

The other major consequence of this bureaucratic-professional pattern of political organization is the *de-activation of rank-and-file members*. The more the organization is geared towards the exploration of and adaptation to the external environment of the political market (in what can be described as a virtually permanent electoral campaign) the less room remains for the determination of party policies by *internal* processes of democratic debate and conflict within the organization. The appearance of internal unanimity and consensus is what any competitive party must try to cultivate in order to become or remain attractive to voters. As a consequence, internal division, factionalism and organized conflict of opinion and strategy are not only not encouraged, but indeed kept under tight control or at least kept out of sight of the public in a constant effort to streamline the party's image and, as it were, to standardize its product. (In this respect, it is tempting to compare the *practice* of some social democratic parties to the *theory* of the Leninist party; I suspect we would find some ironic similarities.) The highly unequal importance of external and internal environments frequently becomes evident when the results of public opinion surveys – nowadays routinely commissioned by party leaderships – suggests positions and strategies that are in conflict with the declared intentions of party members, who then in the interest of 'winning the next election' are called upon to yield to political 'reality'.

A third characteristic of what Kirchheimer has called the modern 'catch-all-party' is the increasing structural and cultural 'heterogeneity of its supporters. This heterogeneity results from the fact that the modern political party relies on the principle of 'product diversification' in the sense that it tries to appeal to a multitude of diverse demands and concerns. This is most obvious in the case of social democratic and communist parties, who have often success- fully tried to expand their base beyond the working class and to attract elements of the old and new middle classes, the intelligentsia and voters with strong religious affiliations. The advantage of this strategy is quite obvious, but so is its effect of *dissolving the sense of collective identity*, a sense which in the case of both socialist and Catholic parties was once based on a cultural milieu of shared values and meaning.

It is easy to see why and how the three consequences of the organizational form of the competitive political party that I have discussed so far – ideological deradicalization, de-activation of the membership, erosion of collective identity – contribute to the com- patibility of capitalism and democracy. Each of these three mani- festations helps contain and limit the range of political aims and struggles and thus provides a virtual guarantee that the structure of political power will not deviate far enough from the structure of socio-economic power so as to make the distribution of each type of power incompatible with the other. 'The party system has been the means of reconciling universal equal franchise with the mainte- nance of an unequal society,' Macpherson has remarked.[12] The inherent dynamic of the party as an organizational form developing under and for conditions of political competition generates those constraints and imposes those 'non-decisions' upon the political process which together make democracy safe for capitalism. Such non-decisions affect both the *content* of politics (i.e., what kind of issues, claims and demands are allowed to be put on the agenda) and the *means* by which political conflict is expressed. The con- straints imposed upon the possible content of politics are all the more effective since they are non-explicit, i.e., not based on formal mechanisms of exclusion (such as limitations of voting rights, or authoritarian bans or certain actors or issues), but rather consti- tuted as artefacts and by-products of the organizational forms of universal political inclusion. This conclusion, of course, is strongly supported by the fact that no competitive party system so far has ever yielded a distribution of political power that would have been able to alter the logic of capital and the pattern of socio-economic power *it* generates.

In order to avoid any misunderstanding, I should emphasize that what I intend here is not a *normative* critique of the organizational form of the political party leading to a proposed alternative form of political organization. Rather than speculating about the comparative desirability of anarchist, syndicalist, council-democratic or Leninist models of either non-party or non-competitive party organization, let us now look at the future viability of this organizational form itself – its continued potential for constructing and mediating, as it has done in the post-war era, a type of political authority that does not interfere with the institutional premises of the capitalist economy. In other words, the question is whether the institutional link that has allowed capitalism and political democracy to coexist in most advanced capitalist countries for most of the last sixty years is likely to continue to do so in the future. How solid and viable are the organizational forms that bring the 'iron law' to bear upon the process of politics?

One way to answer this question in the negative would be to postulate the emergence of political parties capable of abolishing the above-mentioned restrictions and constraints, thus leading to a challenge to class power through politically constituted power. I do not think that there are many promising indications of such a development, in spite of Euro-communist doctrines and strategies that have emerged in the Latin-European countries in the mid 1970s, and in spite of the recently elected socialist/communist government in France. The other possibility would be a *disintegration of the political party as the dominant form of democratic mass participation* and its gradual replacement by other forms possibly less likely than party competition to lead to 'congruent' uses of state power. As we are concerned with the prospects of competitive party democracy in the 1980s it might be worthwhile to explore this possibility a little further.

Causes of the decline of the party system as the dominant form of mass participation

It is quite possible to argue today that the form of mass political participation based on and channelled through the party system (i.e., according to the principles of territorial representation, party competition and parliamentary representation) has exhausted much of its usefulness for reconciling capitalism and mass politics. This appears to be so because the political form of the party is increasingly bypassed and displaced by other practices and procedures of political participation and representation. It is highly doubtful, however, whether these new and additional practices, evident in quite a number of capitalist states, will exhibit the same potential for reconciling political legitimation with the imperatives of capital accumulation that has been the accomplishment of the competitive party system for a considerable period of time. In a somewhat schematic fashion we can single out three such practices – new social movements, corporatism and repression – as phenomena which tend to bypass, restrict and subvert the party system, with its political practices and reconciling potential.

First, in many capitalist countries new social movements have emerged during the 1970s. For a number of reasons, these are proving very hard to absorb into the practices of competitive party politics. These include various ethnic and regionalist, urban, ecological, feminist, peace and youth movements. To a large extent, all of them share two characteristics. First, their projects and demands are based not on a collective *contractual position* on either goods or labour markets, as was the case, for instance, with traditional class parties and movements. Instead, their common denominator of organization and action is some sense of collective identity, often underlined by ascriptive and 'naturalistic' conceptions of the collective 'self' in terms of age, gender, 'nation' or 'mankind'. Closely connected with this is a second characteristic: they do not demand *representation*, by which their market status could be improved or protected, but *autonomy*. In short, the underlying logic of these movements is the struggle for the defence of a *physical and/or moral 'territory'*, the integrity of which is fundamentally non-negotiable to the activists of these movements. For the purpose of this defence, political representation and parliamentary politics is often considered unnecessary because what is requested of the state, as can be illustrated in the issues of abortion or nuclear energy, is not to 'do something' but to 'stay out'; or it may even be considered dangerous, because it is suspected of demobilizing and disorganizing the movement. To the extent such movements attract the attention and the political energies of more and more people, not only particular political parties but indeed the *traditional competitive party system as a whole* will decline in function and credibility because it simply does not provide the arena within which such issues and concerns can possibly be processed. The concerns of these 'new social movements' are not geared towards what is to be created or accomplished through the use of politics and state power but towards what should be saved from and defended against the state and the considerations governing the conduct of public policy. The three most obvious cases of such movements, the peace movement, the environmental movement and various movements centred on human rights (of women, of prisoners, of minorities, of tenants, etc.) all illustrate a 'negative' conception of politics trying to protect a sphere of life against the intervention of state or state-sanctioned policy. What dominates the thought and action of these movements is not a 'progressive' utopia of what desirable social arrangements must be achieved, but a conservative utopia of what non-negotiable essentials must not be threatened and sacrificed in the name of 'progress'.

Second, many observers in a number of capitalist states have analysed an ongoing process of the 'deparliamentarization' of public policy and the concomitant displacement of *territorial* forms of representation by *functional* ones. This is most evident in 'corporatist' arrangements, which combine the function of interest *representation* of collective actors with policy *implementation vis-à-vis* their respective constituencies.[13] The functional superiority of such corporatist arrangements, compared to both parliamentary-competitive forms of representation and bureaucratic methods of implementation, resides in their informal, inconspicuous and non-public procedures and the 'voluntary' compliance that they are said to be able to mobilize. Although the dynamics and limits of corporatist forms of public policy-making, especially in the areas of economic and social policies, cannot interest us here, what seems to be clear is that there has been a trend towards such arrangements, especially in countries with strong social democratic parties (such as in Europe, Sweden, Britain, Austria and Germany) and that they have worked at the expense of parliament and the competitive party system. A number of Marxist and non-Marxist political scientists have even argued that 'parliamentary representation on the basis of residence no longer adequately reflects the problems of economic management in a worldwide capitalist system', and that 'a system of functional representation is more suited to securing the conditions of accumulation'.[14]

Third, a constant alternative to free party competition is political repression and the gradual transformation of democracy into some form of authoritarianism. In an analytical sense, what we mean by repression is *exclusion from representation*. Citizens are denied their civil liberties and freedoms, such as the right to organize, demonstrate or express certain opinions in speech and writing. They are denied access to occupations in the public sector, and the like. The expansion of police apparatuses and the observable growth in many countries of the practice of virtually universal monitoring and surveillance of the activities of citizens are indications of the growing reliance by the state apparatus on preventive and corrective repression. More importantly, in the context of the limits of competitive party democracy, there is one other aspect of the exclusion from representation. This is the *de facto* and/or formal limitation of competitiveness within the party system: whether by the strengthening of intraparty discipline and the sanctions applied against dissenters; through the election campaigns from which substantive alternatives concerning the conduct and programmatic content of public policy often seem to be absent; or on the level of parliament and parliamentary government, where the identity of individual (and only nominally 'competing') parties more and more often disappears behind what occasionally is called the 'great coalition of the enlightened', inspired by some vague 'solidarity of all democratic forces'. Referring back to the economic metaphor used before, such phenomena and developments could well be described as the 'cartelization' of political supply and the closure of market access.

If I am correct in assuming that the displacement of the role and political function of the competitive party system is a real and widespread process, as indicated by the emergence of new social movements, increasing reliance on corporatist arrangements, and self-limitation of the competitiveness of party systems in numerous advanced (and not so advanced) capitalist states; and if I am also correct in assuming, as argued above, that the organizational form of the competitive political party plays a crucial role in making democratic mass participation compatible with capitalism, then the decline of the party system is likely to lead to the rise of less constrained and regulated practices of political participation and conflict, whose outcomes may then have the potential of effectively challenging and transcending the institutional premises of capitalist social and economic organization.

Our picture remains incomplete and unbalanced if we concentrate exclusively on those cases in which the 'channel' of political participation that consists of party competition, elections and parliamentary representation is bypassed and reduced in its legitimacy and credibility by the protest politics of social movements or corporatist negotiations among powerful strategic actors, or where this channel is altogether reduced in significance by 'repressive' mechanisms of exclusion. Another alternative, alluded to above, would consist not of the displacement and loss of relevance of the organizational form of political parties, but rather of the successful strategy of 'self-transcendence' of the party moving from 'political' to 'economic' democracy. All models and strategies of *economic* democratization, beginning in the mid 1920s in Austria and Germany and continuing through the current Swedish concepts of wage earner funds and the Meidner plan[15] rely on the notion that the tension between the democratic principle of equal mass participation and the economic principle of unequal and private decision-making power could be resolved through instituting, by means of electoral success, parliamentary legislation and democratic bodies at the level of enterprises, sectors of industry, regions, cities, and so on. The central assumption that inspires such strategies is that 'democracy would explode capitalism (and) that the democratic state, because it could be made to represent the people, would compel entrepreneurs to proceed according to principles inimical to their own survival. . . . The working class, as the spokesman for the great, non-capitalist majority, would enforce the primacy of politics throughout the economy, as well as in politics *per se*'.[16]

Although this alternative means for suspending the incompatibility of democracy and capitalism is part of the programmatic objectives of almost all social democratic/socialist (and increasingly also of communist) parties in Europe (and even of some forces in North America), nowhere has it been accomplished to the point where the private character of decisions concerning the volume, kind, point in time and location of investment has been effectively transformed in the manner of democratic control. The European Left in the early 1980s seems to be divided on the strategic alternatives of either trying to overcome the constraints of political democracy and its oligarchic organizational dynamics by supporting those 'new social movements' engaging in their politics of autonomy and protest, or sticking to the older model of economic democratization. Both tendencies, however, provide sufficient reason to expect a weakening of these organizational and political characteristics that have so far made democratic mass participation safe for capitalism. The extent to which it becomes likely that competitive party democracy is either displaced by social and political movements and corporatist arrangements or is complemented by 'economic democracy' will, however, probably depend on the stability, growth and prosperity the economy is able to provide. Let us therefore now turn to the question of the organization of production and distribution and the changes that have occurred since Andrew Shonfield's book, *Modern Capitalism*, appeared in 1964.

The Keynesian welfare state and its demise

Let me now try in an even more generalized and schematic fashion to apply the analogous argument to the second pillar upon which, according to my initial proposition, the coexistence of capitalism and democracy rests, namely the KWS. The bundle of state institutions and practices to which this concept refers has developed in Western capitalism since the Second World War. Until the decisive change of circumstances that has occurred since the mid 1970s and that has been marked by OPEC price policies, the end of *détente*, and the coming to power of Reagan in the US and Thatcher in Britain (to mention just a few indicators of this change), the KWS had been adopted as the basic conception of the state and state practice in almost all Western countries, irrespective of which parties were in power and with only minor modifications and time lags. Most observers agree that its effect has been, first, an unprecedented and extended economic boom favouring all advanced capitalist economies and, second, the transformation of the pattern of industrial and class conflict in ways that increasingly depart from political and even revolutionary radicalism and lead to more economistic, distribution-centred and increasingly institutionalized class conflict. Underlying this development which constitutes a formidable change if compared to the dynamics of the capitalist world system during the 1920s and 1930s is a politically instituted class compromise or 'accord' that Bowles has described as follows. The accord

represented, on the part of labour, the acceptance of the logic of profitability and markets as the guiding principles of resource allocation, international exchange, technological change, product development, and industrial location, in return for an assurance that minimal living standards, trade union rights, and liberal democratic rights would be protected, massive unemployment avoided, and real incomes would rise approximately in line with labour productivity, all through the intervention of the state, if necessary.[17]

It is easy to see why and how the existence of this accord has contributed to the compatibility of capitalism and democracy. First, by accepting the terms of the accord, working-class organizations (unions and political parties) reduced their demands and projects to a programme that sharply differs from anything on the agenda of either the Third or the Second Internationals. This change of perspective is not entirely incomprehensible in light of the physical, moral and organizational devastations caused by the Second World War, and after the discredit the development of the Soviet Union had earned for communism. Moreover, the accord itself worked amazingly well, thus reinforcing a deeply depoliticized trust in what one leading German social democrat much later came arrogantly to call the 'German Model' (*Modell Deutschland*):[18] the mutual stimulation of economic growth and peaceful class relations. What was at issue in class conflicts was no longer control of the mode of production, but the volume of distribution and growth. This type of conflict was particularly suited for political processing through party competition precisely because it did not involve 'either/or' questions, but rather questions of a 'more or less' or 'sooner or later' nature. Overarching this limited type of conflict, there was a consensus concerning the basic priorities, desirabilities and values of the political economy, namely economic growth and social (as well as military) security. This interclass growth-security alliance does in fact have a theoretical basis in Keynes's economic theory. As applied to the practice of economic policy-making, it teaches each class to 'take the role of the other'. The capitalist economy – this is the lesson to be learnt from Keynesianism – is a positive sum game. Therefore, playing as one would in a zero sum game is against one's own interest. That is to say, each class has to take the interests of the other class into consideration: the workers must acknowledge the importance of profitability, because only a sufficient level of profits and investment will secure future employment and income increases; and the capitalists must accept the need for wages and welfare state expenditures, because these will secure effective demand and a healthy, well-trained, well-housed and happy working class.

The welfare state is usually defined as a set of citizens' legal entitlements to transfer payments from compulsory social security schemes to state organized services (such as health and education) for a wide variety of defined instances of need and contingency. The means by which the welfare state intervenes consist of bureaucratic rules and legal regulations, monetary transfers and the professional expertise of teachers, doctors, social workers, etc. Its ideological origins are highly mixed and heterogeneous, ranging from socialist to Catholic–conservative sources; its character as the fruit of ideological, political and economic *interclass* compromises is something the welfare state shares with the logic of Keynesian economic policy-making. In both cases, there is no fast and easy answer to the zero sum question of who wins and who loses. For, although the primary function of the welfare state is to cover those risks and uncertainties to which wage workers and their families are exposed in capitalist society, there are some indirect effects which serve the capitalist class too. This becomes evident if we look at what would be likely to happen in the absence of welfare state arrangements in a capitalist society. It is fairly clear that the answer to this counterfactual question is this: first, there would be a much higher level of industrial conflict and a stronger tendency among proletarians to avoid becoming wage workers. Thus, the welfare state can be said to partially dispel the motives and reasons for social conflict while making the existence of wage labour more acceptable by eliminating part of the risk that results from the imposition of the commodity form on to labour.[19] Second, this conflict would substantially increase economic costs by its disruption of the increasingly complex and capital-intensive process of industrial production. Therefore, the welfare state performs the crucial functions of: removing some of the needs of the working class from the arena of class struggle and industrial conflict, of providing the means to fulfil their needs more collectively and hence more efficiently, making production more regular and predictable by relieving it of important issues and conflicts, and providing, in addition, a built-in stabilizer for the economy by partly uncoupling changes in effective demand from changes in employment. As in the case of Keynesian doctrines of economic policy, the welfare state too can be seen to provide a measure of mutuality of interest between classes so that virtually no room remains for fundamental issues and conflicts over the nature of the political economy.

The functional links between Keynesian economic policy, economic growth and the welfare state are fairly obvious and agreed upon by all 'partners' and parties involves. An 'active' economic policy stimulates and regularizes economic growth; the 'tax dividend' resulting from that growth allows for the extension of welfare state programmes; and, at the same time, continued economic growth limits the extent to which welfare state provisions (such as unemployment benefits) are actually claimed.

Consequently, the issues and conflicts that remain to be resolved within the realm of formal politics, party competition and parliament, are of such a fragmented, non-polarizing, and non-fundamental nature (at least in the areas of economic and social policy) that they can be settled by the inconspicuous mechanisms of marginal adjustments, compromise and coalition-building.

If all of this still held true, then today's ubiquitous critiques and political attacks directed at Keynesianism, the welfare state and, most of all, the combination of these two would be plainly incomprehensible. They are not. As in the case of competitive political parties, these innovations and their healthy effects seem to have reached their limits today. While the integrative functions of the party system have partly been displaced by the alternative and less institutionalized forms of political participation described above, the Keynesian welfare state has come under attack for some of its less desirable side effects as well as its failure to correct some of the ills of an economic environment that has changed radically, compared to the conditions that prevailed prior to the mid 1970s. Let us look at some of the reasons why there are very few people left, be it in academia or politics, on the Left or the Right, who believe that the Keynesian welfare state continues to be a viable peace formula for democratic capitalism.

My thesis, in brief, is that while the KWS is an excellent and uniquely effective device to manage and control *some* socio-economic and political problems of advanced capitalist societies, it does not solve all those problems. Further, the problems that can be successfully solved through the institutional means of the welfare state no longer constitute the most dominant and pressing ones. Moreover, *this shift of the socio-economic* problematique *is in part an unintended consequence of the operation of the KWS itself*. The two types of problems to which I refer here are the production/ exploitation problem and the effective demand/realization problem. Between the two, there exists a trade-off: the more effectively one of the two is solved, the more dominant and pressing the other one becomes. The KWS has indeed, to a remarkable extent, been able to solve the problem of macro-economic demand stabilization. But, at the same time, it has also interfered with the ability of the capitalist economy to adapt to the production/ exploitation problem as it has emerged ever more urgently since the mid 1970s. The KWS, so to speak, has operated on the basis of the *false* assumption that the problems it *is* able to deal with are the *only*

problems of the capitalist political economy, or at least the permanently dominant ones. This erroneous confidence is now in the both
politically and economically painful process of being disproven and
rectified.

To the extent the demand problem is solved, the supply problem
is considerably widened. The economic situation has changed in a
way that appears to lend support to conservative and neo-*laissez-
faire* economic theory. Far from stimulating production, the
government practice of deficit spending in order to combat unemployment contributes to even higher rates of unemployment.
For this practice, as at least some economists have argued, drives up
interest rates and makes *money capital scarce and costly*. Also, and
possibly even worse, the welfare state amounts to a partial *disincentive to work*. Its compulsory insurance schemes and legal
entitlements provide such a strong institutional protection of the
material interest of wage workers that labour becomes less prepared and/or can be less easily forced to adjust to the contingencies
of structural, technological, locational, vocational and other
changes of the economy. Not only are wages 'sticky' and 'down-
wardly inflexible', but, in addition, the provisions of the welfare
state have partly 'decommodified' the interests of workers, replacing 'contract' with 'status', and 'property rights' with 'citizen rights'.
This change of industrial relations brought about by the KWS has
not only helped to increase and stabilize effective demand (as it was
intended to), but it also has made employment more costly and
rigid. Again, the central problem on the labour market is the supply
problem: how to hire and fire the right people at the right place with
the right skills and, most important, the right motivation and the
right wage demand. The welfare state is, in my view to a large extent
justifiably, seen by business not as part of the solution, but rather as
part of this problem itself.

As small capital as well as big capital has come to depend on the
stimulating and regularizing effects of interventionist policies
applied to both the demand and supply sides, and as labour relies on
the welfare state, the parameters of incentives, motivations and
expectations of investors and workers alike have been affected in
ways that alter and undermine the dynamic of economic growth.
Pressures to adjust to changing market forces have been reduced for
capital and labour alike, thanks to the availability of state-provided
resources that either help to avoid or delay adaptation or to the
expectation that a large part of the costs of adaptation must be

subsidized by the state. Growth industries such as defence, civilian aircraft, nuclear energy and telecommunications typically depend as much on markets created by the state (and often capital provided by it) as stagnant industries (such as steel, textiles and, increasingly, electronics) depend on state protection and subsidized market shelters. Economic growth, where it occurs at all, has become a matter of political design rather than a matter of spontaneous market forces.

The increasing claims that are made on the state budget both by labour and capital, by both the growing and the stagnant sectors of the economy, can only lead to unprecedented levels of public debt and to constant governmental efforts to terminate or reduce welfare state programmes. Hence economic growth not only becomes more costly in terms of the budgetary inputs required to promote it; it also becomes more costly in terms of political legitimation. The more economic growth becomes 'growth by political design', and the more it is *perceived* to be the result of explicit political decisions and strategies of an increasingly 'disaggregated' nature (i.e., specified by-product, industry and location), the more governments and political parties are held accountable for the physical quality of products, processes and environmental effects resulting from such industrial policies. The widespread and apparently increasing concern with the physical quality of products and production, and the various 'anti-productivist' and environmentalist political motives and demands that are spreading in many capitalist countries have so far been interpreted in the social science literature mostly either in objectivist terms ('environmental disruption') or in subjectivist categories ('changing values and sensitivities'). In addition, however, these phenomena must be analysed in terms of the apparent political manageability of the shape and impact of industrial production and growth, a perceived area of political decision- and non-decision-making that gives rise to a new arena of 'politics of production'. The outcomes of the conflicts in this arena, in turn, tend to create additional impediments to industrial growth.

The strategic intention of Keynesian economic policy is to promote growth and full employment, the strategic intention of the welfare state to protect those affected by the risks and contingencies of industrial society and to create a measure of social equality. The latter strategy becomes feasible only to the extent that the first is successful, thereby providing the resources necessary for welfare policies and limiting the extent to which claims are made on these resources.

The combined effect of the two strategies, however, has been high rates of unemployment *and* inflation. At the very least, neither economic nor social policies have been able to prevent simultaneous unemployment and inflation. But one can safely say more than that. Plausible causal links between the KWS and today's condition of 'the worst of both worlds' are suggested not only by conservative economic policy ideologues advocating a return to some type of monetarist steering of a pure market economy; they are equally, if reluctantly, acknowledged by the practice and partly by the theories of the Left. The relevant arguments are:

1 The Keynesian welfare state is a victim of its success. By (partly) eliminating and smoothening crises, it has inhibited the positive function that crises used to perform in the capitalist process of 'creative destruction'.

2 The Keynesian welfare state involves the unintended but undeniable consequence of undermining both the incentives to invest and the incentives to work.

3 There is no equilibrating mechanism or 'stop-rule' that would facilitate adjustments of the extension of social policy so as to eliminate its self-contradictory consequences; the logic of democratic party competition and the social democratic alliance with unions remains undisciplined by 'economic reason'.

While the latter argument is probably still to be found exclusively in the writings of liberal–conservative authors,[20] the other two are hardly contested by the Left. Let me quote just one example of an author who clearly thinks of himself as a social democratic theoretician:

It is unfortunate that those who wish to defend the welfare state . . . spend their energies persuading the public that the welfare state does not erode incentives, savings, authority or efficiency. . . . What the Right has recognized much better than the Left is that the principles of the welfare state are directly incompatible with a capitalistic market system. . . . The welfare state eats the very hand that feeds it. The main contradiction of the welfare state is the . . . tension between the market and social policy.[21]

We cannot concern ourselves here with whether these increasingly frequent accusations against the KWS are entirely 'true', or whether in addition, they are the result of paranoic exaggerations or a conscious tactical misrepresentation of reality on the part of capital and its political organizations. For what applies in this context is a special version of a law known to sociologists as the 'Thomas-theorem': what is real in the minds and perceptions of people will be real in its consequences. The structural power position of the owners, managers and associational representatives of capital in a capitalist society is exactly their power to *define* reality in a highly consequential way, so that what is perceived as 'real' *by them* is likely to have a very *real impact* for other classes and political actors.

Without entering too far into the professional realm of the economist, let me suggest two aspects of what I consider a potentially useful (if partial) interpretation of this change. One is the idea, already alluded to, that the Keynesian welfare state is a 'victim of its success', as one author has put it:[22] the side effects of its successful practice of solving *one* type of macro-economic problem have led to the emergence of an *entirely different problematique*, one which is beyond the steering capacity of the KWS. The familiar arguments that favour, and indeed demand, a shift of economic and social policy-making towards what has been baptized 'supply-side economics' are these: the non-productive public sector has become an intolerable burden upon the private sector, leading to a chronic shortage of investment capital; the work ethic is in the process of being undermined, and the independent middle class is suffocated economically by high rates of taxation and inflation.

The other set of arguments maintains that, even in the absence of those economic side effects, the political paradigm of the KWS is now undergoing definitive exhaustion for *inherent* reasons. The relevant arguments, in brief, are two. First, state intervention works only as long as economic actors do not *expect* it to be applied routinely, and therefore does not enter into their rational calculations. As soon as that happens, however, investors will postpone investment because they can be reasonably sure that the state will intervene by special tax exemptions, depreciation allowances or demand measures, if only they wait long enough. The spread of such 'rational' expectations is fatal to Keynesianism, for to the extent it enters the calculations of economic actors, their strategic behaviour will *increase* the problem load to which the state has to respond or at least will not contribute, in the way it had been naïvely anticipated, to resolving the unemployment and state budget problems. This pathology of expectations, of course, is itself known to (and expected by) actors in the state apparatus. It forces them to react either by ever higher doses of intervention or, failing that possibility for fiscal reasons, to give up the interventionist practice that breeds those very problems that it was supposed to solve. This would lead us to conclude that state intervention is effective only to the extent it occurs as a 'surprise' and exception, rather than as a matter of routine.

A further inherent weakness of the KWS resides in the limits of the legal-bureaucratic, monetarized and professional mode of intervention. These limits become particularly clear in the areas of personal services, or 'people processing organizations', such as schools, hospitals, universities, prisons and social work agencies. Again, the mode of intervention generates more of the problems it is supposed to deal with. The explanation of this paradox is well known: the clients' capacity for self-help and, more generally, the system of knowledge and meaning generating it, are subverted by the mode of intervention and the suppliers of such services, especially human service professions and higher level bureaucrats (referred to by neo-conservatives as the 'new class') who take a material interest in the persistence and continuous expansion and redefinition of – rather than the solution to – the problems with which they are supposed to deal.[23]

Thus, for reasons that have to do both with its external economic effects and the paradoxes of its internal mode of operation, the KWS seems to a large extent to have exhausted its potential and viability. Moreover, this exhaustion is unlikely to turn out to be a transient phenomenon that will disappear with the next economic boom. This boom itself is far from certain. Why is this so? First, because it cannot be expected to occur as the *spontaneous result* of market forces and the dynamics of technological innovation. Second, it apparently cannot be *generated* and manipulated either by the traditional tools of Keynesianism or by its 'monetarist' counterpart. Third, even to the extent it *does* occur either as an effect of spontaneous forces or state intervention, the question is whether it will be *considered desirable* and worthwhile in terms of its inevitable side effect for the 'quality of life' in general, and the environment in particular. This question as to the desirability of continued economic growth is further underscored by what Fred Hirsch has called the 'social limits to growth', by which he means the decreasing desirability and 'satisfaction potential' of industrial output, the use-value of which declines in proportion to the number of people who consume it.

Conclusion

We have seen that the two institutional mechanisms on which the compatibility of the private economy and political mass participation rests – namely, the mechanism of competitive party democracy and the paradigm of the Keynesian welfare state – have come under stress and strain, whose order of magnitude is unprecedented in the post-war era.

One plausible hypothesis is that, as the political economy turns from a growth economy into a 'zero sum society',[24] the institutional arrangements of conflict resolution will suffer from growing strains and tensions. These tensions are probably best described within the conceptual paradigm of 'organized capitalism'[25] as threats of *disorganization*. Such threats are likely to occur on two levels: on the level of *inter*organizational 'rules of the game', and on the level of the organization of collective actors. Under positive sum conditions, it has not only been a matter of legal obligation or traditional mutual recognition, but also of evident *self-interest* for each participant to stick to the established rules of interaction and negotiation. As long as one participates, one can be at least certain of not losing, of receiving future rewards for present concessions, and of having one's claims respected as legitimate, because the process of growth itself provides the resources necessary for such compensation. Stagnation and, even worse, recession or expected no-growth conditions, destroy the basis for co-operative relations among collective actors; confidence, mutual respect and reciprocity are called into question, and the organizational elites involved begin to consider the previous coalitions, alliances and routinized networks of co-operation problematic and needing revision. Crucial as these 'social contracts' (i.e., subtle 'quasi-constitutional' relations of trust, loyalty and recognition of the mutual spheres of interest and competence) are in a complex political economy,[26] the interorganizational relations required for the management of economic growth tend to break down under the impact of continued stagnation. This is manifested in a number of Western European countries, and even in the EEC itself, by strains within party coalitions, between unions and parties, employers' associations and governments, states and federal governments, etc., all of which find the principle of 'relying upon one's own strength' increasingly attractive.

The second type of disorganization that follows from stagnation has to do with intra-organizational relations within collective actors such as trade unions, employers associations and parties. Such organizations depend on the assumption, shared by their members, that gains achieved through collective action will be achieved at the expense of *third* parties, not at the expense of some groups of members themselves. As soon as this solidaristic expectation is frustrated, the representativeness of the organization is rendered questionable, and 'syndicalist', 'corporativist' or otherwise particularistic modes of collective action suggest themselves. The consequences of this internal disorganization of collective actors include either increasing 'factionalism' of political and economic interests within the organization following the logic of '*sauve qui peut*' and/or a shrinking of the social, temporal and substantive range of representation the organization is able to maintain.[27] The political and economic forms of the interclass accord that has gradually developed in all advanced capitalist states since the First World War and that has helped to make capitalism and democracy compatible with each other are clearly disintegrating under the impact of these developments and paradoxes.

Does that mean that we are headed back to a situation that supports the convergent views of Marx and Mill concerning the antagonism of mass political participation and economic freedom? Yes and no. I think yes, because we have numerous reasons to expect an increase of institutionally *un*mediated social and political conflict, the expression of which is not likely to be channelled through parties or other avenues of representation, and the sources of which are no longer to be dried up by effective social and economic policies of the state. But I also think no, because there are strict limits to the analogy between the dynamics of 'late' and 'early' capitalism. One of these important limits derives from the fact that the forces involved in such conflicts are extremely heterogeneous in regard to both their causes and socio-economic composition. This pattern is remarkably different from a bipolar 'class conflict' situation involving two highly inclusive collective actors defined by the two sides of the labour market. But, in spite of the highly fragmented nature of modern political conflict, its outcomes may well involve fundamental changes in either the economic or the political order of society: changes that have, for just a limited period of time, been inconceivable under the unchallenged reign of competitive party democracy and the Keynesian welfare state.

Notes and references

1   cf. for instance J. S. Mill's argument on the necessary limits of the extension of *equal* voting rights as developed in Chapter 8 of his *Considerations on Representative Government* (Oxford 1975).

2   This idea is stated in all three of Marx's major political writings on France, namely *Die Klassenkämpfe in Frankreich von 1848–1850* (1850), *Der achtzehnte Brumaire des Louis Bonaparte* (1852) and *Der Bürgerkrieg in Frankreich* (1871).

3   G. Therborn, 'The rule of capital and the rise of democracy', *New Left Review*, **103** (May–June 1977), p. 28.

4   I follow this procedure on the basis of the rather trivial, if not uncontroversial, idea that compatibility, stability, continuity or 'self-reproductiveness' of any social system is not sufficiently accounted for in terms of its 'inertia' or its presupposed 'adaptive capacity' and that, rather, the continuity of any social system can and must be explained as a *process* of reproduction in which integrative tendencies outweigh those of change or disruption; cf. C. S. Maier, 'The two postwar eras and the conditions for stability in twentieth century Western Europe', *The American Historical Review*, **86** (1981), pp. 327–52.

5   B. Hindess, 'Marxism and parliamentary democracy', in A. Hunt (ed.), *Marxism and Democracy* (London 1980), p. 34.

6   Lenin writes in *State and Revolution*: 'The democratic republic is the best possible political shell for capitalism, and therefore capital, once in possession . . . of this very best shell, establishes its power so securely, so firmly, that *no* change of persons, of institutions, or of parties in the bourgeois democratic republic can shake it'. Following the Leninist tradition of thinking of the state as a mere reflection of socio-economic power structures and the corresponding theorem of the eventual withering away of the state after the revolution, the Italian political theorist Norberto Bobbio has rightly asked whether there is anything at all like a 'Marxist theory of the state' which would be conceptually equipped to grasp the 'specificity of the political'; cf. N. Bobbio's contributions to *Il Marxismo lo Stato* (Rome 1976), quoted after the German translation, *Sozialisten, Kommunisten und der Staat* (Hamburg 1977), pp. 15–61.

7   It is only on the basis of the *real* assimilation of the practices of political parties to market behaviour that the 'economic paradigm' in democratic theory (as formulated in the famous works of Schumpeter, Downs and Olson) could become so plausible and influential.

8   Max Weber, 'Parliament and government in a reconstructed

Germany', in G. Roth and C. Wittich (eds), *Economy and Society* (Berkeley 1978), vol. 2, p. 1460.

9   R. Luxemburg, 'Massenstreik, Partei und Gewerkschaften', *Gesammelte Werke*, vol. 2 (Berlin 1924), pp. 163–5 (my translation – ed.).

10   cf. R. Michels, *Soziologie des Parteiwesens* (Stuttgart 1925); W. J. Mommsen, 'Max Weber and Robert Michels', *Archives Européennes de Sociologie* **22** (1981), pp. 100–16; D. Beetham, 'From socialism to fascism: the relation between theory and practice in the work of Robert Michels', *Political Studies*, **25** (1977), pp. 3–24, 161–81.

11   cf. the brilliant analysis of this problem by A. Przeworski, 'Social democracy as an historical phenomenon', *New Left Review*, **122** (1980).

12   C. B. Macpherson, *The Life and Times of Liberal Democracy* (London 1977), p. 69.

13   The most comprehensive accounts of recent theorizing and discussion on 'corporatism' are the two works edited by P. C. Schmitter and G. Lehmbruch, *Trends Toward Corporatist Intermediation* (London 1979) and *Patterns of Corporatist Policy-Making* (London 1982).

14   B. Jessop, 'The transformation of the state in post-war Britain', in R. Scase (ed.) *The State in Western Europe* (London 1980), pp. 23–93.

15   For a detailed account of current Swedish debates surrounding these plans see U. Himmelstrand *et al.*, *Beyond Welfare Capitalism?* (London 1981), especially pp. 255–310.

16   D. Abraham, ' "Economic Democracy" as a Labour Alternative to the "Growth Strategy" in the Weimar Republic', unpublished manuscript, (Princeton 1982), pp. 16ff.

17   S. Bowles, 'The Keynesian Welfare State and the Post-Keynesian Political Containment of the Working Class', unpublished manuscript (Paris 1981), p. 12.

18   This slogan has since become a technical term in comparative politics; cf. A. Markovits (ed.) *The Political Economy of West Germany. Modell Deutschland* (New York 1982).

19   For a detailed formulation of this argument see essay three in this volume, 'Social policy and the theory of the state'.

20   cf. N. Luhmann, *Politische Theorie im Wohlfahrtsstaat* (Munich 1981); S. Huntington, 'The United States', in M. Crozier *et al.*, *The Crisis of Democracy* (New York 1975), pp. 59–118; B. Cazes, 'The welfare state: a double bind', in OECD, *The Welfare State in Crisis* (Paris 1981), pp. 151–73. See also the powerful critique of the 'economic reason versus political irrationality' argument by J. Goldthorpe, 'The

current inflation: towards a sociological account', in F. Hirsch and J. Goldthorpe (eds.), *The Political Economy of Inflation* (London 1978).

21   Quoted from a paper by Harvard sociologist, G. Esping-Anderson, 'The incompatibilities of the welfare state', *Working Papers for a New Society* (January 1982).

22   cf. J. Logue 'The welfare state – victim of its success', *Daedalus* **108** no. 4 (1979), pp. 69–87; also R. Klein, 'The welfare state – a self-inflicted crisis?', *Political Quarterly* **51** (1980), pp. 24–34.

23   On this problem of the new 'service class' and its (partially converging) critique from the Left and the Right, see I. Illich (ed.), *Disabling Professions* (London 1977); a penetrating and influential economic analysis of the rise of 'unproductive' service labour is R. Bacon and W. Eltis, *Britain's Economic Problem: Too Few Producers* (London 1976).

24   cf. L. Thurow, *The Zero-Sum Society. Distribution and the Possibilities for Economic Change* (New York 1980).

25   cf. J. Kocka, 'Organisierter Kapitalismus oder Staatsmonopolistischer Kapitalismus. Begriffliche Vorbemerkungen', in H. A. Winkler (ed.), *Organisierter Kapitalismus* (Göttingen 1974).

26   cf. E. W. Böckenförde, 'Die politische Funktion wirtschaftlich-sozialer Verbände', *Der Staat* **15** (1976), pp. 457–83.

27   cf. for the case of German and Italian unions, R. G. Heinze *et al.*, 'Einheitsprobleme der Einheitsgewerkschaft', *Soziale Welt* **32** no. 1 (1981), pp. 19–38; and M. Regini 'Repräsentationskrise und Klassenpolitik der Gewerkschaften', *Leviathan* **10** (1982).

9 Political culture and Social Democratic administration*

Democratic stability and political culture

The political stability of democracy in developed, industrial-capitalist societies presupposes a certain form of political culture. Richard Löwenthal, one of the most influential social-democratic intellectuals of the older generation, has emphasized the importance of this connection. He outlines a distinct dilemma with which he sees Western democracy to be confronted. The one horn of the dilemma is the 'danger of totalitarianism', namely, the attempt to postulate 'scientific' knowledge of the course of history, the 'correct' understanding of public welfare and the strategies of its realization, and to make the knowledge thus acquired the basis for political activity. This attempt, in the view of theorists of totalitarianism, necessarily leads to the abolition of political and social freedom. The other horn of the dilemma, according to Löwenthal, is the danger that political competition for state decision-making positions will degenerate into a pure conflict of interests between social groups and political organizations. If citizens and political elites competitively pursued only their particular interests, democracy could deteriorate into a state of affairs that would render generally acceptable decisions and governmental functions impossible.

The dilemma is clear: a *substantive* definition of public welfare leads to totalitarian structures, while the competitive-democratic *renunciation* of such a definition, the equation of the 'public

* This is a shortened version of an essay which first appeared in *Das Argument*, **128** (1981), pp. 551–64. It was written with Volker Gransow. The argument anticipates the subsequent defeat of the German Social Democratic Government (in October 1982), and engages the widespread discussion of political culture in West Germany. This discussion was prompted in the late 1970s by the phenomenon of 'terrorism' and the growing uncertainty within the Social Democratic Party about how to engage the politics of the new social movements, such as feminism, environmentalism and pacifism.

interest' with any empirical *outcomes* of competition, can lead to instability and ungovernability. The task of solving this dilemma is assigned to the political parties. Their attempts to define the 'public interest' must be restrained and, whenever necessary, they must accept defeat in accordance with the rules of democratic competition. According to Löwenthal, parties must orient themselves equally towards political substance and form, their programmes as well as the rules of competition. 'Liberal democracy can only solve the problems of advanced industrial society if parties . . . are willing and competent to propose and realize conceptions of the public interest by means of the public control of general economic and social development.'[1]

Clearly, this kind of party would have to steer a course between the two poles of party systems familiar to sociologists: first, that of the '*Weltanschauung*' or 'class' party which defends a material definition of the public interest and is unwilling to yield to the procedural rules of democratic competition, instead seeking to conquer the state *and* – following Lenin – transform it so that its power becomes unquestionable. Second, the 'vote maximizing' or 'catch-all' party, which can, and indeed must, renounce any consistency in its platform and any independent conception of the public interest in order to win and defend a majority in the never-ending electoral campaigns of modern mass democracy. Rejecting both of these poles, Löwenthal recommends that party elites 'must appeal increasingly to citizens' social awareness' and thereby 'stop behaving as mere coalitions representing different interest groups; they must increasingly present themselves as the bearers of alternative concepts of collective social development and win citizens' votes primarily on the basis of community interests'. A 'growing social awareness of citizens' should be considered as 'a basic condition for the survival [of democracy] in advanced industrial societies'. According to Löwenthal, this kind of political culture – one which parties must appeal to, rely upon, and develop and advance if liberal democracy is to survive – consists in a 'feeling of unity between people', an 'obligation towards people', the 'consciousness of collective forms of life and institutions', and 'common values'. The foundation and source of this solidarity – which is directly mediated by values and norms, and not by interests – are historical processes and the awareness gained from 'the historical identity of concrete community'.[2]

In view of these claims, the overall questions to be examined are the following: after achieving parity with the Christian Democratic Union in 1966, and since assuming a leading role in 'governmental responsibility' in 1969, has the policy and programme of the Social Democratic Party (SDP) lived up to these criteria outlined (for other parties as well) by one of its own leading theoreticians? Did the SDP derive its policy and programme from a specific interpretation of 'the historical identity of concrete community'? Conversely, did it contribute to the dissemination and sharpening of this community's consciousness? Did it succeed in engaging with a 'collective political identity' (Glotz) of citizens, thereby consolidating this identity?

Nation, class, culture and the SDP

In what follows, I shall defend the view that SDP policy has failed and, consequently, that it has not enhanced the conditions of stability of liberal democracy, as postulated by Löwenthal. This thesis does not underestimate the fact that, in the face of the exceptionalism of twentieth-century German history, *all* political parties, though especially the SDP, find it particularly difficult to relate to any consciousness of a collective identity, whether conceived in national, class or cultural terms.

To begin with, any attempt to refer to the 'national question' for an understanding of the public interest is impossible, and not only because of the chauvinist and racist perversions of the term 'German Nation' during the Third Reich. Since the 1950s, the economic, political and military integration of Western Europe (NATO, EEC) has firmly tied German politics into transnational relations of dependency. Moreover, under the leadership of Willy Brandt in the early 1970s, the SDP in particular could therefore only succeed in carrying through its project of normalizing foreign policy and economic relations with the Soviet Union, Poland and the German Democratic Republic *against* the cultural-political remnants of 'national identity aspirations' (i.e., the desire for the political reunification of Germany). Today, the 'German Nation' can only be considered as a marginal reference point in the justification of any political programme; one may recall the abortive attempts during the election campaigns of the 1970s to reactivate the old misgiving about 'national unreliability' against the Social Democrats.

Second, if one refers to categories of class positions and their structural conditions, that is, to the possibility of relating a political programme to a collective identity defined in *socio-economic* terms, it must be remembered that, as a consequence of the liquidation of workers' organizations by National Socialism and the post-war prosperity which induced changes in the West German social structure, the expression 'worker' carries less the connotation of a collective identity or a common awareness of social life, and more a social statistic or, at best, a category of political organization. As with the expression 'German', the term 'worker' is of relatively little significance as a source of shared past experiences or future aims, to which state policy could refer as a normative foundation. Because the category 'worker' has a diminishing political-cultural relevance for those who are compelled to sell their labour power, the SDP, as is well known, decided in 1959 to rid itself of the electoral label, 'workers' party', thereafter declaring itself a 'people's party'.

The same problem ultimately applies, third, to collective *cultural* identities, of which religion has always played a decisive role as a standard for political action. Even though the political consequences of a general 'secularization effect' have often been overestimated, and while the considerable weight of religious factors is still evident in electoral analyses (as, for instance, in the usual under-representation of Catholics within the total of workers who vote SDP), it must be remembered that, as a consequence of its national partition, West Germany is a country structured on approximately equal religious lines. This means in turn that the party system (in contrast to the Netherlands) has been structured, from the outset, above and beyond religious concerns.

In comparison with other Southern and West European countries, then, West Germany has a very limited fund of 'pre-political' – national, socio-economic or cultural – collective identities which the policies of parties and governments could deploy as a repertoire of justifications and commonly-shared definitions of the public interest. This state of affairs is reinforced by the fact that – again in contrast to most of the Federal Republic's neighbours – there are no 'sub-nationalist' collective identities, such as ethnic, linguistic or religious minorities or quantitatively relevant regionalist movements. It is therefore difficult for any of the political parties to draw upon any given collective identity, politically relevant structures or lived forms of political culture. Löwenthal's thesis that this democracy without historical roots requires an awareness of its historically-developed identity in order to secure its long-term stability and development therefore implies, under German conditions, an especially formidable task.

Social Democratic political culture

Social Democratic policy in the 1970s was not merely a passive victim of this characteristic vagueness of West German political-cultural structures. It has also actively and causally (although not 'consciously') participated in their further disintegration. Therefore, it does not seem unrealistic to expect that in the near future the SDP could become a 'victim of its own policy', that is, of its renunciation of hegemonic political demands and of the concrete formulation of the political-cultural basis of such hegemony.

This danger results from the fact that, first, German Social Democracy represents an extremely *statist* version of reformism. It is certainly characteristic of all modern social democratic parties that they defer to the welfare state and party democracy as the definitive political order, and that they programmatically renounce changes in the constitutional guarantee of freedom (of the private ownership of property, for instance) and in the procedures for formulating political objectives and decisions (say, in the sense of 'council democracy'). Serious theoretical reasons and historical experiences could be cited to show that this political-strategic decision by no means forces the SDP to switch from an *unconditional recognition* of the parliamentary-democratic, constitutional order to a *restriction* of *all* reform policies to statist forms and procedures. Crudely speaking, the methodical premise of social democratic policy is 'Rely on us, we'll do it for you!' In return for loyally having cast their vote for the SDP, voters are offered a 'quality of life' which takes the form of organized and institutionalized welfare, universally arranged and administered by the state.

At this point, I do not wish to produce once more a balance sheet of the *substantive* outcomes and achievements of statist reformism during the 1970s. It is well known that reforms in the domains of education and social policy were anything but impressive.[3] Of greater interest are the consequences of a form of policy that always conceives of changes in terms of administrative intervention and legislation, as the exclusively statist reorganization of living conditions. This peculiar form of state-mediated and, to a certain degree, 'other-determined' emancipation has the merit of partly compensating for the (structural or conjunctural) lack of social power of wage-dependent workers and other 'disadvantaged' categories through politically enacted and legally enforced demands and regulations. Yet the statist correction of the social relations of power has the negative effect of turning into its opposite, so that its beneficiaries are not only *unburdened* but at the same time *deactivated*, that is, are prevented from autonomously conceiving and realizing their own notions of what is necessary for improving their conditions of life. The citizens become objects of administrative care not only in the positive sense, but also in this thoroughly negative sense – their *own* struggle is put to one side and even prohibited. Consequently, as Ulrich Preuss has stated, we face the problem of 'being unable to dispense with sovereign power [i.e., the statist concept of reformism] because it supports the weak, the unorganized and the general social interest . . . while also being forced to recognize that this power is at the same time an obstacle to the development of less alienated forms of social life and norms of action'.

The statist administration of social problems, generally cut off from the experiences, forms of action and values of the social base, becomes entangled in the problem that it can never be certain whether its solutions to problems will be experienced and accepted as such by those who are affected. Every act of modernization not only has the positive aspect of improvement; it is often also marked by the equally ambivalent aspect of restructuring living conditions through brutal and irritating interference and encroachment. Citizens are confronted with new circumstances whose utility or contribution to an 'improved quality of life' could only become manifest if the results of restructuring were guided explicitly by norms of political culture. The less this is the case, the more the danger arises that the results of reform and planning will be experienced as the work of modernist and meddlesome administrators and 'experts' who contribute nothing to the improvement of the quality of life. Every strictly statist conception of reformism not only renounces the driving forces and social resonance that could be decisive for its success; it also blocks its capacity for self-correction by the needs of those affected by its reforms. The contradictions and subsequent problems produced by this rigorous and one-sided social democratic statism are not only presently brought to light by the Right's successful demagogic criticism of bureaucracy, the welfare state and the general 'tutelage' of citizens under the state. They are equally expressed in the widespread hostility of representatives of the 'alternative' economy and culture towards the social democratic defenders of statist rationality. Considering both of these factors, the prospect of a self-paralysis of social democratic statism is not altogether unrealistic.

This possibility is reinforced by the distinct *loss of a normative perspective* of the political culture of the ruling Social Democratic Party and its coalition partners. The 'basic values' officially canonized by the party – 'freedom', 'justice' and 'solidarity' – have not been widely translated into concrete conceptions of the 'good life' or 'quality of life' in the realms of work, the urban environment or family life. Interestingly enough, the aims associated with the (negative) value of 'peace' – negative in the sense of *détente* and the *prevention* of war – are still the most successful symbols of Social Democratic policy. Otherwise, only a programmatic arbitrariness prevails – an abstract and blind will to modernize that can be described as 'embarrassed liberalism'. This fact is today acknowledged and deplored by leading Social Democrats themselves: 'One of the cardinal mistakes of the SDP since Godesberg is its displacement of questions of meaning into the isolated private sphere, according to the motto: "People must deal with their own emotional problems themselves".' Glotz concludes this analysis with a diagnosis: 'The workers' movement . . . must redefine its old task anew: it must win over people for worldwide social struggle and not underestimate the significance of the ethical-political moment of history.' Admittedly, Glotz does not ask further about the political, organizational and theoretical conditions under which this could be achieved. Were he to do so, he would realize that the present condition of Social Democratic political culture simply prevents it from responding to such recommendations. The positive 'SDP culture' that Glotz wishes to regenerate cannot be reconciled with the organizational and administrative practices of the SDP. The objective nature of this discrepancy – which Glotz discloses with a rare clarity – *is* the 'SDP culture'.

By comparison with Christian, communist and even liberal or radical parties, social democratic parties suffer to a very marked degree from the dilemma of being unable to draw programmatically upon a traditional fund of value-orientations, a militant class culture, a Christian ethic or upon bourgeois liberal pathos. Compared with all other parties, they are more vulnerable to the 'dilemma of modernity'. The diversification of its constituency which accompanies its transformation into a type of 'people's party'

intensifies this vagueness of its value-premises. This is further reinforced in the case of German Social Democracy by the poverty –
unparalleled in Western Europe – of the country's collectively-
respected political symbols. Such symbols are rare in the Federal
Republic. The political holidays (17 June and 20 July) refer to
events that lie beyond the geographical or historical boundaries of
West Germany – in itself this is quite rare – and not to its foundation
as a Republic. The 'capital', Bonn, owes its status to nothing more
than coincidence. The people who could symbolize social democratic traditions are either dead or, if they survived fascism, too old
for political activity. They have been replaced by a 'team' of
younger 'operators' who are virtually indistinguishable in respect to
their appearance, speech, biography and educational background,
and are therefore useless as personal bearers of symbols. The
'poverty of meaning' of Social Democratic policy and its actors is
not rectified – but instead harshly parodied – by ghastly attempts to
cultivate militaristic traditions (or by the much more harmless
custom of the Social Democratic Chancellor choosing a hat that
reveals his north German origins). In the context of German
history, the SDP has at its disposal virtually no serious symbols
which would make it capable of demonstrating who it is and what it
stands for.

The symbolic and normative obscurity of the ruling Social
Democratic Party is consistent with the 'openness' which is a basic
feature of its domestic policy. There is no discernible or even
programmatically definable socio-political project, no desired
model of social life comparable to those associated with the
Christian or communist adversaries of the Social Democrats.
Instead, there are *formal* goals: the electoral-political strategy of
appealing to *all* social groups, strata and classes; the methodological
premise of promoting diversity, mobility and innovation; and the
principle of not 'limiting' options, but of 'keeping them open'. The
Social Democratic political process – as is repeatedly explained by
its theoretical protagonists like Peter Glotz – takes place in an
atmosphere of willingness to communicate and co-operate with all
groups. If this explicit rejection of dogmatism and socio-political
discrimination seems at first sight to be unexceptionable, it subsequently becomes clear that this 'openness' is an alibi for the almost
unconditional willingness to react to the given social-economic
relations of power and blackmail. Those who are in principle 'open'
are less resistant to the influence of economic, political and cultural

structures, within whose boundaries the chances of capitalizing on this 'openness' are very unequally distributed. This is why the SDP becomes captive to almost nothing but 'openness' and a type of policy that can be described as simultaneously 'power-obsessed' and 'power-blind': 'power-obsessed', because in the interest of preserving Social Democratic 'administrative responsibility' almost every normative programme must be placed at its disposal; and 'power-blind', because the actual consequences and useful opportunities arising from this 'openness' must be forcibly suppressed and ignored.

The abstract, normatively and politically diffuse, and purely statist will to modernize that is more typical of Social Democratic administrative action than any other party has latent consequences that reveal a third feature of Social Democratic political culture: the forced *destabilization of the institutional parameters of all spheres of social life*. During the recent election campaign, the conservative and reactionary forces in the Federal Republic made much of this theme: the fact that they *could* do this with great resonance is due to the statist will to modernize and its unintended side effects. The broad historical perspective of the socialist workers' movement formerly imbued the technical–industrial modernization process of capitalism with an historical significance. It did this by simultaneously conceiving the destruction of the old as the construction of the new, and by grounding the project of a peaceful and just social order within the development of the human and non-human forces of production. The modern SDP, by contrast, has no conception of the relationship between destruction and construction, modernization and liberation – a relationship that today can no longer be considered simply in 'productivist' terms. The SDP pursues and legitimates technical, industrial and bureaucratic modernization without endowing it with a positive practical significance – it merely vindicates this modernization process negatively, by referring to the ubiquitous *fear* of unemployment and the stagnation of economic growth. While the imperative of modernization has lost its perspective, it has also dramatically increased the relative significance of those institutions, values and conditions of life that bear the costs of modernization: the sense of individual identities based on age and sex roles; the importance of regional and ethnic communities; and the value of an intact natural and urban environment. It is certainly difficult to unravel the mixture of 'progressive' and 'reactionary' motives that is currently growing into an 'anti-modernist' protest movement. It is none the less certain that a 'modernist' Social Democratic policy concerning education, family life, technology and regional and economic growth neither checks the process of modernization nor guides it towards plausible goals. This modernist policy even encourages this protest tendency and its 'post-modern' structures and values. To the degree that the constructive, emancipatory aspect of the process of modernization becomes impalpable, its costs – the experience of its destructive aspect – become much more apparent. Those costs are politically attributed to the SDP as the political advocate of modernity by both the new social protest movements and the Right-wing populist forces.

A fourth characteristic of what can be described as the 'syndrome' of Social Democratic political culture – its typically abstract desire for modernization – is linked in a contradictory way with its claim to 'openness'. I am referring to the *repressive* character of Social Democratic policy. This repressive policy is generally deployed against all those who intransigently follow an 'independent line', and in all situations where 'co-operation', the 'willingness to compromise', 'mediation' and technocratic management are rejected in favour of autonomous forms of life, experience and judgement. The connection between 'openness' and 'repression' is not at all mysterious: a party (and the government policy it represents) that parades its 'openness' and has shown considerable skill in balancing all relevant social power groups naturally must be carefully concerned with controlling those forces – within and outside its own ranks – that could disturb that balance. The SDP – and the majority of its trade union allies – are consequently dominated by a suspicion of those political forces that could damage either their electoral image or their ability to negotiate and form coalitions. Furthermore, to the degree that a *positive* integration of party members, voters and followers can no longer be achieved because of the absence of a discernible hegemonic project and normatively distinct socio-political goals, the problem of mass integration is solved in a *negative* manner, through the exclusion of social minorities and 'deviants'.

Both considerations clarify how and why the 'openness' principle of a political force like the SDP must lead almost inevitably to extremely illiberal forms of repression. From the infamous agitation of Berlin's Social Democratic mayor, Schütz, against the student movement in 1967 ('Look at these Types!') to the no less notorious '*Berufsverbote*' resolutions in 1972, the reform of criminal procedures in 1977, to the latest technocratic fantasies of Herold – the Social Democratic director of criminal prosecution who wants to transform the reactive functions of the police into those of prevention and 'social sanitation' – Social Democratic domestic policy is marked throughout by an almost unthinking repressiveness, a repressiveness that is always explained away through reference to one formula ('symbolic confirmation of its own invulnerability to militant ideas and practices') or another ('mass integration through images of an enemy'). Consequently, the distance and mistrust between many of the supposedly 'deviant' intellectuals and artists and exponents of 'sub-cultural' values and forms of life and the Social Democratic administration is correspondingly great – and, for the time being, perhaps unbridgeable. The official government and party practice of defining and exluding, of symbolically and repressively discriminating against 'deviant' elements expresses a remarkable mistrust of the level and solidarity of popular political convictions. These official campaigns – frequently assessed by foreign observers as 'hysterical' – to eliminate 'terrorists' from society, 'sympathizers' from universities, 'enemies of the constitution' from the civil service or non-conformist writers from the mass media, make sense only if it is assumed that these groups' activities and utterances could fall at any time on fertile ground and 'infect' the political and cultural public sphere to a dramatic degree; that is, only if it is assumed that the population has absolutely no 'autonomous', political and moral powers of resistance to 'deviance'.

These assumptions are directly generated by Social Democratic political culture. The fifth characteristic of this political culture is the negative finding that, despite its educational policy reforms, Social Democratic administrative practice has not successfully destroyed the *hard core of totalitarian and authoritarian, predemocratic traditions and opinions* typical of German political culture since before the fascist period. Social Democratic modernization is an *external* process, one that has not been accompanied by a modernization of values, attitudes and forms of political association. The traces of an authoritarian, aggressive 'political naturalism' founded on categories of age, sex, nationality and race are not much rarer today than in the 1950s. One can indeed accept the claim of the conservative political scientist Hennis that democracy in the Federal Republic has 'become almost emotionally irrelevant'. The 'naturalization' of social power and privilege and the devaluation of socio-political struggles to redistribute power and privilege are the two characteristic features of authoritarianism: what exists is given naturally, and to seek its transformation is to be condemned to 'unnaturalness'. One has to imagine the storm of indignation and anger that erupted when the Berlin police authorities attempted to recruit Turkish residents to the police force – not on the grounds of fully extending (long overdue) civil rights to foreign workers, but simply because of police tactics and considerations of expediency. Turkish people – so this thoroughly unbroken resentment responded – by nature cannot be policemen, that is, bearers of sovereign authority *over Germans*. The force of such political-cultural 'self-evident truths' is also popularly expressed in the thinly disguised wish for the physical liquidation of violent criminals or the psychical separation of 'bright' and 'not so bright' children in different types of schools. Social Democratic political culture cannot counteract the force of these 'truths' through determined and hopeful information campaigns – perhaps not even to the extent necessary for long-term electoral successes against the growing Right–populist mobilization of the authoritarian–naturalistic syndrome.

Conclusion

Social Democratic government policy has not only failed to enhance the democratic stability of the Federal Republic. Because of its combination of statism, lack of normative principles, its openness towards existing relations of power and repressive exclusion, the SDP is increasingly becoming a party based only upon a stratum of power administrators. Shedding its 'opposition' elements without being able to integrate new 'alternatives', traditional social democracy is thus eroded. This development appears to be tragic, only because another type of reformism is conceivable: a reformism that is programmatically based on *social* forces and struggles, one that is open to alternative and opposition cultures and, hence, to the recovery of normative perspectives.

Notes and references

1   R. Löwenthal, *Gesellschaftswandel und Kulturkrise* (Frankfurt 1979), p. 219.

2 ibid., pp. 219, 221.
3 cf. M. T. Greven, 'Sozialliberalismus und Reformismus', in Werner Goldschmidt (ed.), *Stamokap-Theorie/Staat und Monopole (III)*, special issue of *Das Argument*, **36** (Berlin 1979).

10   Alternative strategies in consumer policy*

Most sociologists would agree that the principle of continuous *structural differentiation* both underlies the development of modern societies and constitutes the essence of their 'modernity'. According to one interpretation of modernization, social action that formed part of a (supposed or real) 'original' unity undergoes a division into functionally related structural components. The separation of the domestic household from the sphere of work is an example of this structural separation of formerly integrated patterns of life. The same principle is evidenced in such processes as the division of labour, and in the separation of manual and mental labour, labour and capital, state and society, law and morality, and state and church. As is well known, the fact that spheres of action that were once structurally related become separated from each other involves the important advantage of 'setting free' the elements of a system. The process of differentiation opens up an enormous range of possibilities: the domestic household can consume commodities which it cannot produce; among members of the household, there may emerge moral convictions that are not at all prejudiced by their capacity as citizens of a specific political system; and so on. According to this first interpretation, then, the evolutionary sequence of differentiation/increase in liberty and welfare/further differentiation is celebrated as the crucial advantage of, and the reason for, the superiority of 'modern' societies.

Within academic social science and political movements during the past few years, the question has been raised as to whether continuous differentiation leads to new problems and bottlenecks in development. Some sociologists are already troubled by the

* This paper was first presented to the conference on 'Applied Consumer Research', organized by the West German Federal Ministry of Research and Technology, Bonn, February 1981. It was published as 'Ausdifferenzierung oder Integration – Bemerkungen über strategische Alternativen der Verbraucherpolitik', *Zeitschrift für Verbraucherpolitik*, 5 (1981), pp. 119–33.

possibility that modern society may have been undergoing a process of *'excessive'* differentiation,[1] while others focus upon the concept – and the implicit political programme – of *'de*-differentiation'. This controversy within sociological theory is of great relevance to the study of consumer policy. For only in societies having undergone the process of differentiation does the concept 'consumer' make any sense. In societies such as our own, the concept of 'consumer' designates an array of actions, interests and situations that are clearly delimited from other interests, situations and actions. In so-called primitive societies, but also in medieval societies divided into estates and, therefore, already affected by processes of differentiation, the concept of 'consumer' is simply not meaningful. There, the concept of 'consumer' has no distinct basis in social reality, because the sphere of action related to consumption is not yet clearly delimited from other spheres of action such as work, politics and family life. Only modernized social structures, with their differentiated systems of action, make possible relatively clear-cut distinctions between individuals acting 'as' consumers, workers, voters, heads of the family, and so on.

Actors and rules in consumer policy

If the 'welfare' of consumers is taken as the normative and strategic reference point of consumer research and consumer policy, it can readily be shown that this welfare is influenced either positively or negatively by three types of actors. These three categories of actors are in a relationship of 'differentiation', in the sense that they are relatively independent of each other. These actors include manufacturers or suppliers of goods and services consumed within the domestic household; the state, especially in its capacity as a judicial and legislative power; and, finally, individual consumers and their organizations.

Each of these three actors pursues certain interests, is subject to certain restrictions and strategic chances, and, in order to improve its strategic position, strives to enlarge its own sphere of action at the expense of other actors. If consumer policy is considered as an empirical process or 'game' that unfolds over time, it is immediately obvious that the respective (provisional) results of this game must be understood as the composite outcome of the interdependent and relatively autonomous actions of the three players. That is to say, not one player alone – be it the consumer, the manufacturer or the state – is in a position to determine outcomes unilaterally. Let us, therefore, try to briefly outline the main characteristics of the three actors participating in the 'game' of consumer policy.

Manufacturers/suppliers

To the extent that they are engaged in the private sector, these actors endeavour to influence the welfare of consumers in manifold positive and negative ways, for instance through market research, marketing policy, product design and voluntary self-regulation of suppliers' associations. However, their economic interest in profits and profitability is a primary goal, and they therefore engage in consumer policy only to the extent that the (positive or negative) influencing of consumer welfare serves this goal of profitability. Only in the case of competitive relationships which favour or even exact a consideration of consumer interests are manufacturers and suppliers compelled to positively take account of consumer welfare. This compulsion is not operative, however, in every relationship of competition. Moreover, by means of a variety of strategic measures (for example, the formation of a cartel), many retailers can escape the conditions of competition which they face within the market-place. Manufacturers or suppliers of goods and services are in general, therefore, interested in the welfare of the consumer only in an indirect and secondary way. They are in a position to modify, within certain limits, the conditions which might otherwise force them to have 'consideration' for the consumer. In accordance with these facts, an important strategic advantage accrues to the manufacturer/supplier side in the 'game' of consumer policy. This advantage consists precisely in the fact that, to a certain extent, and without prejudicing its interests, the manufacturer/supplier side can afford to be disinterested in the increase of consumer welfare.

State/law

The judicial and legislative powers of the state, together with its regulatory apparatus of public policy, also actively influence consumer welfare through, for example, market regulation, measures of consumer protection, provision of concrete assistance to consumer organizations, and the public promotion of consumer information. Government, political parties and parliaments tend to support consumer welfare for obvious reasons: many consumers are also voters who may well refuse their political support if their interests are not considered to some degree by the organs of state policy. At the same time, the self-interest of state bodies is limited by the fact that no 'unreasonable' demands may be imposed on the manufacturers and suppliers. If this happens, state authorities must reckon with the possibility that manufacturers and suppliers will withdraw their economic activity, which, in turn, may severely encroach upon the specific interest of the state in economic growth, employment and revenue from taxation. In this respect, state policy is caught within a structural dilemma. If it is to avoid seriously infringing its own interests, it may neither engage 'too much' nor 'too little' in consumer policy.

Individual consumers and their organizations

It can safely be supposed that consumer organizations have an unlimited, immediate and positive interest in consumer welfare. This interest varies from consumer to consumer, since almost nobody is 'only' a consumer. Individuals perform a variety of different 'roles': at the same time, they may be consumers and employees, or they may be consumers and parents. This implies that individuals may experience conflicts of interest which reduce their determination to exercise their interests as consumers. In addition to this conflict, the collective actors of consumer organizations have to endure a number of well-known difficulties which can only be briefly enumerated here. For instance, these organizations are always at a time disadvantage compared to manufacturers and suppliers, and can thus only respond *ex post* to the already existing supply of goods and services. Faced with enormous variations in the supply of, and demand for, consumer goods, they also find it difficult to formulate and maintain a consistent conception of what constitutes 'the' interest of consumers. Due to the aforementioned fact that hardly anyone is *only* ever a consumer, finally, consumers' associations are faced with the organizational problem of mobilization; that is, with the actual difficulty of stimulating and preserving *motivation* among their potential members, and thus with generating the material and personal resources necessary for the operation of their organization.

If we summarize these considerations, the following picture emerges. Three different groups of independent social actors participate in consumer policy as a political process, namely, suppliers, states and (organized) consumers. Concerning the *intensity of interest* in the welfare of consumers, it can be said that the interest of suppliers is weak and indirect, that of state authority is ambivalent and caught within a dilemma, while the interest of consumer organizations is strong and immediate. The strategic chances of *actually influencing* the welfare of consumers are distributed in precisely the opposite way, however. Manufacturers and suppliers are endowed with considerable and direct chances because of their 'producer's sovereignty'; by contrast, state policy has a limited and indirect capacity to influence consumer welfare; finally, due to their organizational and resource problems and their dependence upon either manufacturers or the state, consumer organizations are endowed with limited and only indirect influence. Within the field of consumer policy, in short, the interested party is weak and the strong party is disinterested.

Two difficulties concerning consumer 'welfare'

This suggested model of the structural chances of success of consumer policy becomes even more sobering when the concept of consumer welfare is itself examined. According to one approach, consumer welfare is maximized when the *subjectively-perceived* needs of economic subjects acting as consumers are satisfied to the maximum possible extent. However, two objections must be made against such an understanding of consumer welfare.

First, while we certainly 'have' needs, it is often questionable whether they are really our 'own' needs. To indicate this is not merely to allude to the obvious and trivial fact that needs can be 'manipulated' and 'artificially induced'. It is rather to indicate that a large number of needs for consumer goods which consumers express on the market are directly linked with their *living conditions* which, in turn, may not be in accordance with the needs of the consumers.

A hypothetical example of this latter possibility might be the medicaments individuals require in order to ward off illness which would otherwise result from the poor environmental conditions at their place of work or residence. Obviously, these medicaments could only be considered as means of satisfying 'needs' if the need to work or live within poor environmental conditions is itself assumed. The need for medicaments would then be considered as a subsidiary need generated by the satisfaction of the primary need to live and work in exactly these conditions and nowhere else. However, the fact that individuals live and work under conditions detrimental to their health can only be interpreted as being in accordance with their needs if they had the objective possibility of living and working elsewhere. Where this is not the case, it can be said that the choices made by consumers within the market-place are not always actions for the satisfaction of their 'own' needs, but are in fact responses to a situation where certain needs are 'structurally imposed'.

Another example of this 'structural imposition of needs' is furnished by the consumption of automobiles. Consumers often regard automobiles not as a means of satisfying a 'need' (such as the desire for mobility or the pleasure in driving) but, rather, as a response to urban living conditions which often make it 'impossible to live without a car'. In such frequently heard expressions, there is the suggestion that the apparently paradoxical need for an automobile is a need we could, in fact, do without: there is, in other words, a more or less vague awareness of the gap that exists between our needs and the demands forced upon us by the conditions in which we live. While this distinction opens up very difficult theoretical terrain, it is impossible to establish a relatively precise concept of consumer welfare if one simply ignores this phenomenon of 'structurally imposed needs'. In this context, it is interesting to note that steps in this direction have been taken in the recent literature on the theory of the household and in critical studies of consumption.[2]

This point is related to a second objection to the model of subjectively-perceived needs. A concept of consumer welfare which is neither merely naïve nor ideological must not only distinguish between 'genuine' and 'imposed' needs and include the former in the concept of consumer welfare. It should also seriously consider the *ways* in which consuming subjects become aware of their consumption needs; that is, how a need as such stabilizes over time and comes to be permanently associated with an individual. This question can scarcely be avoided by stating that needs simply 'exist'. On the contrary, consideration must always be given to the fact that the acknowledgement or recognition of a need is always a *cognitive* and reflexive process which is regulated by cultural norms and social relations. Not only may needs be objectively imposed; we may also be subjectively *mistaken* about our needs. If such deception is to be avoided, we require a certain degree of knowledge and a capacity to self-reflect which, in turn, are dependent upon socio-structural pre-conditions. The methods of ascertaining one's own needs are quite precarious under modern conditions characterized by a high degree of 'differentiation'. Deluged by 'options',[3] modern consumers find it difficult to choose, recognize and maintain needs *as* their own. This difficulty becomes greater the less recourse can be made to traditional habits and conventional standards of 'normality'. Accordingly, in consumer research there is a growing concern with encouraging the possible 'autonomous determination of needs' and with developing forms of organization and communication which 'help consumers to reflect upon their own desires and needs'.[4]

Considered together, these two objections to a theory of subjectively-perceived needs specify two requirements within a theory of consumer welfare. The first objection points to the distinction between 'genuine' needs and imposed conditions of living and survival, while the second objection emphasizes the need to consider the socio-structural pre-conditions of the autonomous self-determination of individuals' needs. There is much evidence that the proportion of structurally-imposed needs is increasing in complex and highly differentiated societies and that, at the same time, the pre-conditions for the cognitive consideration of individual needs and their integration into personal identity are diminishing. The biases and distortions of a theory of consumer welfare will be the more substantial the more it naïvely clings to the premise that the choices made by economic subjects on the consumer goods market *do* accurately express the real needs of consumers and that these subjects *are* actually in a position to adequately recognize their needs.

On the other hand, these two objections undoubtedly disturb the pillars of liberal economics and psychology by challenging their axiomatic equation of 'empirical' and 'real' needs. Of course, this equation has the unquestionable and essential advantage of resisting political or cultural regimentation and of defending the liberty and sovereignty of the consumer. Today, however, it is an open question whether this liberal equation has exactly the opposite effect, namely, of cognitively 'repressing' and ideologically screening out the numerous and clear indications that many consumer choices have nothing to do with the satisfaction of needs, that they are merely a reflex action to the conditioning of needs by actual social conditions, and that modern social structures restrict the development of the capacity of choosing, establishing and questioning needs.

The arguments briefly summarized above suggest two findings: first, that the structural power and interests of the 'players' involved in the 'game' of consumer policy are distributed in such a way that the chances of realizing consumer interests are very poor; and, second, that our knowledge of these consumer interests, as well as our conceptual tools for investigating consumer welfare are such that severe self-criticisms of conventional economic doctrines and very fundamental controversies are called for. Considered together, these two findings stimulate research into alternatives in consumer policy that might have some chances of success. Two different sets of alternative strategies can be identified.

Consumer policy as the increase of 'consumer power'

The first of these can be described as an attempt to increase the countervailing power of consumers. This strategy is based on the idea that consumers' capacity to act must be increased within the framework of the existing differentiation between suppliers, state power and consumers. This can be achieved, for instance, by increasing the right of consumer organizations to participate in the legislative and administrative process. It can also be achieved by improving the information and education of individual consumers, by research into consumer behaviour, and by other ways of providing information as a resource for increasing the power position of consumers. It can also be effected by weakening the dominant position of manufacturers and suppliers through legislative action or policies which regulate economic competition. Or, finally, this goal can be achieved through the development of new models of organization which improve the effectiveness of consumer organizations in activating existing or new members. It is neither possible nor necessary at this point to exhaustively describe the various ideas and concepts usually associated with this global strategy for developing the countervailing power of consumers. However, it can be shown that any strategy of this type meets with at least one of the following two difficulties.

The first of these difficulties is derived from the fact that consumer interests always conflict to a certain degree with interests related to economic growth or, at any rate, with the specific economic interest in profitability. This implies that there is a continual danger of satisfying interests that individuals have *as* consumers at the expense of their interests as *employees*. In view of the worsening conditions in the contemporary labour market, it can be assumed that consumer interests will be weakened in relation to the prevailing interest of both employees and manufacturers in retaining jobs and profits respectively.

The other structural obstacle before which a strategy of mobilizing countervailing power is relatively powerless is the fact that 'consumers' do not constitute a clearly delimitable and organizable complex of individuals. Rather they constitute an abstract category which defines certain *aspects* of the social actions of almost all individuals. Everyone and at the same time no one is a 'consumer'. The concept of 'consumer' does not apply 'segmentally' (i.e., consumers versus non-consumers) but, rather, 'functionally', that is, with reference only to *certain* spheres of action of *all* individuals. It is precisely the magnitude of the clientele of consumer policy – and the 'fuzziness' of the social domain of collective action of consumers – which render the efforts of consumer organizations so difficult and relatively ineffective. At the same time, this problem of size also implies problems of social, technical and temporal heterogeneity. Different individuals consume different goods and services at different times and purchase them from different producers and suppliers. The common denominator of 'consumer' is too abstract to facilitate the development of consumer organizations. Exceptions merely confirm, but do not invalidate this rule. Indeed, in the light of the experience of the Federal Republic and other highly industrialized countries, the general rule is that it is possible to organize consumer interests especially, and usually only, if:

1   the common interest of collectively acting individuals is not increased utility but the *avoidance of (physical) damage*. The relatively great mobilization success of consumer movements and organizations that concentrate on the constructional defects of automobiles or harmful chemical additives in food are examples; the chances of successful consumer mobilization are less if these movements and organizations are concerned with the *price* of goods and services, and especially so if their actions focus upon the *quality*, or positive use value, of goods;
2   the collective action is preoccupied with objects of *homogeneous mass consumption*, especially with such 'basic needs' as communication and transport services, petroleum, housing or rents, and foodstuffs;
3   the collective action is opposed to *highly visible* monopolies or

oligopolies of supply, such as petroleum companies or energy utilities;

4   in addition to their 'exit' option, consumers are provided with the possibility of increasing their influence (or of discrediting political leaders) through *political participation*, especially in state or public monopolies such as postal services, television authorities and public transportation;

5   the consumer movement can identify with political or cultural *symbols of collective identity* (for example, youth or women's movements), so that the consumer interest does not constitute the only point of initiation and crystallization of collective action, but rather merges with other concerns, such as anti-sexist, anti-imperialist or ecological ones.

These conditions probably increase the chances of consumer mobilization and organization in a cumulative way. In the Federal Republic, the only example of the confluence of all five conditions is the uninterrupted mass movement against the further expansion of nuclear energy which, since the middle of the 1970s, has, as a result, been able to develop beyond the scope of a mere consumer movement. The example of the anti-nuclear movement is instructive: besides indicating the very special conditions necessary for the lasting mobilization of consumers, it also still suggests (cf. above) the obstacles encountered by consumer movements in relation to the dominant interests of manufacturers, suppliers and workers in profits and jobs.

The organizational 'reintegration' of consumption and production

In view of the scepticism generally associated with the strategies of countervailing power, a number of theorists working on 'alternative' models of economic organization and activity have concretely delineated a quite different strategy for the realization of consumer interests. The aim of this second type of strategy is to overcome the structural differentiation between manufacturers and suppliers, the state and consumers, upon which the strategy of countervailing power is based. In other words, the aim is not to strengthen or weaken actors' positions within the 'game' of consumer policy but rather to *reorganize* or reconstitute the game and its actors. This strategy seeks to reinforce the chances of de-differentiation, that is, of remixing or partly *integrating* social functions which have become separated as a result of the differentiation process at work in modern industrial society. The hopes and expectations associated with this conception of de-differentiation in consumer policy rest upon a paradoxical formula: consumers can only acquire the power necessary for the realization of their interests *as* consumers by structurally combining their interests in consumption with productive *and* political functions – and thereby transcending their identities as mere consumers. Theoretically speaking, there are three possible variants of this combination strategy:

1   the fusion of production, administration and consumption into a centralized, regulatory apparatus;
2   the reabsorption of productive functions into the realms of the domestic household and domestic consumption;
3   the incorporation of consumer functions and interests into the sphere of production.

A discussion of the first variant would go beyond the scope of this essay and, in any case, appears to be of little promise in view of the performance and development of Eastern European economic systems. The second variant, which is of greatest interest to proponents of 'alternative' or 'self-help' models of economic organization, pushes consumers beyond the limits of their specialized consumer functions by integrating them with some production functions in the (extended) household domain; for example, in the form of self-help, autonomous craft labour, and co-operative self-support. While the dilemma of consumer policy might be expected to be overcome by this strategy, its proponents often tend to one-sidedly and over-optimistically minimize several of its negative consequences. In the remainder of this discussion, I should like to draw particular attention to the limits and shortcomings of this approach. This will in turn shed light on some of the strategic advantages which, in my opinion, are offered by the third variant which is concerned not with the integration of production functions into the spheres of the household and consumption but, inversely, with the reabsorption and integration of consumer interests into the sphere of production. It may well be, of course, that these two complementary processes of integration can be combined and thereby mutually stabilize each other.

With regard to the shortcomings of the second variant, the strategy of more closely integrating production into the household domain, it is important to emphasize three points. First, the model of productive self-help through the household (or collectives of households) must face doubts about whether the objective and subjective dispositions for 'self-help through grass-roots organization' are actually so widespread – and so evenly distributed throughout the social structure – that production activities taking place within or close to the household domain (for example, the non-market and non-public production and distribution of food, the construction and repair of durable goods, the provision of a wide range of social services) could become quantitatively important. Second, as is generally known, the alternative of self-help is often burdened with losses in efficiency (the key word here is 'self-exploitation') which, in turn, must be considered a real obstacle to the expansion of this form of merging production and consumption at the level of the household. Third, concerning the political motivation and mobilizing potential of self-help activities, one must consider the negative implications of the very compelling argument that, in the final analysis, self-help initiatives (of parents or tenants, for instance) function as stop-gap measures for deficient public service programmes. Supported by cost-saving 'voluntary work', governments strive to control their financial bottlenecks without seriously being interested in the autonomy of the participant consumers or the quality of their services. To sum up, it can be said that self-help initiatives are limited in terms of social and technical resources and that they are frequently of a short duration. They are marked by considerable difficulties of internal organization and unification, and they readily experience severe legitimation problems *vis-à-vis* both the state and their own members. These problems will persist so long as their right to exist, their autonomy, and their resource needs are not supported, acknowledged and guaranteed by public authorities. To appraise self-help initiatives in this sceptical way is not to deny that, as spearheads of social movements, they constitute a form of action which – as the squatters' movement indicates – can fulfil important functions of innovation and protest which signal the need for *political* action and reform. However, self-help will fail to be an effective and permanent institution for organizing 'consumer' interests until its 'informal', 'autonomous' and 'alternative' character is institutionally acknowledged and protected – and thus to a certain extent formalized.

Let us, therefore, consider the inverse solution, that of integrating consumer interests into the sphere of production. In my opinion, a basic problem which must be faced by the theory of consumer policy is the ever-widening gap between the 'institutional' and the 'functional' definition of 'consumption' and 'consumer' in modern, welfare capitalist society. Briefly, according to an *institutional* definition of the consumer, consumption consists of the choices made by private households on the commodity markets. Economic citizens are viewed as acting as 'consumers' whenever they make such choices. This definition suggests that an increase in the rationality of choices can and must have a substantial effect on the 'welfare' of the consumers and domestic households. This 'consumer welfare' is central to a *functional* definition of consumers and consumption, for it includes within the sphere of consumption not just purchase-related acts but all those conditions and actions that have a positive or negative influence on the welfare of households.

It appears that these two definitions are by no means congruent and that the 'overlap' between the phenomena encompassed by each is even diminishing. Nowadays, it is becoming quite evident that private households acquire a high proportion of the goods and (especially) services which are of vital importance for their 'welfare' – regardless of how welfare is defined – not through rational *individual purchases* of goods and services, but through state-regulated provisions, or through such collective 'compulsory purchases' as social security and social services. That is to say, consumer *'welfare'* is only partly, and probably decreasingly, determined by consumer *behaviour* (i.e., choices and purchases); the consumer *as* a consumer is increasingly subject to the decisions and parameters established by the state or large firms and their long-term investment strategies. The consumer movement (for example, Naderism in the United States) and much of the current consumer research have for some time extended and even concentrated their activities and interests on the domain of *public services*; that is, upon those goods which cannot be acquired by way of purchase, but which nevertheless are of great relevance to consumers' welfare.

A further aspect of the fact that the *well-being of consumers* is only partially determined by their *choices and acts of consumption* becomes visible if we look at how the household is related to work. The welfare of the private household depends not only on public services, but also on the conditions encountered by wage earners within the work-place. As is generally known, a special characteristic of the labour market is that – in contrast to all other markets – it depends upon the trading of a 'commodity' (labour power) which, nevertheless, *cannot* be separated from its physical owner and thereby placed at the exclusive disposal of its buyers. In the labour market, in other words, workers certainly exchange income for the work they perform, but they are never fully divorced from the concrete process of the utilization of their labour power by its buyers. It is undeniable that the experience of this utilization process is of considerable relevance in negatively or positively influencing the welfare of working individuals. This holds true irrespective of the amount of household income which they receive from 'selling' their labour power. Because it is impossible to fully separate labour power from its individual owners, the theory of the household must, as it were, project itself into the territory currently occupied by the theory of production. The household is always 'present' and necessarily affected when labour power as a factor of production is set in motion. This seems to suggest that the 'separation' of household and production that is often thought to be *the* dominant characteristic of industrial society is in fact quite incomplete and only apparent. In this respect, it certainly is meaningful to distinguish between the 'investive' and 'consumptive' elements of the labour process. The investive aspects of the labour process refer to the relationship between the energy expended on labour and the income derived from labour, whereas the consumptive elements comprise all the concomitants and side effects of the labour process which positively or negatively influence the welfare of individual workers. However complicated this distinction may at first appear, it has exerted a strong influence on the practice of industrial relations and their development during the 1970s. The whole trade union and political debate on the aims and methods of the 'humanization of work' is concerned to emphasize more strongly the consumptive aspect of the industrial labour process. Similarly, evidence furnished by opinion surveys suggests that, in addition to the investive criterion (i.e., estimates of how 'difficult' or 'well paid' work is), the consumptive criterion (i.e., how 'meaningful' or 'interesting' work is reckoned to be) is gaining in importance.

In so far as empirical evidence suggests that labour power is simultaneously oriented to the goals of business firms *and*, increasingly, to the direct (i.e., non-monetary) securing of the welfare status of household members who work, a new theoretical and political strategy of consumer welfare becomes conceivable. This new strategy would seek to expand 'autonomy' not by integrating production within the household but, rather, through attempts to bring the consumption-related welfare interests of the household into the sphere of production. If consumer research conceptually frees itself from the rigid and increasingly implausible 'institutional' definition of consumption (i.e., consumption = market choices of private households), and provided that it also becomes more willing to focus on those welfare components that are *not* allocated through markets, but instead through state administration, there is no reason why the theoretical frame of reference of consumer policy research should not go one step further by including the consumption aspects of work and production. After all, the latter are at least as relevant for the well-being of consumers as the outcomes of market transactions of private households; the *purchase* of goods and services is only one of several links (and probably a decreasingly important one) that allocate positive or negative use-values to private households. There is, therefore, no reason to restrict the attention of consumer research to this particular institutional link, the market.[5] It is well recognized nowadays that consumers of public goods and services confront the suppliers of these goods and services, i.e., state authorities, in their capacity as voters and bearers of rights and that these consumer-citizens are therefore capable of exerting a considerable influence on the quality, price and safety of these goods and services through appropriate forms of organization, communication and co-operation. The same principle applies to the consumptive dimensions of the production process, in so far as certain steps have been made in the direction of regulating the welfare-related aspects of the work process through enterprise, trade union or state intervention. This development considerably expands the possible scope for stimulating political imagination, which is an acknowledged and legitimate goal of social scientific research on consumption issues. Indeed, three interrelated points of departure of a production-centred consumer policy can be systematically distinguished: work policy, process policy and product policy.

Work policy   Given that the consumption of such public goods as health or education systems is already the subject of contemporary research on consumer policy, there is no conceivable reason why this research should not also concern itself with the positive and especially the negative (for example, health-related) consequences of the labour process. It is unfortunately true that contemporary consumer research and research on the humanization of work do not yet have a common conceptual frame of reference which might guide their inquiries. Nevertheless, the consumptive interest of workers in improving their working conditions has become a topic on the agenda of labour movements at the firm, trade union and political levels. As the example of 'innovation counselling' conducted by the German Industrial Metal Workers' Union (IG Metall) suggests, there is also a growing awareness that the problem of humanizing work cannot successfully be tackled only at the level of work relations within the business firm, or at the level of the state's promotion of scientific-technical research and development, but that a *third* level – the managerial control over investment – must become an additional point of departure for controlling and improving the 'consumptive' aspects of work. In this strategy, it is essential that the works councils within both the manufacturing enterprises and their customer firms co-operate with each other beyond the level of the single firm. For example, manufacturing enterprises which produce office machinery also 'simultaneously' produce the working conditions within the business firms using these machines, which implies that influencing the product policy of manufacturers of investment goods constitutes an appropriate step in the direction of effective control over the developments of working conditions in the user firms.

Process policy Industrial processes of production have (negative) consumptive consequences, not only for the individuals directly involved, but also for all others who do not participate in these production processes. Examples of these negative effects include the pollution of air and water, problems of noise accompanying production, or the ecological and aesthetic degradation of the environment. In many cases, these effects become so important that they begin to have repercussions within the internal structure of the business enterprises as, for instance, when large manufacturing plants have difficulty recruiting senior personnel because the latter hesitate about living within an area negatively affected by the firm's production. Just as poor working conditions and the resulting difficulties and additional costs of hiring labour sometimes tend to stimulate firms' (opportunistic) sympathy for 'humanization' measures, so these problems of recruiting management personnel might be expected to lead to parallel initiatives for the 'restoration of the environment'. Clearly, these 'automatic' corrections within the calculus of the firm will remain limited in their social, technical and temporal scope and highly dependent upon economic developments unless appropriate forms of countervailing power are developed within the enterprise itself. This would facilitate the effective articulation of the consumptive interests of households (including even those not linked directly to the firm through labour contracts). By instituting such organs of countervailing power within the firm, 'consumer protection within the sphere of production' would become a real possibility.

Product policy   In as much as decisions about the production schedule and the quality, price and side effects of products presently fall outside the sphere of influence of unions, works councils and state regulatory policies, the chances of success of product policy strategies are for the time being uncertain. Nevertheless, Cooley's discussion of the initiatives and successes within the Lucas Aerospace firm suggest a very promising model of product policy controlled by workers and oriented by criteria of use-value.[6] This model of socially useful production is also anticipated in the recent statements of the Industrial Metal Workers' Union on the pro- duction and export of armaments ('U-boats for Chile?'). There are also signs of an increasing awareness of the problems likely to be generated as a result of the growing economic concentration of some markets for such durable consumer goods as automobiles and electronic entertainment equipment. The smaller the number of manufacturers engaged in producing a certain product, the greater the statistical probability that the workers of a manufacturing firm will also be the final consumers of the products they themselves have produced. This effect is reinforced by the widespread practice, for instance in the European automobile industry, of companies granting a discount price on products for their own employees, a practice that has even led workers to protest against the reduction of the quality of 'their' products (for example, thinner car-body sheets) because of product or process innovations.

Given the problems associated with process and product policies, there are strong indications that use-value-oriented interests will be pursued only with difficulty and that, in cases of conflict, use-value concerns will be subordinated to that more or less reluctant alliance of labour and capital which reflects the interests of suppliers. Strategies of consumer policy that are based upon the integration of consumptive concerns into production are, however, no more burdened by this difficulty than the conventional type of strategy oriented to increasing the leverage of the consumer within the market-place. This difficulty may even apply less to the former strategy, especially considering that all efforts at consumer organization which focus on the fuzzy identity of 'the consumer' have to face well-known and enormous difficulties – those of overcoming the technical, social and temporal heterogeneity of consumer action by generating the resources and establishing the autonomous forms of organization necessary for collective action. If we compare the two different types of strategy delineated here – defending an 'independent' consumer interest and integrating consumption and production – the strategy of linking together the spheres of production and consumption is evidently more promising because there already exists within the spheres of production trade unions and organizations of workers upon whom consumer interests could depend more strongly than has until now been the case.

In view of the need to overcome the present rather considerable opposition to the type of consumer policies based on the strategy of integration, the further development and securing of an 'autonomous' sector of production and consumption – comprising such household-linked activities as autonomous work, self-help, neighbourhood co-operatives and community work, the co-operative system and squatters' actions – could come to play an important role. As long as they were recognized as socially 'normal' and vital for certain individuals or age groups, these household-linked forms of activity could help break up the power of the individual and collective imperative of wage-labour and 'full employment', an imperative that presently enables the industrial sector to insulate itself against consumer and use-value interests.

Notes and references

1 N. Luhmann, *Gesellschaftsstruktur und Semantik: Studien zur Wissenssoziologie der modernen Gesellschaft*, vol. 1 (Frankfurt 1980).
2 cf. the critical study of William Leiss, *The Limits to Satisfaction* (Toronto 1976); the distinction between comfort and pleasure introduced by T. Scitovsky, *The Joyless Economy. An Inquiry into Human Satisfaction and Consumer Dissatisfaction* (Oxford 1976); and A. Hirschman's distinction between 'preferences' and 'metapreferences' in his *Shifting Involvements* (Princeton 1982), pp. 70ff.
3 Ralf Dahrendorf, *Life Chances* (London 1979).

4   G. Scherhorn, 'Die Entstehung von Verbraucherproblemen im Spannungsfeld von Konsum und Arbeit', *Zeitschrift für Verbraucherpolitik*, **4** (1980), p. 112.

5   ibid., p. 113.

6   M. Cooley, *Architect or Bee?* (London 1983).

11 European socialism and the role of the state*

Problems of a theory of socialism

A theoretical discussion about socialism encounters problems similar to those of talking scientifically about the future: *by definition*, this future does not constitute a 'present reality' and is therefore but an imaginary object of reflection. No one in the tradition of Marxist theory has talked about socialism *as such*, but only about the present reality as a history out of which socialist social formations are *real* (as opposed to merely imagined) *possibilities* – if only one among a number of possibilities, as Rosa Luxemburg's formulation of 'socialism *or* barbarism' reminds us. As an objectively identifiable possibility inherent in present conditions, socialism requires struggles, the contingencies of which are beyond the capacity of social theory to prescribe or predict. It is only as an objective possibility that we can talk, on the level of theoretical discourse, about socialism.

To do so, two steps are required to substantiate the claim that socialism is an objective possibility and therefore capable of becoming an object of analysis. The first of these steps develops the argument that *capitalist* social relations (relations of production, power relations) are subject to *self-paralysing laws* or tendencies. In the history of socialist thought, we have economic theories trying to demonstrate the self-annihilating nature of the capitalist mode of production (cf. the falling rate of profit debate); we also have theories of class conflict and growing class consciousness, as well as various attempts to link the two together in a comprehensive theory

* This essay was first presented as a discussion paper to the Third International Colloquium of the Interuniversity Centre for European Studies on the theme, 'The Future of Socialism in Europe?', Montréal, 30 March 1978. Earlier versions were published in André Liebich (ed.), *The Future of Socialism in Europe?* (Montréal: Interuniversity Centre for European Studies, 1978), pp. 67–75, and in *Kapitalistate*, 7 (1978), pp. 27–37.

of capitalist crisis and breakdown. Although this argument is not easy to conduct in detail, and with all the theoretical and empirical sophistication it requires, it is still the easier of the two steps to take, partly because everyone tends to accept its correctness and almost no one, least of all liberals, is surprised by it. Although this argument is hard to *develop*, it is even harder to *reject*, given the evidence of social, political and economic disorder, to which liberals have reacted with an almost inflationary use of the concept of 'crisis'. Clearly, however, the impossibility of capitalism does not tell us anything about the possibility of socialism, and it is this second step that one has to argue before we can even start to talk about socialism as an objective and real possibility. Such an argument would have to demonstrate that the crisis of capitalism is *not* a total crisis (a crisis of *history*, as it were), but a crisis that *contributes to* and *prepares* a socialist social formation rather than chaos, stagnation or barbarism.

Along these lines many revolutionary theorists have argued that capitalism is both (partly) bound to be self-destructive *and* (partly) worthy of being inherited by a socialist society which, in fact, derives its very foundations from what survives the decomposition of capitalism. Some of these theorists have proposed, for instance, that the forces of production, highly developed by the dynamics of capitalism, constitute the material basis of a socialist formation. Similarly, we find the argument that the inherent capitalist tendency towards capital concentration creates pre-conditions for socialist forms of management and the 'administration of things' (Engels, Hilferding, Lenin). Some have emphasized that the socialist revolution will redeem the cultural traditions and political values (such as the idea of the nation, democracy and equality) which have been inherited from the bourgeois revolutions but subsequently betrayed and corrupted in capitalism's history (R. Luxemburg). Finally, we find the theory that capitalist relations of production create a large, unified, self-conscious and mature working class capable of organizing and living in a society of 'freely associated producers'. It is exactly this second type of argument – one which develops the point that capitalism is not only *destructive of itself*, but at the same time *constructive of a socialist formation* – that would have to be elaborated to counter the presently abundant crisis rhetoric and all those apocalyptic visions suggested by radically disillusioned liberal cynics.

The definition of socialism is itself affected by such dialectical tension of continuity and discontinuity with capitalism. If socialism means the abolition of the domination of capital over wage-labour, and thus the abolition of the *commodity form of wage-labour*, including the political and cultural structures supportive of this commodity form, it also means that this is accomplished *within* the economic, political and cultural framework of the society that is to be transcended. Rupture and continuity *together* define any concrete instance of socialism, of which consequently no abstract, permanent definition is possible. This unavoidable component of inheritance and continuity that is to be found in movements, parties and societies that describe themselves as socialist has often given rise to the critical question of whether any particular politics or social arrangements do in fact constitute a break with the past, a liberation of the proletariat. The question, more precisely, is whether *continuity outweighs change*, whether the form of change annihilates its content, or the *means* used obstruct the *end* of liberation. The two major traditions of European socialism, those going back to the Second and the Third Internationals, have both become subject to this kind of criticism which, on the most abstract level, argues that the inherited form of the struggle for socialism has in fact corroded its revolutionary content. Such criticism was first formulated by the Left minority, most notably by Rosa Luxemburg, in its attacks on the reformism, revisionism and 'parliamentary cretinism' of the pre-First World War German Social Democratic Party. How justified this critique has been becomes all the more evident if we look at post-Second World War Social Democratic and Labour parties, which, due to their commitment to parliamentary forms of transformation, have been forced to abandon more and more of what remained of their radical programmatic intentions. No less important is the analogous critique of Stalinism and Eastern European socialism which argues that the very conditions that have *made possible* the transformations of 1917, namely the overthrow of Tsarist autocracy, or those of 1945–8, namely the imposition of socialist regimes in the aftermath of the War, have at the same time *seriously perverted* the socialist content of these transformations. Vestiges of authoritarian regimes – such as the 'asiatic' mode of production, and military occupation – remain prominent features of these regimes. The decisive theoretical and political problem for all modern socialist politics, on the basis of this critique and its underlying experience, is this: given the unavoidability of the fact that, in the process of transformation, one has to

rely on the institutions, opportunities and progressive and constraining traditions of the system that is to *be* transformed, how can
those links of continuity, and the *forms* and instruments of change
be prevented from turning *against* the purpose and content of the
transformation itself?

The state and socialist transformation

It is in the context of this problem that I want to discuss conceptions
of the role of the state in the process of socialist transformation.
One of the most powerful ideological objections by liberals to a
process of socialist transformation has been the fear that the means
of such transformation, the seizure of state power by a socialist
party, would by necessity turn against the proclaimed ends of the
process, the liberation of the proletariat. Socialism, according to
Max Weber, would not mean something different and progressive
but more of the same – that is, more of the same inescapable
element of bureaucracy that, according to him, capitalist liberal
democracy, at least, is able to curb by institutions securing individual freedom. In view of this almost ubiquitous fear, and amid a
perception of the social and political realities of the Soviet Union
and other Eastern European states which renders this suspicion
highly plausible, socialist and communist parties in Europe have
considered it their major task to develop convincing alternatives to
the statist models of socialist transformation. These theoretical and
programmatic formulations take seriously what the classical
writers. Marx and Lenin in particular, have strongly emphasized:
namely, that state power must not only be *occupied* by the victor-
ious organizations of the working class, but at the same time must be
smashed, that is, fundamentally transformed, so as to be 'appropriated' by society. These formulations confront the problem of
revolutionizing the very means by which the revolution has been
accomplished in order to avoid the inherent danger of the *form*
perverting the *content* of socialist transformation.[1]

   It is thus not only in response to widespread fears, especially
among the middle classes, that some communist parties of the Latin
European countries seem to have partly committed themselves to
strategies which would weaken and disperse state power, broaden
popular participation, decentralize authority and guarantee
democratic freedoms. Such anti-statist commitments, which would
eventually lead to a far more *social* character of state power by

overcoming the separate, autonomous organization of society's repressive and directive capacity, cannot be understood as a tactical consideration of electoral politics. The question remains, of course, whether the structural conditions of socialist transformation in Western Europe are likely to be supportive of such programmatic design or whether, as has been the case in the Soviet Union, the authoritarian bureaucratic form of the socialist state remains unchallenged, thus exacerbating the form/content problem. Most commentators, when discussing this crucial question, have put it in extremely voluntaristic and subjective terms: they have limited the problem to the question of whether or not the leadership of communist parties is *sincere* when committing itself to a far-reaching democratization not only of the social and economic content but also of the *political form* of the socialist state. Putting the question *this* way, however, makes it both largely uninteresting and unanswerable. What I want to do instead is to discuss the question of whether the structural conditions of advanced industrial capitalism are, in fact, conducive to non-statist forms of socialist transformation; that is, whether they facilitate and at least make possible the implementation of the classical idea that the occupation of state power has to be followed by its structural transformation and democratization. In my view, objective conditions will play a much larger role in determining the outcome of the form/content dilemma than the sincerity of politicians and party elites. Correspondingly, the truth of any programmatic statements and commitments of the latter cannot be measured by judgements about the honesty of their intentions, but only by a social analysis of whether there exists the objective possibility for such intentions to *become* true *if* taken seriously by party elites as well as their mass constituency.

My rough outline of such an analysis begins with an observation on the dilemma of the *capitalist* state, on which there exists a surprising agreement among Marxist, conservative and liberal analysts. This dilemma is the following: the interventionist capitalist welfare state (with its institutional framework of party competition and representative democracy) is confronted, as it fulfils the fundamental function of any state (namely, the stabilization and protection of a national social formation), with a multitude of demands and requirements which are impossible to satisfy within the constraining parameters of this *very same* order with its liberal democratic arrangements. The political and the economic structures of advanced capitalism are not in harmony. What the state is *required* to do becomes evidently *impossible* to accomplish unless either the private character of accumulation or the liberal democratic character of the polity are suspended. For our present discussion, it is pretty irrelevant whether we explore this dilemma in terms of the contradiction of capitalism and democracy (Marx's original formulation), or in terms of the antinomy of accumulation and legitimation functions of the modern state (O'Connor, Wolfe), or in terms of the now fashionable theories about the 'economic contradictions of democracy' and the ensuing 'crisis of democracy' (Huntington).[2] The underlying diagnosis, if not the implied therapy, is almost identical: the emergent functional discrepancy, or 'lack of fit', between the economic and political substructures of advanced capitalism. The demand 'overload' cannot be absorbed by the state without its simultaneous undermining, for example, via inflation, or by the rule of profit that it supposedly protects. Conversely, a 'healthy' growth rate cannot be achieved without imposing restrictions on democratic freedoms and political mass participation, the right to strike, and on the various accomplishments of the welfare state. This, of course, is what the neo-conservative proponents of this crisis-analysis are less and less reluctant to advocate.

The constraints that the capitalist economy imposes upon the state, thereby disorganizing its capacity to maintain 'order' by responding effectively to political demands and requirements, are based upon capital's *power to obstruct*. As long as investment decisions are 'free', that is, as long as they obey the rule of maximum expected profitability, the decisive variable constraining 'realistic' political opinions is what Kalecki has called 'business confidence'.[3] The ultimate political sanction is non-investment or the threat of it (just as much as the ultimate source of power of the individual capitalist *vis-à-vis* the individual worker is non-employment or termination of employment). The foundation of capitalist power and domination is this institutionalized right of capital withdrawal, of which economic crisis is nothing but the aggregate manifestation.

On the basis of this analysis, one strategy of socialist transformation is guided by the logic of *vetoing capital's use of veto power which forecloses exactly that one option upon which the class power of capital resides*: the option *not* to invest and thereby to withdraw society's resources from societal use. This process would take the form of a thorough nationalization and bureaucratization of at least those branches of industry which could, by using their potential for obstruction, cause damage to, and impose significant constraints on, societal reproduction as a whole. This is the line of reasoning that I consider an ideal-typical model of statist solutions of the problem of socialist transformation in Western Europe.

Today, no socialist group of any significance advocates such a statist type of strategy, but it is not immediately evident what is wrong with it. It appears to me that three types of objections can be raised against such a statist strategic orientation. First, from a normative point of view, we could run into the aforementioned form/content problem; although this solution would, at least in the short run and within the confines of a national political economy, eliminate the constraints to which the political system is subject in capitalist societies, such *liberation of policy-making* is by no means necessarily identical to any notion of the *liberation of the proletariat*. Second, in an industrially advanced society there exists a highly differentiated social structure which implies a great number of partial divisions and conflicts of interest according to such criteria as occupational groupings, regional interests, branches of industry. The very fact of such differentiation would preclude a degree of homogenous mobilization that could serve as a solid basis of support and legitimacy for a unified command structure of political and economic decision-making, as soon as the 'party in struggle' has become a government party; nor could repression and exclusion – regardless of its normative incompatibility with any notion of 'liberation of the proletariat' – conceivably operate as a functional equivalent to legitimation, because the fact of structural differentiation increases the vulnerability of the bureaucratic apparatus to non-compliance or resistance. Third, the fact of differentiation and complexity affects the political balance sheet not only on the support side, but also on the policy side; once the profitability criterion is eliminated as the ultimate guideline of allocating decisions, the complexity of industrial economies precludes any immediate shift to an alternative and substitutive mechanism of allocation, certainly not within tolerable limits of time or efficiency. We would conclude, then, that not only on the basis of normative considerations, but also from the point of view of effectiveness criteria (obedience to commands) as well as efficiency criteria (rationality of commands), the feasibility of any statist model of socialist transformation would appear as something beyond the realm of objective possibilities. Seen this way, the recent commitment of socialist theoreticians and Euro-communist parties to nonstatist conceptions of the process of socialist transformation would not appear as a major political 'concession' (to say nothing about deception), but as a reflection of the insight that statist roads to socialism, a societal transformation performed through bureaucratic planning, is no longer a realistic option in advanced capitalist systems.

This leaves us with the inverse dilemma, compared to the one which I have described as the structural problem of the capitalist state. Whereas the capitalist state suffers from an 'overload' of demands and requirements which it cannot *satisfy* without destroying the capitalist nature of the economy nor *ignore* without undermining its own democratic institutional set-up and the regulation of class conflict provided by it, any socialist state *can* solve this dilemma only by exposing itself to a different one: the new dilemma of a state apparatus that can maintain its directive capacity only to the extent that it gives itself up *as a state* – that is to say as a *separate* organization of the ultimate power of collective decision-making – ultimately by negating its identity as an 'apparatus' and eliminating the categorical distinction of 'state' and 'civil society'. Briefly, whereas the capitalist nature of civil society constrains the capitalist state, the statist nature of any socialist state constitutes its major barrier.

The dilemma can be described as the contradiction between two insights or assumptions shared by almost all socialist parties and groups in Western Europe. First, the insight that winning state power, gaining control over institutionalized political decision-making positions, using the directive capacity of economic, social and foreign policy-making, etc., is an absolutely indispensable element in the struggle for socialist transformation, or class struggle on the political level. The second insight is that what is to be won in this struggle, namely the control over state power, is itself in need of transformation and eventual negation. Socialism in industrially advanced societies cannot be built *without* state power and it cannot be built *on* state power.

State power, both in its directive and repressive capacities, is needed in order to consolidate political changes and protect institutional accomplishments against countermeasures initiated by elements of the capitalist class. Such resistance, or manifestations of the lack of 'business confidence', can take many forms, ranging from acts of strategic disinvestment, boycott, sabotage and capital flight to secessionist movements and to the organized intervention of transnational corporations, banks or social democratic parties and retaliatory acts of supranational economic and military organiz-ations. Obviously, only a regime that is able to insulate itself against the disorganizing impact of such measures and to maintain a minimum of autonomy *vis-à-vis* such pressures can hope to continue the process of socialist transformation. The decisive case is when the strategies of retaliation do not consist only of economic pressures coming from national or international actors or in military threats, but when, in addition, they involve strategically important elements of the *domestic* constituency, such as the intelligentsia, the military or other segments of the middle class (cf. the case of Chile) which become part of a capitalist 'popular front'. In such cases, a socialist regime, whether or not it resorts to more far-reaching repressive measures, thereby compromising its commitment to political freedom and democracy, will soon succumb to interna-tional pressures and its domestic repercussions. This is the reason why the state as a *national* organization of power is unlikely to be the scene of a process of socialist transformation in the absence of strong *supranational* alliances of socialist parties and governments such as those which seem to be developing in the Latin European countries – an alliance that eventually might serve to make depend-ence on the Soviet Union avoidable as well. The structural weak-ness of a socialist *national* regime, its extreme vulnerability to international pressure, does also explain why a 51 per cent majority is not strong enough to absorb the foreseeable measures of retali-ation. It is exactly under conditions of international and domestic resistance to incipient processes of socialist transformation that the weakness of the state as the guarantor and agent of such transfor-mation becomes apparent.

The powerlessness of state power as a means of transformation appears to render any statist solution, whether a traditional social democratic or a communist one, clearly unrealistic. But it does not by itself suggest practicable non-statist solutions. Almost all concepts and strategies of social struggles that have been discussed in European communist, socialist and labour parties have in common an emphasis on the need to extend the *concept of politics* beyond the sphere of the state and its institutional channels (*auto-gestion*). Gramsci, whose work and particularly his much debated concept of 'proletarian hegemony' is experiencing a tremendous renaissance, refers to a level of politics and alliance based not on formal organizations of group representation in the state apparatus, but rather on the spreading of values and the proclamation of collective identities transcending both the state apparatus and class lines. (Even the German Social Democratic Party, during its brief period of active reformism between 1969 and 1973, entertained the idea that extraparliamentary mobilization might be as important a way to accomplish reformist projects as electoral politics.) And the practice of most European communist parties demonstrates that the conditions of struggle are most favourable and the chances of political penetrability are greatest not at the centre, but at the *margins* of the state apparatus, in city governments and universities, for example, where there are likely to exist sustained communications and mobilizations network plus a relatively remote threat of retaliatory countermeasures.

A non-statist socialist strategy?

One major change that occurred in the politics of most European countries (as everywhere else, certainly in North America) is the appearance of movements which are activated neither by specific *interests* and status-related demands nor by *ideological* orientations, but by *moral, political* and *cultural values*. These movements have defined new concepts of autonomy and collective identity that neither correspond to the categories of the market-place nor to those of institutionalized political conflict, in which they often are left without any formal representation. Such movements, which base themselves on *causes* rather than interests or ideologies (i.e., feminist, environmentalist, nationalist, regionalist, cultural movements), play at best a peripheral role in the political process as it is defined by the state structure. Their mobilization is directed against state-initiated or state-supported measures and institutions (abortion and divorce laws, nuclear energy programmes, centralized government). Equally *negative* is the reaction of state agencies towards these movements: non-recognition and repression. In this situation socialist political forces have been consistently the only ones to succeed in providing some organizational and theoretical coherence to these new movements, thus reconnecting the economic, cultural and political levels of struggle and broadening their own political base. The effort to reach to the margins and beyond of what the capitalist state admits as *its* highly selective definition of politics has in the recent past been a much more successful and promising road to the renaissance of European socialism than the focus on central positions of state power itself.

Let me conclude with a hypothesis. A disillusionment with statist conceptions of the road to socialism is to be found in the theory and practice of both socialist and communist parties in Europe. This development, unbalanced and inconclusive as it certainly still is, leaves us with the question whether the commitment to parliamentary forms of socialism *plus* extraparliamentary tactics of struggle do not make the socialist movement particularly vulnerable to the repressive and ideological counter-attacks of the capitalist state. This appears to be a particularly pertinent question in view of recent German developments which have greatly increased the repressive potential of the state apparatus. Is it not more than likely that the extension and utilization of the powers of the capitalist state will hopelessly encapsulate and marginalize the socialist movement both in its electoral and non-electoral politics? I wish to suggest that this is not necessarily the case. My hypothesis is that the capitalist state, under the impact of economic crisis, undergoes structural changes of a corporatist kind which could favour and facilitate a non-statist socialist strategy.

What I mean by corporatism could also be described as an *increase of the social character of politics within capitalism*, a dissolution of the institutional separateness, or relative autonomy of the state, the withering away of the capitalist state as a coherent and strictly circumscribed apparatus of power. What we find instead is a process in which policy-making powers are 'contracted out' to consortia of group representatives who engage in a semi-private type of bargaining, the results of which are then ratified as state policies or state planning. To be sure, such corporatist arrangements, as they become manifest in state-instituted bodies of social and economic councils, social partnership, concerted action, macro-codetermination, investment planning boards, etc., are significantly class-based in two aspects. First, not only do the representatives of *capital* participate in the negotiations on (at least) equal terms, but also their private power remains unchallenged; as a consequence, they not only negotiate, but *they also determine the limits of negotiability* by use of the indirect threat of non-investment (i.e., they define the scope of 'realistic' issues and demands). Second, working-class (*union*) representatives, in order to be admitted to corporatist policy-making bodies and to be licensed as participants of policy bargaining, are subject to legal and factual restrictions which are designed to severely limit their bargaining power.

Nevertheless, the shift from representative to 'functional' forms of representation breaks down the bourgeois definition of politics as the struggle for institutionalized state power. As the realm of *politics* transcends *state* institutions, new arenas of resistance are opened up. Moreover, the class harmony which is supposed to be instituted within such corporatist bodies of policy-making is clearly limited by constraints. First, agreement and peaceful accommodation presupposes growth rates which allow for a permanent positive sum game. Second, a co-operative attitude of unions and other working-class organizations within such corporatist modes of decision-making can only be achieved by means of the *exclusion* of issues, groups and interests of the working class which are made 'non-negotiable' by existing conjunctural power relations. Third, the legitimacy of corporatist arrangements is extremely feeble, relying only on their empirical results rather than any form of democratic theory or ideology. Consequently, these arrangements are generally not held to be binding. The fact that the centres of political power have more and more visibly moved away from the official institutions of the state (such as parties, parliament, the presidency or bureaucratic policy-making) and rather have assumed, within the boundaries of a corporatist politics of group accommodation, an increasingly social character, seems to increase the potential leverage of non-statist strategies of socialist transformation aimed at the breakdown of the limitations of corporatist institutions. At a time when capitalist societies themselves, under the pressure of social and economic crises, are forced to give up their own fundamental distinction of state and civil society, the insistence upon statist strategies of socialist transformation is rendered both unrealistic and anachronistic.

Notes and references

1   A brilliant overview of the history of this *problématique* and the main varieties of argumentation is to be found in Martin Shaw, 'The theory of the state and politics: a central paradox of Marxism', *Economy and Society*, 3 no. 4 (1974).

2   James O'Connor, *The Fiscal Crisis of the State* (New York 1973); Samuel P. Huntington *et al.*, *The Crisis of Democracy: Report on the Governability of Democracies to the Trilateral Commission* (New York 1975).

3   Michat Kalecki, *Studies in the Theory of Business Cycles, 1933–1939* (New York 1976).

12 Reflections on the welfare state and the future of socialism

An interview*

DH   It would be very helpful and interesting if we could begin this
JK   discussion of the welfare state and the future of socialism by
asking you to say a little about some of the most important
political and intellectual influences on your theoretical
work.

CO   I might start by mentioning that from 1960 until 1965 I was a
student at the Free University in Berlin, which at that time
was something like the Berkeley of German university life. It
was a highly politicized place that had the highest concentration of Left intellectuals and students sympathetic to the
German SDS. It was there that questions relating to univer-
sity·reform and scientific and technical 'progress' first became
of central political importance. This experience in Berlin
greatly influenced me, and in fact the first book upon which I
collaborated, *Hochschule in der Demokratie*, was concerned
with the relationship between university reform and socialist
politics. In 1965 I moved to Frankfurt to work with
Habermas, with whom I remained in close working contact
for about the next ten years. The Frankfurt School of the mid
1960s provided a very important intellectual background for
my own work, although I was never very close to either
Horkheimer or Adorno, both of whom were still teaching at
the time. After Frankfurt, I applied unsuccessfully for a
lectureship in sociology in Birmingham and then was lucky
enough to be offered a fellowship in the United States.
Between 1969 and 1971 I worked at Berkeley and Harvard,
and travelled a lot throughout the United States. Since the

* The following interview was conducted by David Held and John Keane in London
and Wassenaar during November and December 1982. The interviewers wish to
express their gratitude to Claus Offe and Liz Dodd, who transcribed the discussions.

mid 1960s, I had had a strong interest in American and British sociology and the growing critique of the assumptions of structural-functionalism. My interest in these most advanced forms of liberal social theory was strengthened by the fact that earlier traditions of German social theory, which included such figures as Max Weber, Simmel, Lederer and Mannheim, had to be reimported into post-Second World War Germany by way of America and its European émigré intellectuals who lived there. It was, in other words, absolutely essential for German intellectuals to read American social science because this was one of the really important sources of our own classical tradition. I should finally mention one exception to this. In Berlin, the sociology programme had been initiated in the late 1950s by one of the most important German political sociologists, Otto Stammer. He had been in personal contact with many writers of the 1920s and had also participated in the underground political struggle against Nazism. He therefore provided a direct link with some of the sociological and political traditions of the 1920s.

DH   It is evident from your writings that you draw upon a variety
JK   of theoretical and methodological perspectives: Marxism, critical theory, systems theory, empirical social research. Do you consider yourself to be an advocate of any one theoretical tradition?

CO   These days I think it comes as neither a surprise nor a shock to describe many sociologists' work as eclectic. I have certainly been critically labelled in this way by others, but I remain persuaded that this is not a particularly strong criticism. Within theoretical and empirical sociology, eclecticism is certainly legitimate, if by this we mean a willingness to learn from both the Marxist tradition and traditions that include Weberians, Durkheimians and others. While I often find myself in the slightly embarrassing position of being able to argue from both sides of a particular methodological debate, I am convinced that there is no single paradigm within the contemporary social sciences that is sufficiently developed and coherent and therefore able to dispense with other paradigms. I do not think there are clear-cut oppositions that today divide sociologists into well-defined and incommensurable camps.

DH Does this mean that you do not consider yourself today, if you
JK ever did, first and foremost a Marxist?

CO In the past, I have certainly thought of myself in this way. But
this labelling process is somewhat of an ironical routine
within German social science. While I am greatly indebted to
classical Marxism and the very important sociological traditions that emerged from the Second International, I would
challenge anybody's right to monopolize definitions of
Marxism and its limits.

DH Could we ask more about your interest in Marxism? Does it
JK stem from an early confrontation with certain problems
posed by classical Marxism, or with the critics of this tradition
– notably the critical theory of the Frankfurt School?

CO One thing that is important to realize is that, in the Federal
Republic, Marxism was the only theoretical tradition that
was not imported from the United States, where the reception of Marxist social theory has in any case been for the most
part extremely deficient or distorted. In post-war Germany,
interestingly enough, the study of Marx's early writings was
stimulated by a group of intellectuals within the Protestant
Church, including Iring Fetscher. In 1961, I was introduced
to the *Economic and Philosophic Manuscripts* by Peter
Christian Ludz, who had himself been associated with these
Protestant circles. I was greatly impressed, to say the least.
My interest in Marxism has also been stimulated by the
continuous efforts within twentieth-century social science to
intellectually refute Marxism. As Ralf Dahrendorf's *Class
and Class Conflict in Industrial Society* correctly pointed out
at the time, the hidden agenda of social science since Marx
has been its attempt to demonstrate what was correct and
incorrect in Marx, as well as to indicate what social changes
since the nineteenth century could not have been known by
Marx. Because of this hidden agenda, the Marxist tradition
has been essential to theoretical sociologists of my generation
– it provided a background for very fruitful readings of
twentieth-century social theory.

DH   In what precise ways do you consider yourself indebted to the
JK   first generation of critical theorists, especially Horkheimer,
      Adorno and Marcuse? In addition, what have you learned
      from your work with Habermas? What is the heritage and
      significance of critical theory today?

CO   The contemporary significance of the tradition of critical
      theory is very widely debated among German social scientists
      and I am convinced by this debate that there is no fast and
      easy answer. Classical critical theory was of course deeply
      sceptical about the possibilities of emancipation proclaimed
      by the Second and Third Internationals. It attempted to
      explain why the working-class movement had failed to
      accomplish its revolutionary historical mission. This non-
      event was explained with reference to what classical Marxism
      had called the 'superstructure' – aspects of life such as mass
      communications, science, family life, popular culture and the
      state. By emphasizing the repressive and disciplinary effects
      of these superstructural elements, the Frankfurt project was
      crucial for understanding and explaining both fascism and the
      post-fascist period of political normalization. Today, this
      project is less than convincing. I do not wish to deny the
      importance of its enormously fruitful and very exciting
      analyses of the mechanisms of domination. But I do think
      that these analyses are of less relevance for the contemporary
      period. Classical critical theory is evidently a species of
      victimization theory, in that it represents the populations of
      welfare state countries as objects of near-total administra-
      tion. This thesis is nowadays misleading and perhaps danger-
      ous, and must in my view be questioned.

DH   How significant has Habermas's break with this 'victimiz-
JK   ation' model of classical critical theory been for your work?

CO   It is true that Habermas breaks decisively with the Frankfurt
      tradition by emphasizing the self-paralysing tendencies of
      late capitalist systems. Habermas's work nevertheless con-
      verges with the main authors of that classical tradition by
      emphasizing 'superstructural' elements as the decisive level
      of societal dynamics. Habermas traces these dynamics to the
      antagonism between the mechanisms of system integration
      and social integration. The central contradiction is between

the structures of instrumental and strategic rationality within the economic and political spheres and the development of motivation and legitimation. Unable to contain the motivational energies of people, the late capitalist system is also confronted with new and contradictory legitimation problems. Of central importance within Habermas's analysis – a point which first brought us into contact – is the system of higher education and its ability to deepen these legitimation and motivation problems by promoting moral–practical knowledge and understanding. I might also add that Habermas differs from the earlier Frankfurt tradition in his questioning of several basic theses of Marxist political economy, such as the labour theory of value, the falling rate of profit and the law of value. As he explained in *Theorie und Praxis*, the earlier Frankfurt School relied too closely upon what he called a 'tacit orthodoxy', in that they presumed the Marxian economic and class analysis as already proven and not worthy of further consideration. I very much agree with Habermas on this point. The revision of the economic assumptions of both classical Marxism and the Frankfurt authors was a very urgent task, and an important part of what happened at the Max Planck Institute in Starnberg, where I worked with Habermas from 1971 to 1975.

DH   We would like to turn now to your appropriation of systems
JK   theory. In your earlier writings in particular, for example *Strukturprobleme des kapitalistischen Staates*, you analyse late capitalist systems as comprising three subsystems, and advance the thesis that the political subsystem cannot secure a 'balance' in the functions it performs without endangering its own existence or the existence of its 'flanking' subsystems, the capitalist economy and the legitimation subsystem. What were the theoretical advantages you saw in this systems-theoretical approach, particularly as it had been formulated at the time by the leading systems theorist in the Federal Republic, Niklas Luhmann? Related to this, why is it that your more recent writings on the welfare state do not use the conceptual language of systems theory? Does your more recent interest in social movements and your consequent reliance upon a conflict model of social and political power indicate that you are now prepared, at least in part, to

abandon the systems-theoretical approach? Or is this shift of
emphasis one of convenience, allowing you to address a
different range of problems both from a systems-theoretical
and a social and political conflict perspective?

CO   Well, I don't see much difference between these two
approaches. I consider systems theory to be a very helpful set
of conceptual tools by which phenomena can be ordered,
classified and their interrelation studied. It has been argued
that contemporary capitalism differs from any earlier form of
capitalism in that it has become, to use a very problematic
phrase, a 'system for itself'. In other words, the managers of
the political, economic and cultural subsystems have become
aware of their interrelatedness. To the extent that this is true,
and particularly in as much as the interventionist, welfare
capitalist state assumes responsibilities for the maintenance
of the entire social order, I would argue that the systems-
theoretical approach is an adequate tool of analysis because it
corresponds to the way the managers of the system conceive
it.

DH   This conviction is part of your more general thesis that
JK   systems-theoretical categories are applicable to certain social
systems and not others. . . .

CO   Exactly, and this is why the use of systems theory is justified
at the present time. It is basically wrong to assume that
contemporary capitalist society continues to be the kind of
anarchic liberal society considered from Mandeville to Marx.
Welfare capitalist society has less the character of an anarchic
interplay of unconscious forces, in which order is an unintended by-product. Order, in the sense of a complex and
integrated coherence between different subsystems, is something that is consciously pursued by agents within the system.
Of central importance is the capacity of state power to
regulate and integrate discrepancies and conflicts. Whether
state power is able to manage and reproduce the highly
oppressive, irrational and self-contradictory capitalist system
is of course an open question. I must say that in trying to
address this question, I have learned a lot from Luhmann. In
spite of his sometimes cynical views on the potential for social
change, I have worked on the assumption that several of his

insights can be very fruitfully connected with Marxism. I was particularly attracted by Luhmann's earlier writings, because the distinction between subjective motives and objective functions and consequences is central to them. Objectively organized functions and outcomes of social activity are, in his view, necessarily and increasingly uncoupled from the motivations of subjects – this is a central feature of Luhmann's view of society.

DH   Doesn't this view nevertheless beg questions about the
JK   precise relationship between so-called objective effects and subjective motives, or between structures and agents? Recalling our discussion of the Frankfurt School, your reasons for employing systems theory seem, to some extent, to echo Adorno's view that the rational moment of systems theory and empirical research is their conceptual reflection of a standardized world that eliminates human agency. Systems theory supposes, in other words, that agency has been thoroughly destroyed: the only remaining agents in this anonymous world appear to be Madame Economic Subsystem and Messieurs Political-Administrative and Legitimation Subsystems!

CO   I did not mean to imply that systems theory celebrates the superior rationality of systems over actors, as Luhmann sometimes tends to do. While this assumption is hard to defend and prove, I think that the ordering activities of administrative, political and economic elites are always insufficiently rational and, therefore, self-paralysing, and that is why they set free agents whose actions are by definition not part of the ordering system. In this respect, I would follow Habermas's general thesis that agency is the by-product of a specific process of alienating and oppressive rationalization. Agency forms as a response to those mechanisms of social and political control that, first, are separated from the motives of action in an abstract and 'reified' way and, second, 'invade' and consequently destroy those spheres of life in which individual and collective identities are constituted and defended.

DH   You frequently distinguish liberal social science from critical
JK   social science. In general, what are the unique features of the

critical social science enterprise in which you are engaged? How is a critical social science possible?

CO   There are two distinctive characteristics of liberal social science. One of these concerns its attempts to model its propositions about society after the objectivistic view of science that one finds within the natural sciences. Its truthful propositions are supposed to be non-partisan and as uncontestable as the laws of mechanics. Related to this assumption, second, liberal social science conceives itself as being distanced from social practices. Consequently, it accepts the given patterns of differentiation within any society: liberal social science understands itself as science and nothing but science. In doing so it forgets that all great social and political theorizing in the nineteenth and early twentieth centuries received its problematic and inspiration from social movements and contested social conditions. In the past, this existential rootedness of social and political theory has always been a source of analytical strength. By unconditionally accepting the academic division of labour between politics and science, liberal social science sterilizes itself and makes itself vulnerable to the worst kind of partisanship to the status quo. As Weber pointed out, it forgets that non-partisanship can *never* mean that the standards of relevance within social science and its conflict-ridden political and social context are divorced absolutely. In this sense, I would say that the distinguishing feature of critical social science is that it is neither objectivistic nor artificially divorced from social and political conflicts that actually exist. Critical social science knows that the criteria for the validity of statements cannot be determined by the latest press release of a given government. It refuses to elevate the given distribution of power into the status of an object about which lasting truths can in turn be generated.

DH   How important is empirical research for the project of critical
JK   social science? It seems important to discuss this question at this point, because your empirical research – for instance, your studies of the construction industry, or the failures of the vocational training reform policies of the Social Democratic Government between 1969 and 1974 – are hardly known

outside of the Federal Republic. Perhaps, with reference to this work, you would briefly summarize what you take to be the scope and importance of empirical social research within the critical social sciences?

CO   If the critical function of social science consists of its attempt to demystify ideology, then empirical research is vital, for it can help to prove the invalidity or, at least, the limited validity of certain assumptions that the system promulgates about itself. In my view, empirical research is a necessary part of a project of demystification. To be sure, empirical research is incapable of proclaiming and prescribing correct and universally valid political norms. However, critical social science, guided by empirical research, can engage in a form of indirect normative criticism by questioning the false empirical assumptions and beliefs upon which the dominant normative images of the social order implicitly rely. Someone has likened this indirect form of normative critique to the activity of mine workers who prepare the mine face for blasting by drilling holes, into which explosives can be inserted.

In my studies of vocational training reform and the construction industry, for instance, I attempted to pursue this kind of indirect criticism by developing empirical arguments against the social democratic, reformist assumption that the state and its agents of public policy are actually in the position of 'ultimate power', a power capable of creating and redefining the terms of social and political order. Somewhat more ambitiously, and in line with some American political sociologists, for example Ted Lowi, my empirical research also attempts to demonstrate the hidden links or correspondences between certain institutional arrangements of decision-making and the issues that can be processed by these same institutional arrangements. For instance, established forms of collective action such as competitive party systems may be appropriate for processing certain issues and programmes and not others. Empirical research can indicate that for certain issues, for example environmental degradation, the established and apparently universally accessible means of decision-making are in fact inadequate because they produce decisions that are systematically biased either towards certain interests or in favour of certain solutions that are less than rational. I should therefore like to emphasize that empirical research can make tentative proposals for revising the institutional frameworks of economic and political decision-making. Empirical inquiry does not simply question the false universality of certain institutional arrangements such as party systems. It can also develop models and proposals which broaden the political repertoire of society in order to provoke institutional innovations. Although critical social science and empirical research cannot legitimately prescribe the one best way of acting, it can stimulate social actors' inventiveness and fantasies about alternative and more adequate decision-making arrangements.

DH Within the English-speaking world, the reception of your
JK   writings on politics seems to have paralleled the reception of other forms of state theory developed within the Federal Republic – for instance, the 'state-derivation' controversies. Arguably, this process of 'parallel reception' has produced one-sided interpretations of your own contributions. Would you therefore briefly say something about this theoretical context within which you have attempted to develop a theory of the structural problems of welfare capitalist states?

CO After the climax of the German student movement in 1969, there was a strong turn towards a Marxist theoretical orthodoxy in the subjects of economics, law and political science. Concerned to overcome both their own political isolation and the social democratic orthodoxies of the time, many middle-class radical intellectuals attempted to form links with the working class by embracing ultra-orthodox formulations. The written controversies were quite bitter, and often sprinkled with the 1907–11 vocabulary of opportunism, revisionism and Left radicalism. I think that most of us who were active in that post 1969 theoretical debate would agree today that the controversies drew too heavily and selectively upon some of the holy writings of classical Marxism. The crudeness and lack of sophistication of this new orthodoxy can be partly explained by the virtual absence in Germany at that time of any established tradition of

Marxist scholarship and research. With the exception of a
very few people like Wolfgang Abendroth, Left intellectuals
seemed to temporarily forget the high-level Marxist theorizing of the 1920s that had, of course, been forcibly interrupted
by Nazism. This amnesia had quite disastrous consequences,
and was reinforced by the tendency of the proponents of the
new orthodoxy to orient their research on the state to the
currently available East German theories.

DH   In other words, your earliest work on the structural problems
JK   of the capitalist state is best interpreted as a negative
      response to this developing orthodoxy of the early 1970s?

CO   Very much so. I was very unhappy with the strange Hegelian
      tones of this new orthodoxy and its emphasis on self-enclosed
      and deductive forms of reasoning. Drawing upon what I
      learned during my stay in the United States and from my
      readings of the works of Poulantzas, Miliband and others, I
      tried to develop what I considered to be a more adequate
      approach to the analysis of the state and public policy. Fortu-
      nately, the ultra-orthodox project of the early 1970s came to
      an end within five years. Little of it remains today, and
      theoretical research on the state has become far more serious
      and productive, and influenced by sophisticated analytical
      approaches deriving from both Marxism and the most
      advanced forms of social science.

DH   Could we now turn to some of the more substantive aspects of
JK   your work on the limitations of the welfare state? To begin
      with, why do you often say that late capitalist systems can
      neither live with nor without the welfare state? Do you
      consider this to be their fundamental contradiction?

CO   A brief definition of a contradiction is that it is a condition in
      which certain indispensable elements of a social structure
      cannot be integrated because they are at odds with each
      other; i.e., the social structure paralyses itself because the
      elements necessary for its survival at the same time render it
      impossible. In applying this concept of contradiction to the
      welfare state, I was greatly impressed by Karl Polanyi's
      reformulation of the classical Marxist interpretation of the
      wage-labour process. As is well known, Polanyi argues that,

although wage-labour is treated as if it were a commodity, it is in fact not a commodity. This is partly because labour cannot be separated from its owner. It is also a result of the fact that unlike all other commodities, the volume, quality, time and place of wage-labour are not predominantly determined by criteria of market rationality. In his studies of the early systems of welfare and social policy, Polanyi points out that a society based on the 'fictitious' commodity form of labour power necessarily depends upon non-commodified support systems. These systems function to preserve and enhance labour power whenever it is not traded in labour 'markets'. I consider this argument decisive. Contrary to the view later associated with the writings of T. H. Marshall, Polanyi suggests that 'welfare' is not a late development within capitalist societies, something that somehow comes into being for philanthropic reasons after the time of the absolute exploitation of labour power. Rather, 'welfare' institutions are a pre-condition of the commodification of labour power. In my view, this relationship between 'welfare' and capitalism is contradictory: under modern capitalist conditions, a supportive framework of non-commodified institutions is necessary for an economic system that utilizes labour power as if it were a commodity.

This contradiction is deepened by the state monopoly of social policy provision. Of course, in the early phase of capitalist society, social policies were provided through traditional forms of organizations, including guilds, families, communities and churches. However, with the disaggregation and mobilization of whole populations, these traditional organizations are themselves undermined and therefore fail to function to the extent that is 'functionally required' – to use a very dangerous phrase – for the development of capitalism. Because of this disorganizing development, non-commodified support systems are increasingly politicized, that is, transferred from private, religious and philanthropic organizations to the state apparatus. This politicization of the provision of welfare was greatly accelerated by three interrelated political developments during the first half of the twentieth century: the parliamentarization of government; the universal extension of the franchise; and the formal recognition of the interests and veto powers of trade unions.

As a consequence of these various developments state institutions which assign legal entitlements to citizens become
relatively 'rigid' or even irreversible. Not constrained by a
definite index or 'stop rule' that would ensure they do not
develop beyond the extent functionally required for the
absorption of the risks and uncertainties connected with
wage-labour, decommodified state institutions tend to
develop an independent life of their own. On this point, I
think that much can be learned from the neo-conservative
argument that the welfare state is becoming an intolerable
burden on the capitalist economy.

DH   In summary form, then, your thesis is that the welfare state
JK   strategy of maintaining the commodity form leads to the
growth of policies and institutions exempt from the commodity form. This seems clear enough. But why do you
consider such organizations as schools, housing authorities,
and hospitals as 'decommodified'? And why do you sometimes consider these organizations as the most *advanced*
forms of erosion of the commodification process? Doesn't
your theory of decommodification also imply the need for
maintaining and extending decommodified state activities?
And, thereby, does it not underestimate the fact that many
state-provided 'use-values' are distorted by their orientation
to capitalist accumulation and, above all, by their *bureaucratic* mode of production and distribution?

CO   I see that these formulations are problematic, because they
tend to create the impression that non-market forms of life
are harbingers of socialism. Let me try to explain more
precisely what I mean. I speak of certain organizations as
decommodified because their provision of use-values is no
longer guided by the form of rationality appropriate to
market behaviour. If we consider the 'products' of the labour
of hospital workers, for instance, it is evident that it is not sold
on the market and that, moreover, its quantity, quality,
timing and geographic distribution are not directly determined by market criteria. This non-market rationality is also
crystallized in many other categories of service labour. In my
view, the continuous growth of decommodified organizations
such as hospitals consequently tends to weaken and paralyse

market rationality. This hiatus between the rationality of commodity markets and activity within decommodified organizations is not only an embarrassing problem for the academic disciplines of public administration and organization theory; it also constitutes a political opportunity for the Left. Areas of social life that have been decommodified by welfare state interventions can be developed, through political struggle, into relatively autonomous subsystems of life oriented to the production and distribution of use-values.

DH The discrepancy in the criteria of rationality between
JK commodified and decommodified systems may be viewed as a political opportunity for the Left, but do you not still underestimate the problem of bureaucratic domination, a problem powerfully raised by Max Weber and one that has increasingly plagued the socialist tradition in the twentieth century?

CO Weber rightly feared a totally bureaucratized, state-dominated society, and in my view his critique of the socialism of the Second International as a one-sided *extension* of bureaucratic domination was largely correct. In opposition to classical liberalism, Weber argued convincingly that the expansion of state bureaucratization and the capitalist form of production are parallel and coextensive, and not necessarily opposed processes. Nevertheless, Weber assumed that, under capitalist conditions, the relationship between the development of market forces and bureaucratic state control could be harmonized. He tended to believe that an uneasy coexistence between these two modes of rationality could be secured by 'responsible' individual leaders at the top of state bureaucracies and capitalist enterprises. The question today, however, is whether private property and market relations continue to constitute a safeguard against bureaucratic domination. It must also be asked whether plebiscitary mass democracy is indeed a check on bureaucratization, as Weber expected it would be. Finally, consideration must be given to whether bureaucratic modes of regulation are as uniquely efficient and effective as Weber assumed. In considering these three areas of doubt, I think that statist and bureaucratic-centralized forms of societal regulation are as vulnerable to criticism in the West as they are – for somewhat different and more obvious reasons – in Eastern European, state socialist regimes.

DH   We can return to this question of the possibility of democratic
JK   socialism later. For the moment, we would like to ask you more about the contradiction that you see between commodified markets and decommodified welfare-state policies. It seems to us that your thesis about the rapid growth of non-market forms of rationality rests upon some unexpressed assumptions about the self-paralysing tendencies of the capitalist economy. In your view, why is it that capitalist processes of commodification constantly tend to paralyse themselves?

CO   I am not myself an economist, and I have only a marginal understanding of technical economic arguments concerning such matters as capital coefficients and falling rates of profit. Bearing that in mind, I would say that there are two essential aspects of the present deep recession of the capitalist world economy. The first of these, which we have already discussed, has to do with the expansion of the decommodifying policies of the Keynesian welfare state. Disincentives to invest and work are unintended side effects of these policies, which clearly block the market mechanism to such an extent that the adaptation potential of capitalism is adversely affected. The present economic recession may, therefore, be seen in part as caused by state interferences with the purgative effects generated by the old business cycles of the capitalist economy. The phenomenon of demand saturation constitutes a second reason why we should not assume that investment outlets for private capital – and therefore full employment and economic growth – will easily be recreated in the near future. Within the highly industrialized economies, investment outlets have been considerably reduced by the exhaustion of demand for certain post-war boom commodities, such as automobiles and refrigerators. In my view, whatever growth potential there is in the near future is likely to be created through forms of investment and consumption that are administratively imposed on the population –

through industries such as defence, energy, transportation and communications. These are the industries that are most likely to flourish and to catalyse any new cycle of capital-intensive accumulation. What is interesting about these industries and their products is that they are developed without direct reference to markets or consumer demands. These industries and forms of consumption are enforced through *political* decisions; questions concerning capital investment and the production and consumption of plutonium reactors, nuclear weapons and transport systems become central within the prevailing political discourse. Given their often negative environmental, military and social consequences, these forms of administratively created investment and enforced consumption meet with enormous resistance from citizens and consumers in our societies. I think that this resistance may signal the emergence of a new politics of production during the 1980s, that is, the rise of forms of struggle that effectively block the opening up of new outlets for private capitalist investment.

DH   In your discussions of the welfare state the concept of
JK   legitimacy is sometimes very prominent. You suggest, especially in your early writings, that the cohesion of late capitalist societies depends upon shared norms and values, that is, upon a pattern of social integration which generates mass loyalty to the political system. You suppose that, without mass loyalty, a political system may be plunged into crisis. There are a number of objections to such a view. First, the evidence provided by industrial and political sociology (in Britain at least) does not support the idea of a widespread system of shared norms and values. Dominant ideologies appear more important for maintaining the cohesion of dominant classes than they are for organizing the dominated. Second, the absence of widespread legitimacy suggests that late capitalist societies do not depend upon legitimacy for their 'cohesion' or stability. How would you assess a view which argued in the following way: political and social order is the outcome of a complex web of inter-dependencies between political, economic and social institutions and activities which divide power centres and which create multiple pressures to comply – whatever the values of

individuals and groups. Political and social stability is related
to the splits between, and the intersection of, power centres,
and to the resultant 'decentring' or fragmentation of political
and economic life, the atomization of culture, and the privatization of people's experience of their social and political
worlds. These fragmentation processes constitute crucial
barriers to the mobilization of opposition movements and to
the formulation of coherent alternatives to existing political
and social arrangements. . .?

CO   Some people have criticized my earlier conceptions of legitimacy for their overly rationalistic and implicitly Parsonian
bias. I think these critics are largely correct and, in response
to their criticisms, I have come to consider the questions of
legitimacy and normative integration in a different way. To
begin with, the concept of legitimacy has a deeply ambiguous
meaning within most writings on the social integration
of liberal democracy. From a sociological or social-
psychological perspective, legitimacy means the prevalence
of attitudes of trust in the given political system. From a
philosophical perspective, on the other hand, the concept of
legitimacy is more applicable to cases in which regime norms
become problematic and are questioned: the legitimacy of a
regime or government depends upon the justifiability of its
institutional arrangements and political outcomes. I think
that these competing meanings of the concept of legitimacy
can be reconciled by understanding them, at the analytic level
at least, as addressed to the following sequence of problems.
First of all, assume conditions in which there is an unprob-
lematic consensus about a regime of power that confirms
itself, as Marcuse put it, by delivering the goods. Under these
conditions, questions pertaining to legitimacy in both senses
are displaced or pushed to one side by the very fact that the
society 'works'. Then comes a second stage of development,
in which empirical attitudes of trust and satisfaction are dis-
turbed by the system's failure to function. This leads to the
development of a sense that society does not work according
to its own established standards of, say, continuous economic
growth, full employment and open and competitive party
government. If even more basic questions are raised, then a
third level of legitimation problem appears. Philosophical

arguments break out concerning the validity of the normative foundations of liberal democratic arrangements. Certain fundamental questions are provoked: do we really need trade unions? What is the role of the mass communications media? Is majority rule justifiable? Must the constitution be altered? Should democracy be understood as synonymous with parliamentary democracy?

In my view, late capitalist systems have entered into this third stage of legitimacy problems. As the political crisis develops along with the economic crisis, popular satisfaction with a system that formerly 'delivered the goods' has turned into dissatisfaction; empirical attitudes of dissent emerge; and the philosophical questioning of the whole relationship between politics and society commences. There is a broadening of the parameters of licence – to employ a term developed in a very interesting study of political integration in Britain by Alan Marsh. In other words, the range of deviation from what is considered by the political culture as positive and normatively binding increases. What many people considered objectionable twenty years ago becomes less objectionable. There has been a 'liberalization' of the parameters of licence in regard to such unorthodox modes of political action as teachers' strikes, factory occupations and citizens' disruption of state ceremonial events. This development is symptomatic of a growing uncertainty about the normative foundations of liberal democratic political systems. It is related to the weakening of certain traditional mechanisms of transmitting cultural values, such as the family. As Habermas has pointed out, this uncertainty is also linked with the fact that the moral infrastructure of society becomes contingent to the extent that it is drawn into the institutional realm of the state. For instance, primary and secondary socialization and education is no longer to any extent the class-specific and 'private' business of the family; these functions are instead delegated to state institutions, and this in turn produces changes both in the form and the content of cultural reproduction. The parameters of licence or level of contingency within the prevailing political culture are expanded. State intervention weakens the processes of privatization and fragmentation. The existing repertoire of values and practices ceases to be 'natural' – it is now subject to political criticism and determination. In conclusion, I have doubts about your thesis that privatization and fragmentation are functional substitutes for normative control. Within such spheres as education, the arts and mass communications, a *de*privatization of moral, cognitive and cultural standards is taking place.

DH   A remarkable feature of recent discussions concerning the
JK   state is their neglect of two factors which Max Weber placed at the centre of his concept of the state, namely, territoriality and the means of violence. If we consider the work of Miliband or Poulantzas or Offe (in fact, nearly all works of contemporary neo-Marxism), it is striking that the 'theory of the state' is caught within Keynesian assumptions, in that it focuses only upon the relation between 'state' and 'economy' within a single, ideal-typical capitalist country. Neither the welfare state's development at the intersection of national and international pressures nor what we might call the overwhelming presence of organizations of violence and coercion seem adequately theorized. Is this a fair comment? If so, why are the questions of territoriality and monopolies of the means of violence striking and peculiar omissions from much state theory in the late twentieth century?

CO   I don't think this is entirely a fair comment. The German student movement, for instance, was motivated by two major issues, and both of them entered into the intellectual scene of the 1960s. These issues were the imperialist war in Vietnam and the repressive emergency legislation of 1968, which provided for the abandonment of democratic rights and procedures under certain conditions. These controversies over imperialism and repression correspond exactly to the two problems you mention: territoriality and the means of violence.

However, your question is very appropriate in as much as, until recently, there has been very little social scientific concern with the problems of repression and violence. These problems can be discussed on three levels. First, with regard to the relationship between the state and the economy, more consideration must be given to the 'dual' relationships that exist between the state and capital and between the state and the working class. If one considers the coercive and social control functions of state institutions *vis-à-vis* the working class, it is evident that the precise and detailed regulation of the conditions under which working-class people are entitled to receive aid and assistance has a definite repressive element. This welfare state system is marked by very strong elements of social control: only the 'deserving poor' are considered as legitimate recipients.

Second, the traditional concept of repression, understood as the use of military or police force, must be enlarged. This would help us grasp the more subtle, comprehensive and sophisticated methods of control embodied within surveillance, computerized criminal investigation and within certain developments in the legal interpretation of the rights of defendants. Very little has been done in this second area until recently, although Wolf-Dieter Narr and others have developed a very helpful sociological approach that relies upon theories of labelling, the sociology of crime, and the relationship between the state apparatus and so-called 'deviant behaviour'. This research was stimulated by the large-scale repressive measures introduced into the German political system in the autumn of 1977, after a wave of so-called 'terrorism'. This short but enormous outburst of state violence resulted – to give a not unusual example – in the stopping and searching of one single driver twenty-two times on the road from Hamburg to Cologne, a distance of about 400 kilometres. The most amazing thing about this period was that people thought this to be normal, that the state was entitled to do such things.

The third level on which the questions of repression and violence should be taken up more than they have been by the Left, I agree, is the problem of counter-violence. The German Left has to a large extent been silent about this problem. The strategy of terrorism and quasi-military fantasies about overthrowing the state have not helped to produce a sophisticated, normative theory of resistance. This silence is reinforced by a basic insecurity in German political culture, which lacks a strong tradition of civil disobedience against unjust state measures, such as one finds within the English-speaking countries. This absence of a tradition of civil disobedience in Germany results in two opposite and equally inadequate reactions: either total willingness to obey orders and comply with repressive measures or nonsensical forms of quasi-military resistance, which clearly lose touch with reality by using the term 'fascism' as if what the state is doing now and what it did forty years ago are somehow analogous.

DH   But surely the theoretical consideration of the problem
JK   of state violence is not exhausted by these three 'levels' of social control, police surveillance and counter-violence? What of the problems of territoriality and nation-state violence?

CO   There have been some interesting theoretical attempts to consider the territorial identities of states. Theda Skocpol's very interesting work helpfully pursues this approach. Her basic methodological point is that states are among other states and cannot, therefore, be analysed in isolation from each other. Nevertheless, we must think more about the contemporary transformation of statehood and democratic institutions as a consequence of the process of supranational-ization. Within organizations such as the EEC and NATO, for instance, many decisions are taken on the supranational level rather than the level of the nation state; the democratic processes that are instituted at the nation-state level thereby lose their grip over such supranational decision-making pro-cesses. It is now becoming very clear to the European Left that there has been a substantial loss of national sovereignty in the spheres of both economics and defence. The new peace movement is partly a reaction to this. There are also strong indications that nationalism both on the nation-state and sub-nation-state or regional levels is a political impulse that can be meaningfully developed by the political Left – in ways quite different from that nationalism of the past 100 years or so, which, especially in Germany, has been an impulse from the Right. These themes have been fruitfully developed by a number of recent critics of supranationalization. According to these critics, economic, political and military moderniz-ation processes have created ever larger units and networks of interdependency, such as nation-state military alliances and the world market. Contrary to liberal doctrines (such as

the law of comparative costs) that justify free trade arrangements, these critics point to the negative consequences of
supranationalization, which is seen to result in certain 'dis-
economies of scale'. These critics do not necessarily suppose
that 'small is beautiful', nor even that national sovereignty is
a value in itself; rather, they suggest that beyond some
'optimal' size, social systems undermine their own capacity
for autonomous, democratic and self-determined development.

I consider this a very important critique of the modernization of the international system: 'modernization' comes to
mean increasing interdependency *and* dependency. This perspective is strengthened by the work of Bahro and others on
ecological questions. Their compelling argument is that the
present system of world markets and international relations
deprives Third World countries not only of their natural
resources but also helps destroy their environmental conditions of survival. The enormous devastation of the environment in countries like Brazil or Indonesia are indeed a direct
consequence of the fact that these countries are forced to
export whatever they can in raw materials, irrespective of the
irreparable environmental damage caused by such export
strategies. This implies that autarky or regional autarky is a
necessary condition of the physical survival of these
dependent countries. The problem of over-centralization is
also discussed in some of the theoretical writings on regionalist movements. Touraine and others in France have shown
that over-centralization is an exploitative relationship which
leads to the devastation and immiseration of peripheral
regions. The internationalization of labour markets, for
instance, has had devastating effects on the countryside of
Turkey, Andalusia, Greece, Yugoslavia and southern Italy.
Not only has the social structure of whole villages been
destroyed, but physical processes of the erosion of the land
jeopardize the possibility of reversing the environmental
damage that has been done. In these regions, centralization
and internationalization produce vast developmental
imbalances and endanger the possibility of future development. This type of argument is by no means a romantic
lament for the beauties of the past. On the contrary, it is a
very advanced economic and ecological critique of the

irreparable damages induced by processes of internationalization and centralization.

DH   You have dwelled on the dependency aspects of North–South
JK   relations. Could we prompt you to say something about
      the general question of territoriality and the means of
      violence in relation to the Soviet bloc and capitalist coun-
      tries? Clearly, East–West relations cannot be understood
      through the categories of interdependence, centralization
      and marginalization. How then can we characterize these
      relationships?

CO   Given my parochialism and domestic orientations, I feel even
      less competent to talk about East–West relations than I do
      about North–South relations. I once spent a short period of
      time in Moscow, and the impression I formed was that state
      socialist regimes are enormously repressive. Two questions
      were constantly on my mind. Why do people accept the
      omnipresence of the instruments and symbols of state
      violence, the enormous privileges of the military, at the
      expense of virtually everything else in the Soviet Union? And
      why is this open authoritarianism and militarization neces-
      sary? One possible answer to the latter question is that this
      militarization is a condition of keeping people at work,
      especially considering that there is such an explosive amount
      of discontent. One possible response to the first question,
      which of course does not apply to Eastern European coun-
      tries, is that the Soviet populations have not known anything
      else in their recent history.
        These are very speculative, tentative approaches to a very
      pressing problem. However, I do think that one very funda-
      mental dilemma faced by both the West European Left and
      West European governments is that *détente* and the policy of
      establishing co-operative relations with Eastern Europe
      involves, at least, implicit recognition of state repression
      within these countries. This dilemma produces very strange
      political alliances. Some intellectuals like André Gorz and
      Cornelius Castoriadis, whom I otherwise admire very much,
      give priority to democratic rights in Eastern Europe and then
      proceed to side with American foreign policy. There are
      others, including figures in the German Social Democratic

Party such as Egon Bahr, who distinguish between the internal and external dimensions of relations with the Eastern bloc. The latter argue that the goal of peace is primary and that political debates over the internal character of the Eastern bloc must be avoided. Only through the securing of economic and military agreements can peaceful relations with the Eastern bloc be maintained. It is further claimed that only if external threats are effectively eliminated will the system of 'real socialism' endogenously develop in the direction of more liberal-democratic arrangements. This old idea of internal change through a relaxation of the Cold War is today very questionable. The Polish events, as they are commonly called, indicate that even after a lengthy period of *détente* the military leaders of the Soviet bloc cannot afford to compromise on such matters as workers' rights and citizen rights. If forced to choose between these two understandings of East–West relations, I would side with those who say that the peaceful stabilization of international relations is more important. My view is very questionable, but I consider that the break-up of state repression in the East is impossible unless *détente* policies are continued and immunized against approaches like those of Reagan and Weinberger.

DH   Doesn't this preference rest on the presumption that the
JK   system of 'real socialism' is not expansionist and that it is, therefore, open to some kind of geo-political compromise with the Western power blocs?

CO   Yes, I am making that assumption. I tend to agree with the argument first suggested by Hannah Arendt and recently utilized by Johann Galtung, who says that the United States and the Soviet Union are the two global imperialist powers. The United States is a typical sea power, and its field of action is the world. The Soviet Union, by contrast, is a typical land power, and its sphere of imperialist action is not the world but its adjacent territories, which obviously, and deplorably, are supposed to include Afghanistan.

DH   One could of course reply that any adjacent territory has
JK   another adjacent territory, and that the horizons of this Soviet land power are the whole world.

CO   That is an argument, although I remain convinced that Galtung's distinction makes some sense. After all, not only Latin America and South-East Asia, but also East Asia, Western Europe and of course Africa have been scenes of massive American intervention. That cannot be said of the Soviet Union to the same degree, although it must be said that its intervention in Africa raises some doubts about this. I do not discount the possibility that the Soviet Union, partly because of the provocations and examples established by the United States, will prove to be the more imperialistic state. It may be that it will come to regard the globe as its territory of action and thus move into Iran and perhaps even the Arabian peninsula. Of course, this would be the scenario for the Third World War which, in my opinion, will have its most likely point of origin somewhere between Pakistan and the Lebanon.

DH   Perhaps more than anyone else recently, Michael Foucault
JK   has highlighted the degree to which the modern state deploys not just forces of coercion like the military, but also forms of disciplinary power, or what he calls a 'subtle, calculated technology of subjection'. His account of this disciplinary power explores the way various agencies (asylums, hospitals, penitentiaries) help sustain 'law and order' and forms of 'governmentality'. You also analyse this process of normalization. You describe it as one in which the state enters more closely into physical contact with individuals' bodies and psyches. What is it about welfare state societies that produce for their own 'security' such dangerous means of surveillance?

CO   At a very abstract level, and drawing upon analogies from biology and cultural anthropology, I would argue that systems tend to become more vulnerable as they grow more complex. It is striking that the most primitive systems are also the least vulnerable systems. For instance, the most primitive Indian cultures survived in the Americas but the advanced Indian civilizations, for example the Incas, were very easily conquered and finally destroyed. On this basis, I would say that modern, complex societies are more sensitive to deviation and, therefore, depend on a very narrow definition of normality; the very complexity of these societies forces them to control, monitor and prevent psychic and physical disorders and 'deviant' modes of behaviour. This type of argument can be complemented with a further consideration, namely, that industrial, high technology, urbanized and densely populated societies such as our own *generate* various forms of mental, physical and ecological disorders that must be contained or remedied before they become threats to the whole social system. As Foucault, Melucci and others have observed, activities relating to eating, sexuality, health and disease cease to be governed by traditional cultural norms and are increasingly taught and controlled by the state. There are many examples of this relationship between complexity, vulnerability, 'deviance' and increasing welfare state control. For example, I vividly remember a programme in New York City that attempted to teach poor people about the superior nutritional value of beans and eggs – something that would never have been a problem for previous generations, but which becomes a problem in the uprooted world of ghetto life. Under modern capitalist conditions, to take a second example, production also becomes highly sensitive to the costly mistakes and failures associated with repetitive and demanding blue-collar and white-collar work. Here again it is evident that there is a genetic relationship between complexity and vulnerability and the generation of 'deviant' behaviour. The forms of labour and machinery are both health-destroying and highly sensitive to the resulting 'deviant' behaviour associated with poor health. It therefore becomes imperative for those who manage the system of production to see to it that people have enough sleep or physical exercise. Nutritional and physical education schemes are complemented by a whole range of programmes of behaviour control – from campaigns against smoking and drinking to sex and drivers' education. These programmes are evidence of a growing surveillance of forms of activity that fifty years ago were still considered as private matters and, therefore, of no interest to the state or employers.

DH   In contrast to Foucault, doesn't your account of the growth of
JK   these mechanisms of surveillance play down the importance

of professionalized forms of power and knowledge in *defining* 'deviance' and disability?

CO   Foucault does indeed emphasize the pre-political power aspects of the professions. I am also interested in this, especially in connection with the growth of forms of service labour. Consider the role of the medical profession within modern health systems. The power of this profession derives partly from the fact that the normal balance of supply and demand within competitive markets does not prevail. Within modern health systems, clients by definition do not know exactly what they demand because the supply side itself defines the treatment required by clients. Market relations of demand and supply are also absent in the sense that customers do not as a rule have to pay individually for what they actually receive. If they are part of a collective insurance scheme, rational individual consumers will want to have as much as possible because they have already paid and, in any case, they don't really know what they need and whether doctors have over-treated them. This endows doctors with an enormous economic power which is virtually beyond control. This monopoly position of the medical profession tends to be reinforced, as Ivan Illich among others has argued, by its destruction of the competence of clients. Popular knowledge about health is indeed destroyed by the professionalization and medicalization of health; clients are made more ignorant about life and death. It is clear from these well-known observations that the medical profession, as well as other health-related and custodial professions, enjoy an enormous economic power position and cognitive advantage over their clients.

DH   May we ask you to speculate briefly about the possible social
JK   or political alternatives to this regulation of populations by welfare state institutions and professions? Might a combination of professionalism and self-help, such as it is practised in sectors of the informal economy or the feminist movement, be viable or desirable? Or does your thesis about the genetic relationship between complexity, vulnerability and deviant behaviour imply the irreversibility of the mechanisms of surveillance and the administration of life?

CO   Let me respond with reference to the widely-discussed

psychiatric reform movement developed by Basaglia and others in Italy. This model of de-institutionalization and de-professionalization is based on the assumption that civil society and its infrastructure of families and communities is capable of absorbing a certain range of 'deviance'. 'Giving the mentally handicapped back to the community' means reabsorbing the handicapped in order to allow them to live meaningfully, without exploitation and discrimination. This proposal is questionable. The sheer complexity of communities may make them intolerant of deviance; what is more, communities have lost the type of popular knowledge necessary for dealing competently with people who have some mental defect. I think this is evident, for instance, when schoolchildren are confronted with mentally handicapped people – these children tend to be frightened, precisely because they and their parents are regularly separated from mental institutions and even mild forms of mental deficiency. The question is, therefore, whether the proposals of Basaglia are in fact utopian because the structural and cultural preconditions for decarceration are simply absent. The very frustrated and disillusioned reports arising out of the Italian legal reforms concerning the mentally handicapped seem to reinforce this conclusion. The point is that certain developments cannot be undone. As soon as systems such as families, cities or labour markets are modernized, they become vulnerable and consequently cease to contain 'space' for deviants. Thus, it appears that the whole social system would have to be transformed in order to make it less vulnerable to, and hence more tolerant of, various forms of deviance and mental illness.

DH   Your work, in contrast for instance to that of Niklas
JK   Luhmann, does not seem to grant much importance to the crucial and specific role that law and legal institutions play in modern society. In view of the recent rise in the level of controversies about law under welfare state conditions – controversies over the explicit 'politicization' of the legal system, concern about the authoritarian potential of the 'medicalization' and 'psychiatrization' of law, and so on – shouldn't one give greater weight to considerations of law within any theory of the achievements and limitations of the welfare state?

CO   Together with the subjects of repression and imperialism, law is insufficiently treated in my work, I agree. Only in my study of vocational training reform and an earlier discussion of the limits of bureaucratic forms of policy-making do questions concerning law appear to any extent. This might be explained by a paradoxical development: while many Anglo-Saxon countries have, in recent years, tried to imitate some of the legalistic frameworks adopted by Continental welfare states in the 1950s and 1960s – this has been the case, for instance, in the field of industrial relations – the reverse development seems to have occurred in Germany. That is, the assumption that law is an adequate and effective mechanism for changing situations and actors has been called into question.

This has happened for two reasons. One of them has to do with the fact that modern law is 'positive' law; that is, it becomes law not by virtue of its moral rightness but because some legislative body has decided that it should be the law. The significance of this point is the following: although law has indeed to a large extent become separated from its moral foundations, it is still not flexible and independent enough to deal with the complexity of the social and economic problems processed by the welfare state. As is evident in attempts to regulate the investment, production, pricing and distribution of primary products, such as coal or milk, making a law is often synonymous with making rules that are in need of revision as soon as they are printed. Legal regulation is appropriate for programmes and issues of a medium-range complexity, that is, for events that do not change very rapidly. In other cases, there seems to be a definite limit to the legal form of intervention itself. The law becomes a series of empty and abstract general phrases that have to be inter- preted in an *ad hoc*, context-dependent fashion – thereby violating the principle of the rule of law. In both cases, *ad hoc* rules and procedures can be said to be superior. This is one reason why I am very interested in studying corporatism, for one of the allegedly great virtues of informal and non-legal corporatist arrangements is their capacity to deal with rapidly fluctuating conditions and events.

Let me turn to the second reason for doubting the effective regulatory potential of law. If we consider the example of the legal surveillance and control of very elementary forms of activity, say, within familial relationships, it seems evident that the very existence of legal rules within these contexts becomes counterproductive. This is because the effectiveness of legal rules always depends upon positive or negative incentives, upon legally established threats or premiums for doing or avoiding certain things. The individual is thus interpellated as a rational maximizer of utilities. But it is exactly this exchange-like, rational-calculating mode of relating to incentives that itself undermines the process of informal interaction regulated by intersubjectively shared (if often repressive) norms. Let me give an hypothetical example of this paradoxical effect of legal intervention: a husband and wife quarrel about how to spend some part of their income. There are of course no legal rules concerning how to settle such a conflict. Yet if the conflict is transferred into the realm of legal regulation, and if one of the partners says, 'According to the Fourteenth Amendment to the Family Act, husband and wife are equally entitled to . . .', the conflict is not resolved. It may well be made *unresolvable*. The very recourse to legal regulations violates principles of mutual recognition, encourages cynicism between actors, and may even encourage them to retaliate by 'escaping' the consequences of the law. I have not researched this, these are only speculations. But the general argument I want to make is that as soon as legal regulations invade the private life–world of people, they fail to develop a regulatory capacity because people want to relate to each other as 'reasonable persons'. They do not wish to place themselves under the threat, authority or tutelage of the state. This is why many problems within welfare state societies are not amenable to what has been called 'legalization' or *Verrechtlichung* – the transformation of informal rules and situations into formal-legal regulations. By encouraging calculative modes of problem-solving, which do not necessarily produce the desired outcomes, this type of formal-legal regulation is self-undermining. Indeed, if everything were to be translated into the language of legal steering, then pure anomie would result.

DH   Your doctoral thesis, published in English in 1976 as *Industry*
JK   *and Inequality*, is well known, but much of your more recent
      work on trade unionism, labour markets, white-collar

workers and the disadvantaged is unfamiliar to most English-speaking readers. Would you briefly summarize and explain the significance of this research?

CO   I think this can best be done by contrasting it with two underlying assumptions within the model of classical Marxism. This model claimed, first, that wage labour is an equalizing and homogenizing process, on the basis of which a politically conscious proletarian 'class for itself' would be formed. Second, this model was founded on the assumption that the work role made for a fundamental equality of individuals as workers and that, therefore, all other roles such as those of consumer, man/woman, citizen, client, inhabitant of a territory or ecosystem were either less relevant or directly derivable from the fact of individuals being workers. I think both of these propositions about the homogenizing effects of labour and its centrality can and must be questioned. At least, their questioning is a recurrent theme within my work.

Concerning the homogeneity assumption: we know from studies of labour market segmentation and sociological accounts of the intermediate and 'new middle' classes, that wage-dependent labour is by no means the same everywhere, and that there is an internal structuring within the working class. Contrary to some Marxist writers of the Second and Third Internationals, this differentiation is not some remnant of the feudal past. It is rather something that is *increasingly* reproduced. Wage-labour does not homogeneously determine social existence. There are numerous categories of differentiation – including the distinctions between the primary and secondary labour markets; skilled versus unskilled labour; gender-based divisions of wage-labour; differences between traditional proletarians and workers who have recently come from self-employed families; productive labour versus service labour (labour that produces not physical products but things like advice which are immediately consumed); and so on. It has to be recognized that all of these divisions within the working class do not at all conform to the ideal-typical figure of the classical Marxian analysis, namely, the productive wage-labourer. This increasing heterogeneity constitutes a serious problem for the collective action of the working class and its political and economic organizations. As we know well in Germany, the great divergency within the work-force makes it very difficult for the system of unitary unions to unify and articulate its constituencies *as* workers.

The assumption about the centrality of labour within classical Marxism must also be questioned. Here I would follow many of the detailed arguments developed by Habermas in his most recent book, *Theorie des kommunikativen Handelns*. My thesis is that under modern capitalist conditions there is no one central condition that causally determines all other conditions in a base–superstructure or primary–secondary manner. The work role is only partly determinative of social existence. For instance, workers' struggles have no necessary priority over conflicts that in some modern Communist Party doctrines are called 'popular democratic struggles'. Social conflicts arising from the role of citizenship – citizens as both politically active beings and recipients and consumers of state services – can be of great significance and therefore should not be dismissed as superficial or 'superstructural'.

DH The combined effect of your questioning of these two core
JK assumptions of classical Marxism is, clearly, the rejection of its model of classes as homogeneous collectivities locked in conflict. How then do you conceive of the political potential of the present-day wage-labour – capital relationship? Must we bid adieu to the proletariat as Gorz and others propose? Has the emancipatory potential of the labour movement and its 'trench warfare' against capital been exhausted?

CO As I have just indicated, I think that it is sociologically and therefore politically misleading to conceive the proletariat as a unitary and homogeneous force. In much of classical and modern Marxism, this conception rests upon collectivist and objectivist assumptions, which have been very effectively criticized in André Gorz's marvellous book, *Farewell to the Working Class*. In spite of these criticisms I have always been, and remain, fascinated by what I think is the core argument in Marx's own analysis, namely, that processes of commodification, in which labour is illegitimately treated as if it were a commodity, presuppose the existence of power relationships. For the sake of simplicity, power in this connection can be defined as the ability or inability to outwait one's opponent. Because the suppliers of labour power cannot afford to wait as long as capitalist actors on the demand side, capital can, to an extent, impose conditions on those who supply labour. Marx describes this difference in a number of places through the metaphor of 'living' versus 'dead' labour. Living labour must eat and therefore cannot wait, whereas something that is dead in fact has a different time structure. I consider this point to be the central idea in the theory of exploitation. Owing to this differential ability to wait, power and blackmail mechanisms are inherent in market relationships between employers and workers. This is why labour is forced into having the by no means 'natural' quality of producing surplus value.

I consider this elementary Marxian thesis to be still important, and essential for any macro-sociological account of late capitalism. On the other hand, this exploitative mechanism based on unequal resources of market power is, in my view, a phenomenon that is shrinking in its potential for determining both relations of social and political power and collective identity. This power mechanism both remains basic and contracts, so that an ever smaller part of the entire social structure is directly determined by it. One doctoral student has expressed this point very nicely by distinguishing two types of interpretations of capitalism. One of them, the domination model, implicitly compares capital to an all-powerful father who has the capacity to positively determine everything that occurs in society. The other version, the constraint model, draws upon the metaphor of capital as a dying old man who still controls some ultimate sanction and can therefore rule over his family and relatives, all of whom know and secretly hope that he will soon die. Jim O'Connor has similarly distinguished two models for analysing capitalism. The victimization model (Braverman is an example) supposes everyone and everything is controlled and exploited by the superior and far-sighted powers of capital. This is a highly implausible argument these days. By contrast, the class struggle model emphasizes the enormous opposition of forces to capital, whose ultimate power to set constraints is nevertheless seen to derive from certain resources and powers still under its control.

In pursuing this second type of argument, I think it important to understand – this is the point of the theory of decommodification – that the development of capitalism leads to a diminution of the organizing potential of capital. Analogous to the fragile old man who requires protection and support, capital increasingly depends upon non-capitalist support systems such as schools, militaries and hospitals. Although capital's power and blackmail mechanisms remain central to the functioning of the commodification process, there are more and more spheres of social life from which capital has withdrawn or been excluded. So, in response to your question concerning the potential of the labour movement, I think its potential has been exhausted to the extent that it ignores the fact that the wage-labour–capital relationship is not the key determinant of social existence, and that the survival of capitalism has become increasingly contingent upon non-capitalist forms of power and conflict. Any labour movement that ignores this and avoids trying to make links with conflicts generated by consumers, clients, citizens or inhabitants of an ecosystem becomes solipsistic. In my view, the crucial problem for the labour movement is how to become *more* than a labour movement.

In the present period, this problem has been made more acute because the vision of full employment has been undermined by capital itself. This means that the goal of absorbing the entire life energy of society into labour markets and industrial production has been rendered utopian. A more plausible scenario is that of the emergence of a bifurcated society organized around a shrinking capitalist core and an expanding periphery of non-market institutional arrangements and conditions of life. Within the productive capitalist core, workers will be relatively privileged. Fewer and fewer workers – mainly those who are fully-employed, skilled, male and domestic (i.e., non-foreign) – will get higher and higher wages. Within the peripheries, by contrast, the old and the young, women, foreigners and mentally or physically handicapped people will become increasingly marginalized and, so to speak, accommodated by institutions other than labour markets. Larger periods of their lives will be spent in non-capitalist institutional frameworks, such as families, schools, hospitals, pension systems, militaries and other total or semi-total institutions. This bifurcation process is, in my view, not random or accidental. It is a process strategically promoted by the logic of the development of capital – by its drive to develop new products, increase exports, improve labour productivity, and so on.

DH   Could you say something more precisely about the implica-
JK   tions of this bifurcation process for trade union strategies? Is your argument that the labour movement can survive only by becoming more than a labour movement close to the proposals of Bruno Trentin?

CO   That's exactly whose ideas I have in mind. Some political and trade union organizations of the European working class have discovered that a strategy solely for labour is doomed to failure and that the historical aspirations of the workers' movement can only be continued if they abandon the idea that all immiseration and domination derive from wage-labour. There are interesting experiments under way. For instance, there is the widely discussed Lucas Aerospace model, which seeks to link employment with questions concerning use-values and democratization at the point of production. This model clearly transcends the traditional concerns of the labour movement. This progressive tendency is also evident in the activities of the Italian Metal Workers' Union, and in the theoretical writings of Pietro Ingrao. Since the early 1970s, Ingrao has argued that the Italian Communist Party must broaden its boundaries as a working-class party to include both the middle class and the marginalized or peripheral strata of young unemployed people and part-time women. Unfortunately, almost the opposite tendency is evident in Germany. Under pressure from the deepening recession, German trade unions are likely to adopt the position that all progressive demands are working-class demands, and that any other collective identities and demands are negligible and, at worst, dangerous and hostile to the working-class movement. Some people have even spoken of the Americanization of the German trade unions. Concentrating on wage issues which concern the core male working class, this movement shows signs of conforming to Sam Gompers' classic description of the American working class – what it wants, in a word, is more! It is also fascinating and ironic to observe how, at the end of their long history, Right-wing Social Democrats emphasize that the German SDP should, after all, be a working-class party, and not a party absorbing the pacifism, environmentalism or civil rights concerns that are typically found within the new and old middle classes and the peripheral strata. In their view, the electoral gains generated by Bad Godesberg – the opening up of the party to the middle class – has gone too far. Any Italian Gramscian would rightly denounce this social democratic view as an extreme form of 'corporativist' insulation of the working class from all other social strata.

DH   It is your conviction that the welfare state must be considered
JK   as an irreversible achievement, that any government is now forced to accept the obligation to provide a range of policies and services that are reproductive of both labour power and capital. What precisely are your reasons for this conviction – which, in the present political climate, some might understand as rather optimistic, as wishful thinking?

CO   There are several reasons underpinning the thesis that the welfare state has become an irreversible achievement. In the first place, basing convictions on empirical evidence is always problematic. Nevertheless, I take this risk because I think that although there are many indications that the number of legal claims, services and entitlements organized by the welfare state are being reduced, they have not been *wholly* questioned. In the present period, the typical pattern is that the scope, volume and timing of benefits and services are being reduced and restricted. However, so far there is little evidence that, for example, unemployment benefit programmes or rudimentary forms of health insurance and welfare are being considered as unnecessary and therefore in need of outright abandonment.

Second, and more seriously, I consider that the welfare state is a two-sided protective device. By removing matters of collective consumption from the point of production, and by establishing a division between the primary and secondary distribution of income, the welfare state protects both workers and capitalists in a highly 'economical' manner. It is certainly true that the consequent fiscal problems impinge upon capital as well as labour. Counterfactually speaking, the welfare state can nevertheless be considered as a comparatively efficient conflict-reducing mechanism. If workers' secondary income (for example, health coverage) had to be generated directly from primary income sources, then levels of wage demands and industrial conflict would arguably be much higher than at present. Especially when it is considered that the volume of labour-power capable of being absorbed by oligopoly capital is steadily decreasing, the welfare state must be seen as a highly efficient and effective means of resolving problems of collective reproduction and, therefore, of reducing economic and political conflict. This is one reason why even the most extreme neo-conservative ideologists are unwilling to tamper with the basic institutional arrangements of collective reproduction. These ideologists correctly sense that the 'dismantling' of the welfare state would result in widespread conflict and forms of anomic and 'criminal' behaviour that together would be more destructive than the enormous burdens of the welfare state itself. The welfare state is indeed a highly problematic, costly and disruptive arrangement, yet its absence would be even more disruptive. Welfare state capitalist societies simply cannot be remodelled into something resembling pure market societies.

My final reason for this conviction is that most social needs can no longer be absorbed by arrangements that have fallen victim to the process of modernization, for instance, the extended three-generation family, community networks, or some version of the 'American Dream' of self-help. Present-day Detroit is a case in point. A quarter of its population is close to starving, yet there are no conceivable alternatives to the federal initiatives. The poor of Detroit are made to eat cheese – the excess production of which the state purchased some time ago, and which it redistributes in an arrogant, discriminatory and authoritarian way. The example of Detroit suggests that the conditions under which welfare is presently provided may deteriorate incredibly, becoming authoritarian or even fascistic. It also indicates that the fact of collective reproduction is something which has become irreversible.

DH Assuming that many welfare state policies are irreversible,
JK how should we understand the 'New Right' and its response
to the present contradictions of the welfare state? What
accounts for its present vitality? Is there anything new about
this New Right?

CO I must first of all emphasize that there is a manifest discrepancy between the doctrines and practices of this New
Right. For instance, while it makes no theoretical allowance
for trade unions, and although it is attempting to restrict their
scope of action, the New Right has not made any attempt to
abolish unions along the lines of fascism. In addition to such
discrepancies between its theory and practice, the New Right
and its arguments suffer from a serious logical flaw. Simply,
their predictions are devoid of all time indicators. It is argued
that the restoration of the market will counteract and heal all
the ills of 'quasi-socialism', but no one says when this will be
the case. Failures can always be excused by calling for more
time. The predictions of the New Right are not guided by
time constraints and are thus directly immunized against
fallibility criteria. To my knowledge, the New Right ideologists and strategists such as Keith Joseph have not seriously
considered the absurd possibility that the patient will die
before the cure becomes effective. But to return to the
question: what do we mean by the *New* Right? In Western
Europe, Britain and the United States, its common denominator is its deep aversion to state intervention, control and
regulation. Luhmann correctly points out that this aversion
to *étatisme* is something that the New Right shares, admittedly for rather different reasons, with the socialist Left.
However, the New Right offers the market as the alternative
to bureaucratic domination, and in this respect it is not like
the old fascist Right – which wanted to strengthen and 're-
enchant' the repressive power of the state by invoking irrational and racist conceptions of community and nationhood.
The New Right is oriented to achievement, effectiveness,
efficiency and productivity. It therefore denounces all those
parasitic, hedonistic and counterproductive forces that do
not conform to the allegedly superior rationality of the
market.

DH
JK
But to suppose that what is new about the New Right is its aversion to *étatisme* does not in practice seem to be confirmed, as you have already pointed out. It is also highly doubtful whether its theoretical discourse is so market-oriented as you say. A careful examination of the writings of, say, Nozick or Friedman suggests that the Right is, rather, attempting to redraw the boundaries between state and society, to redifferentiate spheres of activity that have become highly interdependent. It does not seek to defend the simple utopia of a fully emancipated market but, rather, free markets *and* strong states.

CO
That is a very good point. One has only to consider the work of Samuel Huntington to discover the ambivalence within the New Right's theory of the state. Huntington does indeed advocate a strong state by arguing that the authority of the welfare state has been weakened by the continuous expansion of its responsibilities. The corollary of this view is that state authority can only be restored through a diminution of the functions for which the state can in turn be held responsible. In a similar way, Luhmann's recent discussion of the welfare state proposes that the proper function of the state is the making of authoritatively binding decisions against which no legitimate dissent is possible. According to Luhmann, there is a contradiction within the welfare state's distribution of goods and services: the more the state provides, the less it is able to make decisions which are authoritative and binding in the last instance. The ideology of the New Right is thus by no means anarchist. To summarize this point, I think that there are three things that are novel about the contemporary Right: its critique of the over-extended state; its refusal to draw upon the old repertoire of essentialist conceptions of the state; and its grandiose and, to say the least, unsupported hopes for the market-place.

DH
JK
For some time now, as you have already indicated, you have been centrally concerned with the growth of informal, para-bureaucratic processes of bargaining and policy-making among representatives of the state and key social groups, such as labour and capital. Would you explain why you think that these 'corporatist' forms of policy-making are typically

marked by difficulties and why, therefore, variants of corporatism may not be a viable 'solution' to the present difficulties of the welfare state?

CO Many recent publications argue that the Austrian and to some extent the German models of non-state social and economic policy-making, in which organizations of labour and capital assume the character of private governments, are superior modes of creating order between the state and the market. In practice, this view has been adopted primarily by Right-wing social democrats and technocratic policy-makers. Their reasoning is something like: 'Why don't we find flexible ways of getting labour and capital together by forgetting about the overly complicated and rigid mechanisms of law-making and public authority?' I think there are two serious limitations of corporatist proposals of this type.

One of them derives from the fact that corporatist mechanisms of decision-making tend to be exploitative of third parties such as consumers – price fixing and production quotas being familiar examples. Corporatist arrangements simply do not lead to the equitable resolution of social and political problems. Instead, they export these problems, by shifting burdens on to others who did not happen to be present at the bargaining table. The second deficiency of corporatism concerns the asymmetry built into the bargaining relations between capitalist and working-class organizations. Corporatist arrangements are usually considered to comprise 'tripartite' relations between organizations of employers, labour and the state. Of course, in order for these triangular relations to operate in a non-exploitative and non-discriminatory way, it would have to be supposed that agreements are equally binding on all partners. This supposition would only hold under conditions in which the representatives of capital had as much governing power over their constituent member firms and their pricing and investment policies as the representatives of labour had over the wage demands of individual workers. But, under conditions of private property, this is typically *not* the case. In Germany, for instance, the framework of collective bargaining effectively prohibits workers from striking unofficially. In contrast, the promises and proclamations made by employers' associations on behalf of their member investors and employers are not at all legally binding upon the behaviour of those investors and employers; individual elements of private capital remain formally free to do what they want within the market-place.

It is this asymmetry between labour and capital that constantly tends to disrupt the empirical consensus necessary for the viable functioning of *ad hoc*, non-constitutional, corporatist mechanisms of decision-making. Thus, the question for all participants within corporatist arrangements is whether they are actually willing to insist upon the socialization of the means of production as a necessary pre-condition for the fair and proper functioning of those arrangements. If this insistence were forthcoming, a close connection could be identified between corporatist arrangements and syndicalism, or what G. D. H. Cole and the Austro-Marxists in the 1920s called functional democracy – democracy based on functional rather than territorial forms of representation. This democratic socialist version of corporatism would not only signal the abolition of the private ownership of the means of production; it could also allow for the admission of new and multi-faceted forms of representation which would ensure, in turn, that *all* relevant interests and points of view – and not just those of capital, labour and the state – were fed into the negotiating process.

DH   Your recent writings speak of a whole variety of new social
JK   movements, such as feminism, environmentalism and the peace movement. Are these movements symptomatic of an emerging period in which class divisions and political parties are no longer the key determinants of social and political struggle? What is *new* about these new social movements? What feeds their development?

CO   My interest in the new social movements has been prompted by the fact that a new political paradigm has emerged in Germany and several other European countries. By the term paradigm, I mean a constellation of collective actors, issues, values and modes of action. The collective actors within this new political paradigm are often ascriptively defined, and include groups such as young people, females or inhabitants of certain geographic areas. Their demands are to a significant extent non-economic, in the sense that they cannot be satisfied through distributive and productive means; they are concerned less with the quantity of income and wealth than with the quality of the natural and social conditions of life. The mode of action of these groups tends to be unorganized and non-institutionalized, spontaneous and direct. Environmentalism, pacifism, urban movements and various human and civil rights movements (for example, those defending the rights of women, homosexuals and prisoners) all belong within this category.

I think there are basically two things that are new about these social movements. First, their location within the social structure is by no means marginal. Old social movements such as late nineteenth-century American populism typically grew out of social strata whose institutional and material resources of power were being negated or threatened by processes of modernization. Support for the new social movements, by contrast, is derived predominantly not from peripheral or underprivileged strata but from groups who themselves play a rather central role in steering and managing what Daniel Bell has called 'post-industrial' society. These core groups are relatively well-to-do, and include people from the new middle classes and the professional and service sectors who have the highest levels of education and the greatest cognitive skills. This characteristic feature of the new social movements reinforces their second novel aspect, namely, that they do not protest in the name of preserving a traditional past that is presently threatened by modernization and rationalization.

Within liberal and social democratic journalism and political commentary, there has been a strong tendency to describe these movements as Luddites who idealistically yearn for the good old days of simple, communal life. I think this is highly inaccurate. If sections of the new movements appear to idealize past forms of life, they usually do so in a self-mocking and ironical way – for instance, anti-nuclear protestors playfully liken themselves to a now defunct Germanic tribe by declaring a Free Republic of Wendland. The social movements are by no means romantic adherents of some pre-modern view of social order. Rather, they are inspired and motivated by the view that processes of modern-ization that rely exclusively on instrumental and strategic rationality are inherently counterproductive and destructive. They are moved to protest by the fact that greater military 'security' creates and increases the likelihood of war; that the increased production of goods, especially industrial goods, produces negative environmental results; that more and more areas of social life tend to come under state co-ordination and surveillance; and so on. None of this protest normatively adheres to a romanticized past; it is rather a response to a future that is seen as threatening or potentially threatening. In contrast to old social movements, such as the labour movement, the new social movements do not claim to know what the future will look like. Their concerns are in a sense more limited and even conservative. These movements are not in principle opposed to modernization as such. They seek to defend what is worth defending, to check and control the perverse and self-destructive consequences of technical, military, economic, urban and social policy modernization. As I see it, these movements project a *modern* critique of modernization. They constitute an attempt to increase the learning capacity of late capitalist systems by pointing to their systematic blindness and dangerous effects. This links up with their conviction, moreover, that parliamentary, representative, party-based forms of democracy have an insufficient learning capacity and are therefore incapable of anticipating and dealing adequately with the destructive consequences of modernization. The new social movements consequently insist upon the need for *additional* forms of grass-roots politics that can enrich existing political institu-tions, process more effectively the new types of resistance to the defects of modernization and, thereby, increase the learning capacity of the entire social system.

DH Would you follow Touraine's thesis that these movements are
JK likely to coalesce into a single and dominant social movement, just as the workers' movement did during the earlier phase of industrial capitalism? Or would you reject this possibility, on the grounds that processes of structural differentiation prohibit the formation of a unified social movement?

CO   I am not certain about this. I do think that the grand historical
      constructions to be found in some of the writings of Touraine
      are premature, and I doubt whether it is necessary to con-
      ceive of social movements as organizationally and ideologic-
      ally integrated and unified. For what is also novel about the
      new social movements is their resistance to unification, even
      as an ultimate goal. Touraine's method of sociological inter-
      vention is clearly designed to help overcome this tendency by
      promoting their self-awareness and self-unification. It may
      be, however, that the *ad hoc*, fragmented and incoherent
      character of these movements cannot really be overcome.
      Further, as a means of bringing a more complete set of
      criteria of goodness into political life, I have much sympathy
      with the idea that this fragmentation can in itself help to
      increase the learning capacity of political systems by dimin-
      ishing their degree of 'blindness' or unawareness of fore-
      seeable and often catastrophic consequences. I am in fact
      deeply convinced that all future political designs will be
      mixed and to some degree 'eclectic' designs. Political
      development in this sense would take the form of a more
      multi-faceted and pluralistic combination of different forms
      of economic, technological and political rationality, so that
      the old and the allegedly obsolete would be mixed and made
      compatible with the new at a higher level. This abandonment
      of the opposition 'old versus new' is well under way within the
      new social movements. Whereas old social movements, such
      as the youth movements of the 1920s, rejected cities,
      technology and modern music in the name of a whole and
      principled life, the new social movements attempt to accom-
      modate an eclectic range of elements of the old and the new.
      An interesting example of this is the major German 'alter-
      native' newspaper, *Die Tageszeitung*. As something like the
      mouthpiece of the new social movements, it is a very
      amateurish operation. In terms of journalistic practice, it is
      deliberately unprofessional yet, at the same time, it is a high
      technology, computer-based operation which combines the
      new and the old, the highly professional and the absolutely
      non-professional. Apparently it is all a contradictory and
      impossible synthesis – but it works very nicely.

DH   We would like to ask, finally, about the implications of your

JK   theoretical and empirical writings for the democratic socialist
tradition. In spite of the promise of the new social movements, there is in the present context widespread scepticism
about politics, a withdrawal from traditional party politics
and a considerable cynicism about the failures of 'real
socialism'. These developments appear to discredit many, if
not most traditional socialist ideals. The pressing questions
remain: how can socialist politics best be developed in the
present period? What does it mean to be a democratic socialist today?

CO   One recurrent theme in Marx that I have always found illum-
inating is that of the self-valorization of capital. Marx charac-
terizes the logic of capitalism as 'insatiable' and self-centred;
it is an economic system which has blind disregard for any
needs or use-values external to its own purposes. This blind
recklessness of capitalism is as strongly evident today as it was
in the time of Marx, and I would therefore say that any
contemporary socialist practice must question this blindness
of capitalism by applying use-value criteria to the social
developments for which capital is responsible. In this connection, there can be no doubt that the positive ideals of
democracy, justice, emancipation and self-determination
have lost much of their programmatic clarity and even attrac-
tiveness for many people on the Left. Yet I think that the
significance of these old ideals for modern socialist politics
can be productively reformulated if we understand them as
oriented to the goal of negating the reckless characteristics of
capitalism – as attempts, so to speak, to resist the blind logic
of development of the capitalist system by forcing it to
develop greater learning capacities. I see four important
areas in which contemporary socialist politics can do this.

The first, and probably most obvious area is that of employment and unemployment. For reasons I have already given,
the proportion of life activity that is today structured by
wage-labour contracts has been considerably reduced. Given
the extent to which people's lives have become decommodified in this sense, I think that the process of decommodification itself could be turned into something more positive.
There are lots of experiments under way in this area, and
while no really promising programme has been forthcoming,

I think the Left cannot ignore questions of decommodification and their expanded importance. At the same time, it is clear that we cannot demand full employment. This goal is unrealistic and in any case utterly anti-socialist. Any future kind of full employment will be terror: it would make neither economic, political, ecological nor military sense. We must find ways of resisting the unemployment trap, by questioning the curious fact that the working-class movement began as a struggle against wage-labour and is now united in a superficial way in its struggle for employment through wage-labour. One major task of socialist theory and politics is, therefore, to develop forms of useful activity that are not based on wage-labour. The conventional Keynesian argument that these new forms are less productive or detrimental to growth and welfare must be countered by redefining the terms in which productivity is today defined in a very one-sided way that is biased against concrete, useful labour. We must seek to escape the unemployment trap not by demanding a return to full employment, but by creating socially useful alternatives to the ideal of full employment through wage-labour. This is a major task, and I therefore think that the old idea of co-operatives – non-capitalist forms of producing useful things – deserves a contemporary renaissance.

The second area of concern for socialist theory and politics must be the defence of democratic rights. I do not believe that the tighter controls and surveillance of the welfare state are synonymous with the maintenance and expansion of democratic rights. If it is true, as I've argued, that welfare state capitalist systems tend ever more to subject all life activity to detailed regulation, then the learning capacity of these systems, their capacity to check their contradictory and self-paralysing tendencies, can only be preserved through the expansion of democratic rights – and that implies defending rights of democratic participation in areas of life (for example, workers' control of production) in addition to, and beyond, the realm of parliamentary, representative democracy. Learning capacity is the opposite of blindness, and I therefore take it that the most abstract common denominator of the difference between capitalism and socialism is the latter's superior and expanded capacity for learning.

This is why I consider that environmental or ecological

concerns constitute a third and very important component of contemporary socialist theory and politics. The environmental movement can greatly contribute to the socialist resistance to the logic of blindness of modern capitalism by forcing political and economic elites to evaluate the long-term consequences of the operations of the political and economic system. In the present period, the front of technical and economic modernization has become very fragile. The systemic dimensions of environmental problems have produced a deep insecurity and unease within liberal and social democratic political elites; problems arising out of the chemical poisoning of forests, the depletion of raw materials, and the disposal of nuclear waste jeopardize future production and, thus, become understandable even in the language of the system. This insecurity about the blindness of the present system is evidently deepened by developments within established scientific–technical circles. The scientific and technical professions are deeply divided over such questions as scientific rationality and risk assessment technology, and it is therefore not surprising that important elements of resistance to blind modernization come from these professions. The American term whistle-blowing is appropriate here: the bearers of scientific-technical rationality themselves publicize the dirty secrets and irrationality of the practices they are part of. They therefore come to insist on the need for greater learning capacity within the systems of production and administration. Within industrial, political and scientific-technical circles, then, the cognitive potential to overcome blindness is generated by the very same processes of development that reinforce blindness. This cognitive potential has to be utilized by the environmental movement and by socialist politics.

Finally, there is the question of peace. Strongly paralleling the ecology movement, the new peace movement is defined by its critique of the disastrous consequences of modernization – of blind faith in high technology, the arms race and ever more complicated and dangerous strategic planning. This new movement is linked to the Left everywhere, although it is not controlled or dominated by any single political party. In this respect, the old alignments have changed, and the new peace movement cannot so easily be labelled and denounced as before: just as ecologists are no longer nature-freaks, peace movement activists are no longer simply communists. As with the ecology movement, the new peace movement is an alliance of protestors and elite defectors. Both movements have developed their cases by stealing the most powerful arguments from the system itself. In the German peace movement, for example, one of the more prominent and respected activists is the former general, Bastian, who has been very instrumental in clarifying for the public the dangerous inconsistencies and blindness inherent in the defence stratagies that are unanimously adopted by the present political elites.

To summarize: it is my view that democratic socialism is today being transformed into eco-socialism. Eco-socialism emphasizes the need to resist and arrest the further blind 'evolution' of processes of capitalist rationalization. Surprisingly, while this new eco-socialist project is very unclear about what it favours, its real strength as an alliance of forces lies in its clarity about what it opposes. Eco-socialism is defined by its overall resistance to that logic already described by Marx – the blind and self-destructive logic of the self-valorization of capital.

Index